State Crime and Resista

G000135008

'While the scientific study of state crimes has increased over the last two decades, the overall understanding of how to develop counter-strategies has remained underdeveloped in criminology. This book focuses on practices and policies of resistance to many harmful practices committed by states and their agents, such as genocide and war crimes, corruption and fraud, and the failure to provide principled leadership for dealing with climate change. This novel approach is exemplified through a number of excellent case-studies by world-class authors. It should be on the shelf of academics, activists and the media, and of state officials as well.'

> Stephan Parmentier, *Professor at the Leuven Institute of Criminology (Belgium) and Secretary General of the International Society for Criminology*

Within criminology, 'the state' is often ignored as an actor or represented as a neutral force. While state crime studies have proliferated, criminologists have not paid attention to the history and impact of resistance to state crime. This book recognizes that crimes of the state are far more serious and harmful than crimes committed by individuals and considers how such crimes may be contested, prevented, challenged or stopped.

Gathering together key scholars from the UK, USA, Australia and New Zealand, this book offers a deepened understanding of state crime through the practical and analytical lens of resistance. This book focuses on crimes ranging from gross violations of human rights, such as genocide, war crimes, mass killings, summary executions, torture, harsh detention and rape during war, through to entrenched discrimination, unjust social policies, border controls, corruption, fraud, resource plunder and the failure to provide the regulatory environment and principled leadership necessary to deal with global warming.

As the first to focus on state crime and resistance, this collection inspires new questions as it maps the contours of some unexplored territory. It is aimed at students and academics researching state crimes, resistance, human rights and social movements. It is also essential reading for all those interested in joining the struggles to centre ways of living that value humanity and justice over power.

Elizabeth Stanley is Senior Lecturer in Criminology at Victoria University of Wellington, New Zealand. Her research focuses on state crimes, detention, transitional justice and social justice. Her book *Torture, Truth and Justice* was published by Routledge in 2009, and she has written widely on issues of torture, terror and human rights. Most of her work has explored how victims of state violence experience their victimization and their ensuing attempts to seek recognition and justice.

Jude McCulloch is a Criminologist at Monash University. Her research focuses on state terror, state violence and state crime. Her latest book, *Borders and Crime: Pre-crime, Mobility and Serious Harm in an Age of Globalization* (with Sharon Pickering), will be published by Palgrave Macmillan in 2012. Her research includes police use of force, counter-terrorism laws and policing, (in)security and the violence of incarceration. Her work describes and analyses the growing integration of national security and law enforcement under conditions of neoliberal globalization.

Routledge studies in crime and society

State Crime and Resistance

**Edited by Elizabeth Stanley
and Jude McCulloch**

Routledge
Taylor & Francis Group

LONDON AND NEW YORK

First published 2013
by Routledge
2 Park Square, Milton Park, Abingdon, Oxon OX14 4RN

Simultaneously published in the USA and Canada
by Routledge
711 Third Avenue, New York, NY 10017

Routledge is an imprint of the Taylor & Francis Group, an informa business

British Library Cataloguing in Publication Data
A catalogue record for this book is available from the British Library

Library of Congress Cataloging in Publication Data
A catalog record has been requested for this book

ISBN: 978-0-415-69193-2 (hbk)
ISBN: 978-0-415-63807-4 (pbk)
ISBN: 978-0-203-10106-3 (ebk)

Typeset in Times New Roman
by Wearset Ltd, Boldon, Tyne and Wear

This book is dedicated to Acky and Mark

Contents

Contributors

Megan Blair graduated with a Ph.D. in History from Monash University, Australia, in 2008. She was research assistant on the ARC-funded project 'Justice for All: A History of the Community Legal Centre movement in Victoria,' undertaken by Jude McCulloch. She has recently published an article on the history of Community Legal Centres in the *Alternative Law Journal*.

Chris Cunneen is Professor of Justice and Social Inclusion in the Cairns Institute, James Cook University, Australia. His books include *Juvenile Justice. Youth and Crime in Australia* (Oxford University Press, 2011), *Indigenous Legal Relations in Australia* (Oxford University Press, 2009), *The Critical Criminology Companion* (Federation Press, 2008) and *Conflict, Politics and Crime* (Allen and Unwin, 2001).

David O. Friedrichs is Professor of Sociology/Criminal Justice and Distinguished University Fellow at the University of Scranton, Pennsylvania, USA. He edited *State Crime*, Volumes I & II (Ashgate, 1998) and has contributed journal articles and book chapters on state crime.

Penny Green is Professor of Law and Criminology at King's College London, UK. She has written widely on state violence and corruption, with a particular interest in Turkey. She is co-author with Tony Ward of *State Crime* (2004) and the author of *The Enemy Without: Policing and Class Consciousness in the Miners' Strike* (1990), *Drugs, Trafficking and Criminal Policy* (1997), and, *Drug Couriers* (1991). She is Co-Director of the International State Crime Initiative (ISCI) and one of the Editors-in-Chief of the journal *State Crime*.

Michael Grewcock is Senior Lecturer in Law and teaches criminal law and criminology at the University of New South Wales, Australia. His specialist areas of research include state crime and border policing. He is a member of the editorial board for the journal *State Crime*.

David Kauzlarich is Professor of Sociology at Southern Illinois University, Edwardsville, USA, where he has received several prestigious awards for his teaching and research. His primary areas of expertise are state and corporate crime, victimology, music and society, and critical theory. His book *Theorizing Resistance*, an ethnographic study of punk rock music and resistance to state and corporate crime, will be published in 2013 by Routledge.

Ronald C. Kramer is Professor of Sociology and Director of the Criminal Justice Programme at Western Michigan University, USA. His books include *Crimes of the American Nuclear State, State-Corporate Crime: Wrongdoing at the Intersection of Business and Government,* and *State Crime in the Global Age.*

Jude McCulloch is Professor of Criminology at Monash University, Australia. Her latest book, *Borders and Crime: Pre-crime, Mobility and Serious Harm in an Age of Globalization* (with Sharon Pickering), will be published by Palgrave Macmillan in 2012. Her research includes police use of force and counter-terrorism laws and policing.

Raymond Michalowski is Regents Professor of Criminology at Northern Arizona University, USA. His publications include *Order, Law and Crime, State-Corporate Crime* and *State Crime in the Global Age,* along with writings on criminology theory, state, corporate and environmental crimes, and the political reconstruction of memory.

Wayne Morrison is Professor of Law, Queen Mary University of London, UK. He has published extensively on legal theory and criminology, with *Criminology, Civilisation and the New World Order* (Routledge) being a sustained project to bring the history of genocide and colonialism into the criminological imagination.

Suthaharan Nadarajah is Lecturer at the Centre for International Studies and Diplomacy, School of Oriental and African Studies, UK. His research examines how the international community seeks to expand global order through frameworks which combine themes of security, development and liberal governance. He has published in *Third World Quarterly, Security Dialogue* and several edited volumes.

Christina Pantazis is Senior Lecturer in the School for Policy Studies at the University of Bristol, UK. She has co-authored a number of chapters and articles on the UK's war on terror.

Simon Pemberton is Research Fellow at the University of Birmingham, UK. He has co-authored a number of chapters and articles on the UK's war on terror.

Sharon Pickering is Professor of Criminology, Monash University, Australia. She has previously worked in Northern Ireland, on counter-terrorism policing, refugees and trafficking, and human rights and women in South East Asia. She currently leads a series of Australian Research Council projects focusing on the intersections of security and migration and has recently taken up an Australian Research Council Future Fellowship on Border Policing and Security. She is also the Editor of the *Australian and New Zealand Journal of Criminology.*

Dawn L. Rothe is Associate Professor at Old Dominion University, USA, and Director of the International State Crime Research Consortium. She is the author or co-author of four books and over 50 articles and book chapters on various forms of state crime, corporate crime and international criminal justice.

Victoria Sentas is Lecturer in Law at the University of New South Wales, Australia. Her current research examines the criminalization of diaspora and migrants. Her forthcoming book, *Traces of Terror: Counter-terrorism Law, Policing and Race*, will be published by OUP.

Elizabeth Stanley is Senior Lecturer in Criminology at Victoria University of Wellington, New Zealand. Her teaching and research focuses on state crimes, human rights, transitional justice, social justice and detention. Her 2009 book *Torture, Truth and Justice* is published by Routledge.

Tony Ward is Reader in Law at the University of Hull, UK. He is co-author with Penny Green of *State Crime* (2004) and with Gerry Johnstone of *Law and Crime* (2010), and co-editor with Bev Clucas and Gerry Johnstone of *Torture: Moral Absolutes and Ambiguities* (2009). He is Co-Director of the International State Crime Initiative (ISCI) and one of the Editors-in-Chief of the journal *State Crime*. Before entering academic life, he worked for the British NGO INQUEST, which campaigns about deaths in custody and related issues.

Leanne Weber is Senior Research Fellow in the School of Political and Social Inquiry, Monash University, Australia. She has researched the detention of asylum seekers in the UK, studied migration policing networks in Australia and published widely on the practices and consequences of border control in Australia and Europe.

Rob White is Professor of Criminology at the University of Tasmania, Australia. Among his recent books are *Transnational Environmental Crime: Toward an Eco-global Criminology* and *Global Environmental Harm: Criminological Perspectives*.

Acknowledgements

The inspiration for this volume grew out of an increasing uneasiness about a state crime field that paid close attention to the abuse of state power but failed to take into account the various ways in which individuals, social movements and academics have opposed, challenged and resisted state crime. Much of the credit goes to students in state crime courses who were eager to find hope in the face of the reality of state crime.

The foundation for this volume was laid at a roundtable on state crime and resistance held in Wellington, hosted by Elizabeth Stanley and funded by Victoria University of Wellington, in January 2010. We are grateful to all those who attended the roundtable – travelling from Australia, North America and the United Kingdom – and who generously shared the ideas that helped to shape this volume and provide the framework for all of the chapters that follow.

The success of a book such as this depends on the contributors. The originality and quality of the chapters made our editorial role extremely rewarding. When we set out to extend state crime scholarship to encompass resistance, we never anticipated that we would learn so much or travel so far. That the volume exceeded our expectations in shedding light on state crime and resistance is due to the insights and commitment of each of the authors. In particular, we thank them all for being responsive to our suggestions and willing to write to tight deadlines and within the restraints of style and space necessarily imposed in a joint project such as this.

We extend our warmest thanks to our criminology colleagues at Victoria University of Wellington, New Zealand, and at Monash University, Australia. The collegial environment at each of these institutions has provided the support and critique, productivity and distraction, in just the right doses to allow this project to proceed to fruition. We also want to acknowledge the welcome and stimulating contribution of our students, who add immeasurably to the intellectual culture that provides fertile ground for original ideas and research.

Thanks also to the team at Routledge for supporting the project and ensuring it passed muster. A special thanks to copy editor Julia Farrell, whose careful attention to detail made it a much better book. Jude McCulloch is also grateful to the Australian Research Council for Discovery Grant DP0879533.

Finally, thanks to our partners, Mark Minchinton and Andy Atkinson, two fine fellows who always go above and beyond, putting up with the distraction that inevitably attends academic life in general and the writing and editing that goes into a book such as this in particular. Special thanks also to Otis McCulloch; as a member of a (much) younger generation, he will no doubt find ways of resisting that we haven't even begun to imagine.

Acronyms and abbreviations

AAL	Aboriginal Advancement League
ALS	Aboriginal Legal Service
CLC	Community Legal Centre
CSO	Civil society organization
ECHR	European Court of Human Rights
FAIRA	Foundation for Aboriginal and Islander Research Action
FCAATSI	Federal Council for the Advancement of Aborigines and Torres Strait Islanders
FLS	Fitzroy Legal Service
FP	Federal Party
HFC	Hydrofluorocarbon
ICC	International Criminal Court
IPCC	Intergovernmental Panel on Climate Change
ISCI	International State Crime Initiative
JCHR	Joint Committee on Human Rights
MIFEE	Merauke Integrated Food and Energy Estate
MPA	Metropolitan Police Authority
MPS	Metropolitan Police Service
MRP	Papuan People's Assembly
NASA	National Aeronautics and Space Administration
NGO	Non-government organizations
NSA	Non-state actors
NSW	New South Wales
NZ	New Zealand
OPM	*Organisasi Papua Merdeka*
QLD	Queensland
TPIM	Terrorism Prevention and Investigation Measures
TULF	Tamil United Liberation Party
UNEP	United Nations Environmental Programme
UNSC	United Nations Security Council
WA	Western Australia

1 Resistance to state crime

Elizabeth Stanley and Jude McCulloch

In the middle of even the most grotesque of state crimes, such as genocide, there
are extraordinary tales of courage, rescuing and resistance. Acts of altruism, compassion and pro-social behaviour are woven into the social fabric.

(Cohen 1993: 113)

Within most criminology texts, 'the state' is ignored as an actor or represented as a
neutral force. This occurs despite the centrality of the state in crime and justice
issues, including the political acts of defining 'crime' and responding to those identified as 'criminals' or 'victims'. From the perspective of state crime scholars, the
state is also 'criminal'. Moreover, their research demonstrates that state crimes are
far more serious and harmful than other crimes. The capacity of state officials and
state institutions, particularly through the police and military, to kill, maim, exploit,
repress and cause widespread human suffering is unsurpassed.

Over recent years, state crime scholarship has become an increasingly active
area within criminology (see, for example, Barak 1991; the *British Journal of
Criminology* 2005 special edition; Chambliss *et al.* 2010; Friedrichs 1998; Green
and Ward 2004; Grewcock 2008; Kauzlarich and Kramer 2000; Pickering 2005;
Rothe 2009). State crime scholars have critiqued the state by challenging state-
centred definitions of crime. They have illustrated how perpetrators are 'made';
the way bystanders fail to intervene; the frequent disregard of victims; and the
way state violence is typically directed at the least powerful. They have refused
to accept victims of state crime as unworthy of compassion or as deserving of
harsh treatment, punishment or elimination, and have exposed the psychological,
social, cultural, bureaucratic and structural underpinnings of criminal states (see,
for example, Cohen 2001; Huggins 2010; Stanley 2009; Tombs and Whyte
2003). In this positioning, these analyses are imbued with a sense of resistance.
Nonetheless, resistance is underdeveloped and unanalysed as a fundamental
aspect of state crime scholarship (although, for some discussion, see Lasslett
2012; Pickering 2002; Stanley and McCulloch 2011; Ward and Green 2000).
Criminologists have generally failed to consciously consider a number of key
questions related to resistance, such as: how are state crimes contested, prevented, challenged or stopped?

On one level, state crime literature has helped to confront what Stanley Cohen (2001) terms 'denial'. Cohen's seminal work catalogues and describes the various strategies states use to justify, excuse or downplay involvement in atrocities. Naming the state as criminal and exposing the way that states work to hide or obscure state-perpetrated crimes challenges this denial. Cohen, however, is alive to numerous subtleties and the complex ways that observers or bystanders shut out confronting stories and distance themselves from taking action. People may fail to act against state crime because they are unable to conceive of any actions that might be effective. State crime scholarship, by highlighting the power and impunity of the state, without adequate attention to the ongoing history of resistance, paradoxically may consolidate state power by creating a sense of powerlessness, undermining people's confidence to act. The failure of state crime scholars to include resistance as a core aspect of the study of state crime may lead to feelings of despair, disinterest or impotence among students and other audiences and, flowing from this, states of mind that facilitate passivity, even in the face of irrefutable knowledge about state crimes.

A failure to engage with resistance is also a failure to acknowledge history 'from below'. People's struggles against power may, as Milan Kundera (1978: 3) puts it, be 'the struggle of memory against forgetting'. State power and impunity is always opposed in some way and by some people, and through these struggles history is made. In 2011, *Time Magazine* named 'The Protester' as 'Person of the Year'; with the rise of new technologies, protests have been relayed in real time and have inspired others around the world. Yet protest is, of course, not new. Many of the most inspiring and dramatic milestones in the course of human history have involved protests and other acts of resistance (see, for example, Roberts and Ash 2009). It is not only the dramatic and infamous that warrant attention, however. To understand state crime and resistance, criminologists need to include the study of the everyday harms and violence that are embedded within the fabric of society. Focusing on state crimes and resistance exclusively in the context of the foremost exemplars of state crime risks overlooking the pervasive state-perpetrated violence and harms that occur as normalized, hidden or denied aspects of society, including in democratic states.

With this in mind, this collection focuses on resistance to crimes ranging from gross violations, such as genocide, war crimes, mass killings, summary executions, torture, harsh detention and rape during war, through to entrenched discrimination, unjust social policies, border controls, corruption, fraud, resource plunder and the failure to provide the regulatory environment and principled leadership necessary to deal with global warming.

The following three chapters consider the role of criminologists in resistance practices. Friedrichs (Chapter 2) reflects on the revolutions of the 'Arab Spring' and considers the engagement of mainstream and critical criminologists in exposing state harm and violence. Following that, Green and Ward (Chapter 3) detail the importance of civil society as a counterweight to state crime, and the role of criminologists in researching how civil societies are built and maintained in contexts of widespread state violence. Kramer (Chapter 4) calls on criminologists to speak in the 'prophetic' voice about global warming and to work with global movements to confront the denial and normalization of carbon emissions and environmental harm.

The collection then progresses to present a number of case studies that analyse resistance in liberal democratic as well as repressive states. Grewcock (Chapter 5) reflects on the resistance of unauthorized migrants in Australian detention and illuminates how resistance persists in the face of alienation, criminalization and abuse in bleak conditions. Nadarajah and Sentas (Chapter 6) focus on Tamil resistance to Sri Lankan state crime and consider the complicated ways that identities and campaigns are formed and managed through resistance and repression. Stanley (Chapter 7) highlights how West Papuans have resisted Indonesian-led state–corporate crimes while affirming a space for cultural identity and survival in the face of destruction and violence. Cunneen (Chapter 8) explores Indigenous Australians' resistance to systematic state-sponsored fraud in the form of 'stolen wages', noting the consistent failure of governments to provide adequate redress. Pantazis and Pemberton (Chapter 9) detail how the counter-terrorism agenda of the United Kingdom (UK) has been challenged by frameworks of resistance that focus on human rights, freedom and the contestation of community criminalization. White (Chapter 10) considers the tactics and strategies employed by activists in response to environmental harm, as well as the conciliatory and confrontational countermeasures used by corporations and states to deny, disrupt, accommodate or incorporate resisters and their claims. Morrison (Chapter 11) examines the use of photography in witnessing the Holocaust and reflects on the necessity of visualization and empathy in retaining a humane approach to resistance. Kauzlarich (Chapter 12) considers the role of musicians in spreading knowledge about state crimes and supporting and building resistance among audiences in the United States (US).

The final four case studies examine the value of law as a resistance tool. McCulloch and Blair (Chapter 13) illustrate how radical lawyers, involved in the establishment of Community Legal Centres in Australia, have changed the culture of law in ways that enable it to be used as a protective force against state crimes. Pickering and Weber (Chapter 14) demonstrate the capacity of courts to provide a check against state violence and harm, such as the forced deportation of asylum seekers. Rothe (Chapter 15) argues that the development of international law and criminal justice including the 'responsibility to protect doctrine' serves an ideological as well as a control function in relation to state crime, impunity, and the protection of civilians. Michalowski (Chapter 16) reflects on the effectiveness of resistance, arguing that the 'master's tools', such as the courts and law, are incapable of bringing about meaningful change to the core economic, social and political conditions that give rise to state crime. The book concludes with a short chapter by McCulloch and Stanley, as we reconsider the position of intellectuals in relation to state crime and resistance, outlining what has been accomplished and what still needs to be done.

What is resistance in the context of state crime?

Resistance ranges from the small, silent and personal through to the multitud-inous, spectacular and momentous. The scope of activities that might be defined as resistance is broad (Pile 1997: 14; Urquhart 2011: 37). It may be violent or non-violent, passive or active, hidden or open, verbal or physical, spontaneous or strategic, local or global, and frequently a combination of some or all (Picker-ing 2002; White 2010). The contributors to this volume expose the breadth of resistance acts. These include riots, sit-ins, hunger strikes, self-harm, escapes from detention (Grewcock); marches, flag-raisings, armed guerrilla violence, tra-ditional songs, theatrical acts (Stanley); strikes, political lobbying (Cunneen); trespassing, eco-sabotage, petitions (White); art, photography (Morrison); music, radical fashion, occupations (Kauzlarich); self-immolation, suicide, revolutions (Friedrichs); court cases (Pantazis and Pemberton; Pickering and Weber); adop-tion of human rights laws and policies (Pantazis and Pemberton; Rothe); legal representation, creative legal information, street theatre (McCulloch and Blair); Internet campaigns, strategic networking, street demonstrations (Nadarajah and Sentas); mass social movements (Michalowski); and research and education (Green and Ward; Kramer).

In its focus on the nature and dynamics of resistance, this collection extends state crime scholarship, beyond illustrating and reflecting upon the destructive power of the state or the experience of victimization, towards recognition of the power of people to challenge state impunity through acknowledgement, account-ability, redress and prevention. The contributions are designed to provide insight and inspiration without underplaying the enormous challenges and difficulties. The contingent nature of 'successful' resistance is acknowledged, as is the heavy toll it often takes on individuals and communities. There are no easy lessons. History does not repeat itself, although injustice does. Each struggle against state crime is unique and each generation finds new ways to resist. Rapid changes in technology have provided new tools for resistance, exemplified in the 'Facebook revolts' of the Arab Spring (Friedrichs), the use of WikiLeaks to counter state secrecy (Green and Ward) and the role of the Internet in enabling communica-tions among, and the mobilization of, global audiences (Stanley; White). While younger generations can draw upon the experience of those who went before, states and institutions also learn, developing new ways to deny events or to co-opt people and struggles. Tactics, tools and strategies that worked at one time will not necessarily have the same impact when used again (McCulloch and Blair).

What are the criteria for resistance?

The context of resistance to state crime changes not only from place to place but also over time: states differ; socio-cultural understandings of state violence and harms vary; new tools and technologies emerge to victimize, incapacitate or enable people; networks, courts and laws develop to counter as well as facilitate denial and impunity, and so on. Yet the fundamentals remain the same. We identify four essential elements of resistance: opposition, intention, communication and transformation.

Opposition is a central element of resistance. Resistance to state crime may oppose a regime, an economic system, or particular practices, cultures, laws or events that are perceived as unjust, harmful or damaging. Some contend that the word 'resistance' should be reserved only for acts that constitute opposition to something. For instance, Abowitz (2000) contrasts acts that are an *assertion of* something with acts that are a *resistance to* something. In considering resistance to state crime, we argue that it should include assertive or creative acts. That is, opposition linked to resistance is not simply critique as it can also be productive or creative. Resistance can be about *becoming* or *creating* something – it may produce alternatives for harmful products or processes, such as the development of new energies to combat global warming; it may reinvigorate traditions or affirm values, such as cultural identity, integrity or a sense of self (Bargh 2007; Blagg 2008); it can invoke a competing claim of universalism or attempt to set the boundaries of a 'viable' or 'liveable' life (Butler 2000). Alternatives can be imagined, embodied or produced.

For some, resistance allows new forms of subjectivity to emerge beyond those constructed by the state (see Foucault 1982; cf. Pickett 1996). While the state may be viewed, in an Althusserian sense, as the 'site and stake' of struggles, some groups or individuals seek to move beyond the state. In this regard, it is crucial to understand that, as a result of the cultural, social and political shifts of history, divergent meanings attach to state institutions. In addition, some groups hold 'radically incommensurate interpretations' of past experiences (Blagg 2008: 47). Living according to values that have historical, social, cultural and personal resonance may, according to our definition, be resistance; however, for those living by these values, it may be simply living an appropriate life or even just living. For some, to survive – culturally, psychologically or even biologically – may require acts of everyday resistance.

Intention is another central part of resistance. Resistance is opposition with social, moral or political intent (Abowitz 2000). Intention, even if not directly articulated, is crucial. Without it, any act 'against the state' – from opportunistic rioting to tax evasion – could be labelled resistance. We argue that, to be defined as resistance, an 'event' (or an omission) requires some level of consciousness or human agency. In resisting, people act on their conscience and put themselves 'on the line'. Thus, intention reframes mere opposition into morally and politically meaningful acts (Giroux 1983: 106–11).

The third essential element of resistance is that it is a form of communication. Communicating, or sending messages, about state crime is a means to challenge denial and state control over information. Yet resistant communications cover a spectrum from spectacular and obvious, to ignored, hidden and nascent. While some messages are overt – written on placards or unambiguous statements to dominant powers or bystanders – the communicatory nature of resistance may not always be clear. At times, quiet or personal acts of resistance may not be acknowledged or 'read', although they are nonetheless forms of resistance.

Finally, the fourth element of resistance is transformation. Resistance is bound up with the ways in which people understand their capacity to make or oppose changes (Pile 1997). It might take the form of overthrowing a regime; holding the state accountable for its actions; challenging the state's claim to truth; changing the socio-legal landscape to amend unjust laws or provide access to law; 'answering back' to colonizing norms and values; reasserting positive values of care or dignity in society; changing the practices and values of state workers; or presenting individuals with an opportunity to take action and move beyond powerlessness. For resistance to occur, people must have some (even small) sense of agency or hope that things could be different.

What constitutes effective resistance?

The state, despite its destructive power, is not monolithic. Rather, given its institutions and intersecting processes, it has contradictory roles (Michalowski; White). Modern states are intensely complicated, so much so that it is difficult to live beyond the state (Hillyard and Percy Smith 1988). In addition, states are continually entwined with 'social formations that exist in either supportive or oppositional reaction to the state' (Michalowski 2010: 25). That is, while states may be repressive or violent, it 'is also a site (or series of sites) where claims for social justice and "progressive" politics are forged, fought over, resisted and sometimes implemented' (Coleman *et al.* 2009: 14; cf. Scraton 1987). In this respect, the state, state crime and resistance can all be viewed as interlinked processes, rather than as a series of discrete institutions or events.

At the same time, state crimes and resistance to them are facilitated through networks of relationships. For example, as many of the chapters in this volume attest, those who seek to resist state crimes must engage with multiple targets as crimes frequently involve corporations, international financial institutions, the United Nations, militias and other bodies. Strategies need to be multifaceted to take into account these different targets and relationships that are neither static nor impregnable (White). Moreover, resistant messages need to be heard, understood and acted upon by 'bystanders'. Given the powerlessness of individuals relative to state power, resistance is often seen to be most effective when it resonates with a community of resisters who have shared experiences, and who can support and act with each other (Scott 1990; Sivanandan 1990). At certain junctures, the constellation of relationships and interests may be such that resistance becomes more possible or more effective.

As all of the chapters herein demonstrate, many resistance strategies mobilize a movement of concerned others to achieve shared goals. The reformation of criminal states requires an organized civil society – including human rights organizations, religious bodies, trade unions – that can develop coalitions (Green and Ward; Pantazis and Pemberton). Sometimes effective resistance is tied to celebrated leaders who have the capacity to build collective, unified strategies and inspire many to participate. In other circumstances, people are mobilized in the wake of spectacular or shocking events; for instance, the self-immolation of one man in Tunisia sparked revolts across the North of Africa (Friedrichs). Mobilization can occur in the context of intense repression, surveillance and intimidation (Stanley; Grewcock). It can also emerge in conditions where state power is largely legitimate. For example, the production of articulate workers through liberal education can lead to a situation in which states are faced with organized criticisms, sometimes on an international level. The multiple interests, and contradictory relations, of states mean that states produce potential resisters at the same time as they aim to repress, quell or placate them.

In the contemporary context, resisters also often need to recognize and articulate the local and global connections that underpin many state crimes and facilitate resistance. The effectiveness of resistance may be tied to how state crimes are understood as part of a process that has national or international impacts, and how allies can be generated across the globe in ways that work to recognize a shared humanity, resources and environment (White). Increasingly, resisters do not only deal with narrow state interests but also contest fundamental problems within global structural relations of power.

Despite the desirability of collective action and the aim of changing state behaviour, it is too narrow a frame to consider effective resistance only as collective actions or in terms of that which impacts discernibly on the state. Effective resistance can grow unnoticed from a whole range of small, quiet 'unsuccessful' actions carried out by unknown individuals or small numbers of people (Stanley and McCulloch 2011). Resistance may operate as a type of 'off-stage dissent' (Scott 1990), particularly when it is too dangerous to make open claims or demands. In these circumstances, people may engage in actions that create a 'hidden transcript' (Scott 1990) made up of simple acts – such as lighting a candle to remember someone killed by state forces or marking a place of state atrocity with a stone. These acts may be done in secret without an immediate audience, yet they demonstrate an intention to oppose, communicate and transform within contexts of limited power. While (deliberately) difficult for those not directly involved to comprehend, these acts may work to keep the spirit of resistance alive.

What might be deemed effective resistance thus varies and depends 'very much upon the immediate political struggles and social contexts' (White 2010: 50), although some research suggests that non-violent resistance is successful more often than armed campaigns (Stephan and Chenoweth 2008; also see Stanley). Effective resistance is difficult to measure. What may initially be regarded as positive advances or real 'victories' can turn out to be pyrrhic or temporary or to have unintended or unforeseen consequences. Resistance strategies raise 'moral conundrums' (Friedrichs) and, despite altruistic intentions, may adversely impact on people who have few choices and little power. State crime may prove resilient, re-emerging in altered forms as social, political, legal and cultural landscapes shift (Stanley and McCulloch 2011). Indeed, state crimes that may be viewed as having ended may continue in different forms. Slavery, for example, is regularly regarded as a historical phenomenon but it continues unabated in contemporary forms of forced labour, debt bondage, child labour or trafficking (Bales 2004). Contemporary slavery continues to affect millions of people, yet often goes 'unseen', as it functions as part of an advanced global capitalist system in which labour is outsourced and traded across corporate and contractor networks. In many cases, the impacts of historical slavery remain, as states fail to compensate for unpaid and underpaid labour based on racially discriminatory practices (Cunneen). Slavery and its attendant colonial systems have also changed to fit the demands of contemporary conditions, such that the differential policing and mass incarceration of minority populations within liberal democracies such as Australia, New Zealand, the US and the UK have been made socially acceptable (Stanley and McCulloch 2011). In these instances, it is impossible to argue that substantive equality has been achieved. Instead, the progressive eradication of the slave trade from the eighteenth century and an end to formal racial discrimination have been replaced by new forms of economic, political and social control and servitude.

Nonetheless, resistance is not a win or lose activity; 'losses' can be just as important as 'wins'. Progress can be achieved in the face of apparent failure. Resistance is sometimes (re)invigorated through adversity. Even where resistance is thought to have failed, it may succeed 'to influence, mitigate or even constrain state policies and actions related to state crime' (Friedrichs 2010: 9). While changes may often not meet aspirations, they can still challenge state policies and actions. In addition, the lessons learnt through 'unsuccessful' campaigns may form the foundation for future 'success'. The timeframe for assessing the effectiveness of resistance is impossible to set. Changes can occur incrementally over decades (Rothe).

Resistance to state crime therefore requires a long-term strategy. Time and time again, people have shown great resilience in these endeavours. Cunneen's chapter documents Indigenous Australians' campaigns over 'stolen wages' across many decades. Similarly, the West Papuans and the Tamils in Sri Lanka have been engaged in self-determination struggles for over four and three decades, respectively (Stanley; Nadarajah and Sentas). Of course, the state is also resilient and is likewise able to reconstitute itself to absorb challenges while maintaining core structural forces. Yet this is not a *fait accompli* – the state is not coherent or unified; power relations are incomplete, fluid, inconsistent, awkward, ambiguous and liable to rupture.

The dynamic of state crime and resistance

State crime and subsequent resistance 'cannot be understood as cause and effect, but as mutually bound and intimate relations of action and counteraction' (Nadarajah and Sentas) that might be seen as a 'tactical and strategic dance' (White). These actions are simultaneously destructive and productive or generative – creating new hybrid subjectivities that engender resistance and counter-resistance anew (Nadarajah and Sentas). The relationship between states and resisters is a complex one, where the boundaries between action and counteraction, cause and effect, are sometimes difficult to discern.

Foucault (1981) argued that resistance and the subjects who resist are fundamentally implicated in the power relations that they oppose. He argued that power is an infinite force that characterizes all human transactions. For him, power is inherent in *all* relationships, and multiple sites of power are continually open to reformulation, change and redistribution. Thus, resistance is not opposed to power. Instead, '[w]here there is power, there is resistance, and yet, or rather consequently, this resistance is never in a position of exteriority in relation to power' (Foucault 1981: 95; cf. Foucault 1982). In this regard, resistance is created by and reactive to power. The question of whether resistance can be undertaken in ways that do not implicate resisters in the system they are trying to oppose is contested, as is whether resistance to state crime can be effectively undertaken using strategies that involve state institutions and norms (Pickett 1996; Mills 2000).

Some argue that the 'master's house' cannot be dismantled with the 'master's tools' (Michalowski). While these tools may restrain state crimes, they cannot dismantle the system from which such crimes emerge. According to this argument, effectively contesting state crime requires strategies that go beyond the apparatus of the state to challenge the conditions that facilitate state crime. Still, others argue that the institutions and processes of state power, such as law, are malleable and can be used in different and even contradictory ways (White; McCulloch and Blair). While law frequently fails to restrain state crime and often provides legitimacy for human rights violations, it can also provide protection and redress for victims or prevent some state crimes from occurring (McCulloch and Blair; Pantazis and Pemberton; Pickering and Weber; Rothe). Legal processes may change the boundaries of debate or invigorate further forms of resistance. There are, however, limits to such protection and the durability of gains are questionable as states manoeuvre to overcome any limits to their powers.

These competing claims about the potential of various types of resistant strategies to achieve substantive and long-term change are difficult to assess given that what can be defined as effective resistance remains ambiguous and that 'outcomes' may change or be seen differently over time. What might appear to be a progressive state response to resistance strategies may turn out to be merely symbolic (Pickett 1996), or an opportunity for the state to strengthen its legitimacy through the pretext of consent, in that the state (and state actors) can appear to have been effectively challenged or 'talked back to' without any substantive change having taken place (Coleman *et al.* 2009: 15). Claims can be managed, contained or made polite and civilized. Where states move to accommodate and incorporate resisters, the solidarity of resistance movements will frequently come under challenge as people reach different conclusions about the meaning of state actions or the need for continued resistance. Those who continue their opposition are likely to be labelled extremists and the solidarity required to effectively oppose state crimes can be diminished (Pickett 1996).

Using state institutions like the courts to oppose state crime can simultaneously confirm the institutional basis of the state and reinforce the parameters of 'the law', as well as dominant ideologies that states are 'good', protective and democratic (Agamben 1998; McEvoy 2008). Furthermore, resisters continually reiterate power through the act of resistance because the terms of resistance are established and bounded by the powers that are being opposed (Butler 1997). The language used by resisters can merely reassert state principles or be readily subject to appropriation. For instance, building a critique of a state for not living up to certain principles – such as human rights – is an acceptance and potential strengthening not only of those principles but also of the state power behind them (Pickett 1996). Such a route can also be a means for Western states and their resisters to embed power and impose their own norms onto other states and cultures (Green and Ward; cf. Rothe). Similarly, resistance discourses can be reappropriated by bystanders for their own ends – the images and stories of resistance can be drafted onto hip clothing, books and Internet sites, earning their 'sellers' status or money at the expense of those who have been victimized by state crime.

The repercussions of resistance

The direction and consequences of resistance are unpredictable (Friedrichs). While resisters will have ideal objectives, these are set against the social, political and economic realities that impede their realization (Friedrichs; Kramer; White). For example, states will respond to resisters in a host of ways, such as by ignoring them and their claims; downplaying the extent of resistance or the gravity of state crimes; denigrating them and claiming to be the real victim; stifling dissent through propaganda, media 'spin' or threats; co-opting or dividing them; or engaging in litigation against them.

Resisters must contend with the possibility that the state response will initiate or escalate new forms of state crime. Resistance always risks embedding the power of states by emboldening them to pursue savage measures, or providing states with an opportunity to enhance their institutions, discourses and status. Further, state institutions may move to pre-empt the possibility of resistance as well as the identities of resisters. This pre-emption can have a devastating impact on individuals and communities. Justified on the basis of risk prevention, whole groups of people can be targeted as criminals, terrorists, illegal immigrants, subversives or rebel fighters. Beyond direct attacks against resisters, such as death, torture, sexual violence, incarceration or abuse (Cunneen; Grewcock; Stanley), states can also engage in spatial exclusion – expressed through 'no go zones', reservations, exclusion orders against individuals at sites of potential protest, or cyber-censorship and the removal of access to electronic communications. States have at their disposal multiple surveillance and weapon technologies that can be used to devastating effect against protesters and activists.

Faced with such consequences, it might seem surprising that people continue to resist. However, for some, the consequences of not resisting are simply too great. Experience also shows that repressive state responses can solidify resistance movements, encouraging more people to participate (McCulloch and Blair; Stanley). Even though the odds can be stacked against resisters, they understand that their challenge to state practices might bring incremental 'wins', such as a lessening in violence, the recognition of victims, progressive legislation or regulations, prosecutions, reparations, and so on.

Besides, in the midst of their struggles, resisters can experience a sense of justice, honesty and solidarity that they have not experienced elsewhere. In their recognition of suffering, and stance to preserve the future for generations to come, resisters reassert their commitment to the lives of others. This is a route for transformation – it can mean that resisters change their lives through their consumption patterns and levels, civil relationships, media attention or political involvement. Through these seemingly individual processes, resisters propel visions and practices of how societies can be 'alternatively structured' and 'how human relationships might be alternatively organized' to nurture more humane conditions (Mathiesen, cited in Scraton 1987: 38). After all, if terror and violence are an intrinsic part of the state, as some argue, then humanity is an intrinsic part of resistance.

References

Abowitz, K. (2000) 'A Pragmatist Revisioning of Resistance Theory', *American Educational Research Journal*, 37(4), 877–907.

Agamben, G. (1998) *Homo Sacer: Sovereign Power and Bare Life* (trans. D. Heller-Roazen), Stanford: Stanford University Press.

Bales, K. (2004) *Disposable People: New Slavery in the Global Economy*, Berkeley: University of California Press.

Barak, G. (ed.) (1991) *Crimes by the Capitalist State*, New York: State University of New York Press.

Bargh, M. (2007) 'Introduction', in M. Bargh (ed.), *Resistance: An Indigenous Response to Neoliberalism*, Wellington: Huia Press.

Blagg, H. (2008) *Crime, Aboriginality and the Decolonisation of Justice*, Sydney: Hawkins Press.

Butler, J. (1997) *The Psychic Life of Power: Theories in Subjection*, Stanford: Stanford University Press.

Butler, J. (2000) 'Competing Universalities', in J. Butler, E. Laclau and S. Zizek (eds), *Contingency, Hegemony, Universality*, London: Verso.

Chambliss, W., Michalowski, R. and Kramer, R. (eds) (2010) *State Crime in the Global Age*, Cullompton: Willan.

Cohen, S. (1993) 'Human Rights and Crimes of the State: The Culture of Denial', *Australian and New Zealand Journal of Criminology*, 26(2), 97–115.

Cohen, S. (2001) *States of Denial: Knowing about Atrocities and Suffering*, Cambridge: Polity.

Coleman, R., Sim, J., Tombs, S. and Whyte, D. (2009) 'Introduction: State, Power, Crime', in R. Coleman, J. Sim, S. Tombs and D. Whyte (eds), *State, Power, Crime*, London: Sage.

Foucault, M. (1981) *The History of Sexuality, Vol 1: An Introduction*, (trans. R. Hurley), London: Penguin.

Foucault, M. (1982) 'The Subject and Power', in H. Dreyfus and P. Rabinow (eds), *Michel Foucault: Beyond Structuralism and Hermeneutics*, Chicago: Chicago University Press.

Friedrichs, D. (ed.) (1998) *State Crime*, London: Ashgate.

Friedrichs, D. (2010) 'On Resisting State Crime: Conceptual and Contextual Issues', *Social Justice*, 36(3), 4–27.

Giroux, H. (1983) *Theory and Resistance in Education: A Pedagogy for the Opposition*, London: Heinemann.

Green, P. and Ward, T. (2004) *State Crime*, London: Pluto Press.

Grewcock, M. (2008) 'State Crime: Some Conceptual Issues', in T. Anthony and C. Cunneen (eds), *The Critical Criminology Companion*, Sydney: Hawkins Press.

Hillyard, P. and Percy Smith, J. (1988) *The Coercive State*, London: Fontana/Collins.

Huggins, M. (2010) 'Modern Institutionalized Torture as State-Organized Crime', in W. Chambliss, R. Michalowski and R. Kramer (eds), *State Crime in the Global Age*, Cullompton: Willan.

Kauzlarich, D. and Kramer, R. (2000) *Crimes of the American Nuclear State at Home and Abroad*, Boston: Northeastern University Press.

Kundera, M. (1978) *The Book of Laughter and Forgetting*, London: Faber and Faber.

Lasslett, K. (2012) 'Power, Struggle and State Crime: Researching through Resistance', *State Crime*, 1(1), 126–48.

McEvoy, K. (2008) 'Letting Go of Legalism', in K. McEvoy and L. McGregor (eds), *Transitional Justice from Below: Grassroots Activism and the Struggle for Change*, Oxford: Hart Publishing.

Michalowski, R. (2010) 'In Search of "State" and "Crime" in State Crime Studies', in W. Chambliss, R. Michalowski and R. Kramer (eds), *State Crime in the Global Age*, Cullompton: Willan.

Mills, C. (2000) 'Efficacy and Vulnerability: Judith Butler on Reiteration and Resistance', *Australian Feminist Studies*, 15(32), 265–79.

Pickering, S. (2002) *Women, Policing and Resistance in Northern Ireland*, Belfast: Beyond the Pale.

Pickering, S. (2005) *Refugees and State Crime*, Sydney: Federation Press.

Pickett, B. (1996) 'Foucault and the Politics of Resistance', *Polity*, 28(4), 445–66.

Pile, S. (1997) 'Introduction', in S. Pile and M. Keith (eds), *Geographies of Resistance*, London: Routledge.

Roberts, A. and Ash, T. (2009) *Civil Resistance and Power Politics: The Experiences of Non-violent Action from Gandhi to the Present*, Oxford: Oxford University Press.

Rothe, D. (2009) *State Criminality*, Lanham: Lexington Books.

Scott, J. (1990) *Domination and the Arts of Resistance: Hidden Transcripts*, New Haven: Yale University Press.

Scraton, P. (1987) 'Introduction: Crime, the State and Critical Analysis', in P. Scraton (ed.), *Law, Order and the Authoritarian State*, Milton Keynes: Open University Press.

Sivanandan, A. (1990) *Communities of Resistance: Writings on Black Struggles for Socialism*, London: Verso.

Stanley, E. (2009) *Torture, Truth and Justice: The Case of Timor-Leste*, London: Routledge.

Stanley, E. and McCulloch, J. (2011) 'State Crime and Resistance', *International State Crime Initiative*, available at http://statecrime.org/online_article/state-crime-and-resistance.

Stephan, M. and Chenoweth, E. (2008) 'Why Civil Resistance Works: The Strategic Logic of Nonviolent Conflict', *International Security*, 33(1), 7–44.

Tombs, S. and Whyte, D. (2003) 'Scrutinizing the Powerful: Crime, Contemporary Political Economy, and Critical Social Research', in S. Tombs and D. Whyte (eds), *Unmasking the Crimes of the Powerful*, New York: Peter Lang.

Urquhart, B. (2011) 'Revolution without Violence?', *New York Review of Books*, LVIII, 37–40.

Ward, T. and Green, P. (2000) 'Legitimacy, Civil Society and State Crime', *Social Justice*, 27(4), 76–93.

White, R. (2010) 'Environmental Victims and Resistance to State Crime through Transnational Activism', *Social Justice*, 36(3), 46–60.

2 Resisting state crime as a criminological project in the context of the Arab Spring

David O. Friedrichs[1]

Preface: resisting state crime in the context of the Arab Spring

State crime and resistance is an unorthodox topic for criminologists on several levels: first, in focusing on state crime instead of conventional crime; second, in implicitly calling for activist engagement instead of professional detachment; and third, in highlighting the complex relationship between past, present and future. However, my own engagement with the topic is driven by the conviction that it is both an immensely consequential topic and one to which criminologists have something worthwhile to contribute.

An invitation from Elizabeth Stanley in early 2009 to participate in a State Crime and Resistance Symposium at Victoria University of Wellington, New Zealand, in January 2010, prompted my interest in the topic at hand. My paper 'On Resisting State Crime: Conceptual and Contextual Issues' (later published in Friedrichs 2010) was chosen as the opening paper for the symposium, perhaps because it addressed some of the foundational questions underlying any criminological exploration of this subject. The invitation to contribute to this book, also arising out of the symposium, presented an opportunity to explore some further dimensions of the topic. Since the conceptual issues are very ably addressed in the introduction to this book, those issues are not further addressed here. Yet it should be acknowledged that the present chapter is written in a new international political context.

The criminologists who met in Wellington could hardly anticipate that, only a year later (from January 2011), an outbreak of uprisings in a large number of North African and Middle Eastern countries would occur. Even scholars who specialize in the Middle East did not anticipate the 'Arab Spring' of uprisings. The 'sclerotic, illegitimate, and brutal governments' (Byman 2011: B9) in these Middle Eastern countries have endured – and in some cases (for example, Saudi Arabia) continue to endure – due to a combination of factors, especially the vast oil revenues available to these regimes, strong intelligence and military forces funded by these revenues and ongoing foreign support (from the United States [US], among other countries) with addressing security concerns in the region. The weak civil society and democratic traditions and low literacy rates in this part of the world may also have played a role. In those countries in which auto-crats have the means to buy off key supporters, and which have a restive general population, the autocrats are most likely to be able to maintain their hold on power; 'new, decrepit and bankrupt leaders' are most vulnerable to being overthrown (Bueno de Mesquita and Smith 2011). However, the upris-ings are a reminder of the ultimate unpredictability of history. We have recently commemorated the twentieth anniversary of the fall of the Soviet Union, which was hardly anticipated in 1991, and many other such examples could be given (Aron 2011). Beyond the failure to anticipate these historical events, another sobering lesson of the past is that the ultimate course and consequences of such 'revolutions' is unpredictable. There is a long history of events, celebrated in some quarters as liberating, setting the stage for mass violence, fundamental denials and violations of basic human rights and state crimes on a monumental scale: the French Revolution, through to the Russian Bolshevik and Chinese Communist revolutions, and the overthrowing of the Shah in Iran are all promi-nent historical examples. In the case of the fall of the Soviet Union, many of its former republics, including Azerbaijan, Belarus, Kazakhstan, Tajikistan, Turk-menistan and Uzbekistan, are today ruled by autocrats, and Russia itself is no model democracy (Levy 2011). All of this should be borne in mind in relation to present developments unfolding in the Middle East. Yet there is still another, potentially encouraging lesson to be taken from the Middle East uprisings of 2011: they have been characterized, among other labels, as the 'Facebook revolt' (Amar 2011). The Internet played a key role in the swiftness with which young people in particular were mobilized in relation to the uprising. In Egypt, it was estimated that a staggering 20 per cent of the population – or some 15 million people – participated directly in the mass demonstrations and mobiliza-tions that brought down the regime. Those involved represented a broad swathe of the population, going far beyond, but possibly inspired by, the young protest-ers who were initially connected on social websites. Of course, such rapid mobilization need not ultimately be undertaken to advance democratic and freedom-enhancing objectives. In an earlier historical context, the mass media (with radio as a new element) played some role in the rapid rise and dominance of the Nazis.

The Middle East uprisings – in Tunisia, Egypt, Libya, Yemen, Bahrain, Syria and Morocco – can be characterized as collective forms of 'resistance' to ongoing state crimes, including severe repressiveness, massive corruption and grossly unresponsive or stagnant social policies. The severe repressiveness has included brutal military police action against protesters – firing upon and killing large numbers of them – and the imprisonment and torture of dissidents. The massive corruption has involved the grand theft of billions of dollars (in equiva-lent currency) of the collective wealth of countries in which huge sectors of the population live in circumstances of desperate poverty. The grossly unresponsive and stagnant social policies include the failure to provide appropriate levels of economic development, leading to extremely high rates of unemployment (including for well-educated young people), with the policies skewed to the interests of a small, wealthy and closely interconnected political and business elite. Overall, there is a broad perception of a system not serving the interests of the people. The distinguished political scientist Richard Wolin (2011: B8) concisely sums up these issues:

> The basic message of these revolts is that government must no longer exist for the sake of the ruling elites. It must exist for the benefit of all people to whom it must also be held legally and politically responsible.

In 2011, we also witnessed the unanticipated circumstance of former Egyptian president Muhammad Hosni El Sayed Mubarak, some of his cronies and his sons being held in prison to stand charges for crimes against the Egyptian people; the International Criminal Court formally charging the now late Libyan leader Moammar Qaddafi with crimes against humanity; and a Tunisian court sentencing former president Ben Ali and his wife – in absentia – to 35 years in prison for the embezzlement of over US$60 million of public funds (Amar 2011; Kirkpatrick 2011; Simons 2011). The formal charges inevitably reflect only a small fraction of the state crimes actually committed, over a long period of time. The Ben Ali family, for example, is believed to have stolen billions of dollars from the treasury of a country where some 30 per cent of young people are unemployed (Goldberg 2011). In all of these countries, in varying degrees, those who dissented, protested or 'resisted' the state were subjected to state violence over the course of a long period of time.

Altogether, the 'Arab Spring' brings into sharp relief some of the inherent conundrums involved in resisting – or addressing – the crimes of states, including: the tensions between the ideal objectives of those participating in the uprising and on-the-ground political and economic realities impeding the realization of these objectives; the conflict between Western countries' professed support for democracy and human rights and their ongoing support for autocrats engaged in a range of state crimes against their own people; the moral conundrums involved in 'humanitarian interventions', such as the North Atlantic Treaty Organization air attacks on Qaddafi's forces in Libya, in terms of collateral damage and unanticipated consequences; and the uncertain historical trajectory in the wake of such uprisings and revolutions.

The 'Arab Spring' can be framed in specifically criminological terms. The initial inspiration for the first mass protests and ultimate uprising in Tunisia in January 2011 was a singular, dramatic act of 'resistance': a young Tunisian, Mohamed Bouazizi, trying to eke out a living and support his family as a fruit seller, found himself once again contending with a corrupt municipal inspector, authorized to 'police' the activities of such vendors, who cursed (and by some accounts slapped) him and confiscated his scale (according to some, in lieu of a standard bribe) (Coll 2011; Rodenbeck 2011). Bouazizi purchased a can of gasoline, walked to his town's main square and set himself on fire; he died in a hospital 18 days later. This act of self-immolation seems to have 'ignited' the smoldering rage of many of his disenfranchised and disillusioned fellow

Tunisian citizens, leading to a mass uprising and some weeks later their autocratic and corrupt president fleeing the country. In Tunisia and across the Middle East, the autocrats initially characterized the protests and uprisings as the work of 'criminals' (and terrorists), whose activities had to be suppressed in the name of law and order, and societal stability. Military and policing forces were called in for this purpose. The 'policing' response ultimately failed in some countries, although it was at least temporarily successful in others. In some countries, the fact that many police officers and soldiers joined forces with the protesters played a role. At the outset of 2012, much remained unsettled on the ultimate outcome of the Arab Spring uprisings. In Egypt, there was considerable discontent that the military seemed to be consolidating its power rather than moving the country in the direction of authentic democratic and economic reforms, as called for by the Tahrir Square protest demonstrations. In an increasingly isolated Syria, following months of brutal repression against protesters, with many thousands killed, President Bashar Hafez al-Assad was still taking a hard line against 'outsiders' and 'terrorists', as he labelled the protesters. It also remained to be seen whether the Occupy Wall Street protests in the US and elsewhere – inspiring 'Occupy' encampments in many different settings – were the beginnings of a major challenge to the corrupt economic privileges and political dominance of the 'one per cent'. In all of these countries, recognition of the crimes of states – on behalf of political and economic elites – seemed to be growing.

The foregoing discussion of the unfolding (far from settled) developments in Arab countries in North Africa and the Middle East is intended as a reminder of the potent force of resistance to state crime, how swiftly and suddenly it can be mobilized, and the centrality of the role of both crime and policing in such events. Of course it is still too early to determine whether in the long term the events of the Arab Spring will serve as a foundation for more or less state crime in the region. Iran is a case alluded to earlier, specifically in the Middle East, where resistance began as a revolutionary uprising against an autocrat, but did not play out very well. The Shah of Iran was overthrown in 1979, leading to the establishment of a religious dictatorship that killed and tortured thousands of Iranians and is now brutally suppressing the resistance that opposes it. On the other hand, there is the case of South Africa: the anti-Apartheid movement played a key role in bringing about a generally peaceful transition in 1991 to a democratic, albeit flawed, state (afflicted with pervasive corruption and a failure to address economic inequality in a fundamental way), but on balance the locus of a broader respect for human rights. However, it also remains to be seen whether the wave of resistance to state crime across the Middle East and North Africa would inspire parallel uprisings in countries in sub-Saharan Africa (Githongo 2011). Inequalities in terms of wealth and poverty and gross forms of abuse of power and corruption are, if anything, even more extreme in many of these countries (Mullins and Rothe 2008). It is an especially discouraging historical story that these African states arose out of independence movements that overthrew exploitative colonial regimes.

Resisting state crime and the human future

> [Louis Proal's *Political Crime* (1898)] is a starting point for the development of a branch of criminology that is still almost barren, but in which the desperate necessity for more serious work, if we are to save the world from chaos if not disaster, becomes every day more apparent.
>
> (Edward Sagarin 1973: xvi)

> Louis Proal's *Political Crime* (1898) is noteworthy because this type of crime has never received the attention it should.
>
> (David O. Friedrichs 1974: 724)

In 1898, the celebrated novelist and science fiction pioneer H. G. Wells published *The War of the Worlds*. In this novel, Wells envisions a war culminating in the destruction of a large city, with its inhabitants exterminated by the invaders. Wells correctly anticipated that a terrible war and the systematic obliteration of many human beings was part of our human future, but the ruthless warmongers of his novel were Martians, not human inhabitants of planet Earth. In the same year, an English translation of a book entitled *Political Crime*, by French judge Louis Proal (1898), was published. Although this English translation featured an 'Introduction' by a prominent American sociologist, Franklin H. Giddings of Columbia University, there is no evidence that it made any impression on the early American (or British) students of crime during that era, or subsequently. Proal's work was naive and arguably flawed on various counts, but he recognized the great significance of crime that occurs in the political context and of the crimes of powerful, corrupt and hypocritical political leaders. Proal specifically addressed crimes perpetrated by governments for alleged state-based rationales, as well as by politicians for their own pecuniary or political advantage. He also addressed political assassinations and anarchism, and political crimes committed by those without political power. His call for a political world based upon universal ethical and moral principles, free of hatred, violent conflict and corruption, could be regarded as utopian.

Surely neither Wells nor Proal could have anticipated the vast scope of the horrors that occurred during the course of the twentieth century, in relation to war, extermination (or genocide) and political crime, broadly defined. If the early students of crime during this era seem to have largely ignored Proal's book, it was the work of another European, the Italian physician Cesare Lombroso, that attracted a substantial amount of attention (Knepper 2010). Although Lombroso's specific notion of the 'born criminal' was largely repudiated, his positivistic approach and focus on explaining the sources of the behaviour of conventional criminal offenders was highly influential. One might ask: what if it had been the other way around and it was Proal's perspective on crime that had the major influence on the development of criminology? Could criminology have then contributed constructively to anticipating, explaining and – ideally – generating strategies for containing or controlling some of the monumental crimes of states that occurred throughout the twentieth century? If criminology largely 'missed the boat' on this project for the twentieth century, can it not still get on board for the twenty-first century?

What is criminology?

It may seem remarkable that a major anthology, published by Oxford University Press in 2011, has as its title *What is Criminology?* (Bosworth and Hoyle 2011). After all, criminology as a recognizable entity within the academic firmament has been in existence for a century or so, with seminal inspiration going back to the eighteenth century, and more fundamental initiatives emerging during the course of the nineteenth century (Knepper 2010). However, as the editors of that volume contend, despite the fact that criminology is 'booming' as measured by majors, programmes, journals, books and the like, there are ongoing debates around the questions, 'What is criminology for?' and 'How should criminology be done?' (Bosworth and Hoyle 2011: 4–5). In the 'Foreword' to the volume, John Braithwaite (2011: ix) notes that '[a]n American mentor once described the pages of *Criminology* as applying progressively greater rigour to ever more trivial questions'. This observation about a leading American journal gets to the core of a long-standing concern that critical criminologists – particularly those who focus on state crime – have with the 'mainstream' of the discipline. Further on in *What is Criminology?*, Braithwaite's current work on peacebuilding is addressed, but here he makes another observation that provides a central point of departure for the present chapter: 'it surprises me how very useful criminological theory so often proves in the study of peacebuilding' (Braithwaite 2011: x). In sum, despite the immense challenges of bringing 'rigour' to the study of the crimes of states, criminologists should engage with the decidedly non-trivial questions pertaining to resisting state crime. Yet in doing so, I argue, we can potentially make an especially useful (and unique) contribution by bringing to bear upon these questions knowledge drawn from criminological theory and research. Braithwaite (2011: viii) makes another observation – that contributing authors seem to acknowledge that criminology needs to 'take debates about social justice seriously' – which is a core concern of criminological students of resistance to state crime. State crime is a quintessential source of social injustice, broadly defined, but the optimal strategies for addressing it also generate complex conundrums in relation to the promotion of justice.

In their concluding contribution to *What is Criminology?*, the editors Carolyn Hoyle and Mary Bosworth (2011: 531) adopt the notion of 'crossing borders' as a unifying theme of their volume and make the following germane observation:

> In traversing ideological, political, geographical and disciplinary borders, those of us who call ourselves 'criminologists' take with us our own training, tools, and concepts, as well as 'our' seminal texts. We share these with 'foreigners' outside our comfort zones and dip into or pillage their resources to help us to further make sense of our own worlds as well as those beyond our borders.

More specifically, criminologists who engage with issues around 'resisting state crime' should consider applying their 'training, tools, and concepts' acquired as criminologists to these issues, but should also draw into criminology what they learn from 'foreigners': that is, students of international law, politics, history and other disciplines who have engaged with the dimensions of resistance to state crime. For instance, criminologists need to incorporate both the context (a globalized world) and some 'foreign' core concepts (from universal jurisdiction to cosmopolitanism) into our work on state crime and resistance to it (Friedrichs 2010).

Resisting state crime as a criminological project

> It is my view that criminology must meet the challenge of ... [international] crimes if it is to remain a vital and relevant discipline.... [T]here is a significant need to bring criminological knowledge to the analysis and the evaluation of the many strategies for dealing with international crime.
>
> (Stephan Parmentier 2011: 381, 388)

That a focus on 'resisting state crime' is an unorthodox project for criminologists has been acknowledged. More than 15 years ago, I contributed (Friedrichs 1995) to a volume edited by Jeffrey Ian Ross (1995), *Controlling State Crime: An Introduction*. Ross, a criminologist with a political science background and a student of a leading political science specialist on state violence, Ted Robert Gurr, has been a prolific promoter of criminological attention to political crime and the crimes of states. The notion of 'controlling state crime' has an obvious affinity with 'resisting state crime', but the former term incorporates 'state-driven' initiatives, while the latter generally does not. The mechanisms for controlling state crime are stated to include international law, human rights courts, legislative bodies, political parties and the media. The potential role of social movements, for example, was acknowledged in this context, but de-emphasized. Contributors to Ross's book included some criminologists, but most were affiliated with other fields or disciplines. Nevertheless, in his subsequent work – such as *Varieties of State Crime and Its Control* (Ross 2000) – Ross has contributed to putting the broader issues involved in resisting state crime on the criminological agenda.

It seems worthwhile to acknowledge that criminologists who choose to engage with resisting state crime may do so as concerned citizens, as intellectuals and scholars, or as criminologists. If one participates in a protest march directed at some state policy or action that is viewed as promoting state crime, one does so as a concerned citizen, with no necessary invocation of either scholarly or criminological knowledge. Obviously a personal choice is involved here, in terms of a commitment of time and in some cases putting oneself potentially at risk of state violence. In my own case, as a college and graduate student and college instructor, I engaged in such activities – such as civil rights canvassing in Mississippi in 1964, and anti-Vietnam War and anti-Nixon administration marches from 1965 through to 1973 – but for various reasons such activism has not been a significant part of my life subsequently.

Second, some may choose to engage with resisting state crime as intellectuals, writing about or making speeches about the crimes of states, drawing upon a broad range of resources, but with no specific invocation of the framework or substantive knowledge of criminology. In the US, at least, Noam Chomsky is arguably the highest profile public intellectual who has addressed crimes of states (and 'resisting' such crimes), in countless books, articles and speeches, over a period of several decades. Yet Chomsky is also one of the most distinguished and influential linguists, and a professor at the Massachusetts Institute of Technology. In his political writing, Chomsky draws upon a broad range of sources but does not specifically invoke the terminology or knowledge associated with the field of linguistics (Salkie 1990). It is possible to see some connections between Chomsky's work in linguistics and his political work, but he views them as fundamentally separate. Few, if any, of us can hope to achieve the stature and high profile of a Noam Chomsky.

I want to argue here that criminologists should consider addressing the issues of resisting state crime specifically as criminologists, not simply as concerned citizens or engaged intellectuals. When criminologists write about resisting state crime as intellectuals, it seems to me that their work stands at great risk of being disregarded by others engaged with resisting state crime issues – from international law scholars to those in the field of political science – on the premise that, as criminologists, they are not well-qualified to usefully address the issues and, by fellow criminologists who might at least potentially engage with the issues, as not being aligned with criminological concerns. Ideally, if criminologists addressing issues around the resistance to state crime specifically invoke a criminological framework and criminological knowledge, they might be viewed by scholars affiliated with other disciplines as offering something unique to the understanding of such issues. On the other hand, they might also persuade fellow criminologists not naturally attuned to considering these issues that this is a topic that has relevance for criminology and about which criminologists have something useful to contribute. Accordingly, our natural audience – our students and fellow criminologists – should become open to transcending the traditionally parochial parameters of the criminological enterprise and to engaging with immensely consequential issues in the larger world.

Resisting rape as a conventional form of crime and as a form of state crime

> International criminal justice has barely engaged with the discipline of criminology, and vice versa.... International criminal law could benefit from greater openness to the social sciences. Criminologists might break some paths here by developing more sophisticated approaches to the specifics of crime when perpetrated in time of conflict, or by brutal regimes.
>
> (William A. Schabas 2011: 346–7)

Rape is a classic form of conventional crime and the focus of much attention from the criminal justice system and in the popular press, as well as the criminological literature. However, as Susan Brownmiller's (1975) classic *Against Our*

Will documented, this was not really the case through much of history. Feminists – and the growing number of feminist criminologists (both female and male) – played a significant role in generating heightened attention to rape and the adoption of laws that are more sensitive to the largely female victims of this crime. For example, Susan Caringella (2009) has systematically addressed the challenges that arise in the evolving criminal justice system response to rape cases, in the US, Canada, Britain, Australia and New Zealand. She documents the discrepancies between rape laws on the books and as implemented by justice systems, and proposes and delineates the elements of a creative model for more equitably and effectively addressing rape. Martin D. Schwartz and Walter S. DeKeseredy (1997) have explored the many different dimensions of rape and other forms of sexual assault that occur on college campuses, with special attention to the role of male peer support. Many other examples of criminological contributions to the understanding of rape and criminal justice system responses could be cited.

Susan Brownmiller (1975) also addressed the fact that, throughout recorded human history, rape has been part of war and raping the women of the losing side has been seen as a prerogative of male soldiers. Tragically, rape has continued to be a widespread dimension of many contemporary wars and military actions. Some criminologists – such as Biljeveld *et al.* (2009), Hagan and Rymond-Richmond (2009), Lenning and Brightman (2009) and Mullins (2009) – have examined rape in this context. The systematic documentation of rape cases, and their analysis, contributes to the greater visibility of rape as a crime and accordingly promotes more victim awareness and activism as significant forms of resistance. It seems to me that the study of rape is a quintessentially appropriate project for criminologists who engage with the resisting state crime project. Criminologists should have a specialized knowledge of what has been learned about rape and the justice system response to rape in the conventional context that can potentially provide a useful comparative context for identifying the strategies that could be most effectively adopted in resisting or containing rape within the context of crimes of states (and militias). And parallel applications of criminological knowledge about other forms of conventional crime – including murder and theft – and criminal justice responses to such crimes can be applied comparatively to a state crime context. Any such application of criminological knowledge generated in a Western context needs to be complemented with criminological knowledge generated within a developing country context, while remaining mindful of the complex ethical conundrums that may arise in relation to issues of cultural relativity.

Resisting state crime as critical criminology and mainstream criminology projects

[M]ainstream criminologists must begin to place the issue of humanitarian and HR [human rights] crimes high on their agenda and learn from other fields. Simultaneously HR scholars should avail themselves of criminological insights. There is no time to lose.

(Joachim Savelsberg 2010: 116)

Critical criminologists have been at the forefront of criminological attention to crimes of states. The critical criminological engagement with state crime evolved quite naturally out of the radical criminological shift away from focusing on criminal offenders towards attention on the oppressive dimensions of the criminal justice system (Coleman *et al.* 2009). The critical criminological privileging of power – its asymmetric character and its abuse – provides a basic foundation for a criminology of the crimes of states (see Chambliss *et al.* 2010; Rothe 2009; Rothe and Mullins 2011).

In April 2007, a group of European, American and Australian criminologists met in Maastricht to address a range of issues characterized by an emerging 'supranational criminology'. This symposium and the volume that came out of it – Smeulers and Haveman (2008) – seems to exemplify a coming together of criminologists with essentially mainstream and critical criminological approaches to state crime.

John Hagan of Northwestern University was one of the contributors to *Supranational Criminology*. His exceptionally diverse body of scholarly work essentially fits within the parameters of mainstream criminology, despite some less orthodox dimensions. In recent years, however, he has produced several books and many articles that examine the International Criminal Court and the genocide in Darfur (Hagan 2003; Hagan and Rymond-Richmond 2009). In one recent book – aptly entitled *Who Are the Criminals?* – Hagan (2010) delineates a historical shift in American policies towards crime from the F. D. Roosevelt era to the Ronald Reagan era, and the relative neglect among criminologists of the crimes of the powerful – white-collar crime and state crimes – during the course of the twentieth century. Some critical criminologists have been concerned that Hagan's work almost wholly disregards the contributions of critical criminologists to the study of state crime. Moreover, not all critical criminologists are persuaded of the value of the particular form of analysis that Hagan has applied to an understanding of the International Criminal Court and the Darfur genocide. Yet to my mind it is more important to recognize that Hagan surely reaches a large segment of the community of criminological scholars who do not engage with the work of critical criminologists. The March 2011 issue of *The British Journal of Sociology* devotes a large section to the BJS Annual Lecture, by Hagan and Kaiser (2011), on 'The Displaced and Dispossessed of Darfur: Explaining the Sources of a Continuing State-led Genocide', with comments by five sociologists and a response by Hagan and Kaiser. This symposium exemplifies the broad reach of Hagan's work. Ideally, mainstream and critical criminological approaches to resisting state crime, broadly defined, complement each other and become part of a larger collective scholarly enterprise in this realm.

Joachim Savelsberg of the University of Minnesota is a versatile sociologist and criminologist whose work belongs essentially within the mainstream. In his

Crime and Human Rights: Criminology of Genocide and Atrocities (2010), he issues an urgent call for mainstream criminological engagement with state crime issues, as the quote opening this section signifies. In this book, Savelsberg specifically identifies the ways in which criminology can complement the large body of work produced within the framework of other disciplines in its examinations of state crimes such as genocide. Of particular relevance to the resisting state crime project, Savelsburg focuses upon some of the emerging trends relating to the control of state crimes, as well as both the effectiveness of and some of the present limitations of the international criminal courts and other mechanisms (such as treaty bodies) in this realm. Although there is a huge body of literature on the topics addressed in Savelsberg's brief book, he adds some unique dimensions drawn from his criminological knowledge. This book also has the potential of reaching a broader audience within the community of criminology scholars. It is worth noting, however, that Savelsburg focuses on genocide and other exceptionally dramatic and extreme forms of state crime. Less dramatic forms of state crime – such as the mass incarceration of Indigenous peoples and people of colour – also require criminological attention. The worst state crimes tend to be associated with totalitarian and autocratic states, but of course much significant state crime occurs within democratic states (see Cunneen, Grewcock, Kramer and Michalowski, this volume).

There is also the case of John Braithwaite of the Australian National University. Braithwaite defies categorization in terms of disciplines or the 'mainstream versus critical' divide, and in addition to being described as a criminologist, he has also been described as a 'Peacebuilder, Social Scientist and Restorative Justice Activist' (Wachtel 2006). In recent years, his principal project has been a highly ambitious, collaborative project relating to peacebuilding – a key dimension of resisting state crime (Braithwaite, Braithwaite *et al.* 2010; Braithwaite, Charlesworth *et al.* 2010; Braithwaite, Dinnen *et al.* 2010). The view of some of his admirers – that John Braithwaite may well come to be regarded as the single most influential criminologist of our time – will very possibly be vindicated if his promotion of restorative justice and peacebuilding initiatives has a lasting impact. Braithwaite can be regarded as a model for criminologists who aspire to make a real world difference in relation to the resistance of state crime.

Concluding observations

All those who engage with the topic of resisting state crime should do so with a profound sense of humility, but not humility that precludes engagement and action. It is a common complaint that scholarly work is all too often detached from, and has no measurable impact upon, real world conditions. Admittedly, the forces that coalesce to bring into being the worst crimes of states would appear to wash over academic and scholarly discourse like a massive tsunami wave. However, in light of what is at stake in anticipating and preventing – or at least containing – major crimes of states in the unfolding twenty-first century, scholars across academic disciplines should engage with the resisting state crime project. And such scholarly engagement has the highest probability of making an impact if a critical mass of scholars works together cooperatively and collectively. Yet I have also put forth the argument that criminologists who engage with the issues around resisting state crime are most likely to have an influence insofar as they bring their unique criminological framework and body of knowledge to bear on the topic. Ideally, then, they become part of a collective, critical mass of engaged inquiry across the broadest possible range of disciplines. In an ideal world, this collective endeavour ultimately reaches a broad audience, ranging from ordinary citizens to activists to legislators to political leaders. And this endeavour contributes measurably to the immensely consequential challenge of resisting state crime.

Note

1 My thanks to Elizabeth Stanley and Jude McCulloch for their helpful suggestions and amendments to an earlier draft of this chapter.

References

Amar, P. (2011) 'Egypt after Mubarak', *The Nation*, 23 May, 11–15.
Aron, L. (2011) 'Everything You Think You Know about the Collapse of the Soviet Union Is Wrong', *Foreign Policy* (July/August), 64–70.
Biljeveld, C., Morssinkhof, A. and Smeulers, A. (2009) 'Counting the Countless: Rape Victimization during the Rwanda Genocide', *International Criminal Justice Review*, 19, 208–24.
Bosworth, M. and Hoyle, C. (eds) (2011) *What is Criminology?* Oxford, UK: Oxford University Press.
Braithwaite, J. (2011) 'Foreword', in M. Bosworth and C. Hoyle (eds), *What is Criminology?* Oxford, UK: Oxford University Press.
Braithwaite, J., Braithwaite, V., Cookson, M. and Dunn, L. (2010) *Anomie and Violence: Non-truth and Reconciliation in Indonesian Peacebuilding*, Canberra: ANU Press.
Braithwaite, J., Charlesworth, H., Reddy, P. and Dunn, L. (2010) *Reconciliation and Architecture of Commitment: Sequencing Peace in Bougainville*, Canberra: ANU Press.
Braithwaite, J., Dinnen, S., Allen, M., Charlesworth, H. and Dunn, L. (2010) *Pillars and Shadows: Statebuilding as Peacebuilding in Solomon Islands*, Canberra: ANU Press.
Brownmiller, S. (1975) *Against Our Will: Men, Women, and Rape*, New York: Simon & Schuster.
Bueno de Mesquita, B. and Smith, A. (2011) 'How Tyrants Endure', *New York Times*, 10 June, A35.
Byman, D. (2011) 'Why Mideast Tumult Caught Scholars by Surprise', *The Chronicle Review*, 18 February, B9.
Caringella, S. (2009) *Addressing Rape Reform in Law and Practice*, New York: Columbia University Press.
Chambliss, W. J., Michalowski, R. and Kramer, R. C. (eds) (2010) *State Crime in a Global Age*, Cullompton, UK: Willan.
Coleman, R., Sim, J., Tombs, S. and Whyte, D. (eds) (2009) *State, Power, Crime*, London: Sage.

Coll, S. (2011) 'The Casbah Coalition', *The New Yorker*, 4 April, 34–40.

Friedrichs, D. O. (1974) 'Historical Reprints on Crime and Criminal Justice', *Choice* (July/August), 723–30.

Friedrichs, D. O. (1995) 'State Crime or Governmental Crime: Making Sense of the Conceptual Confusion', in J. L. Ross (ed.), *Controlling State Crime: An Introduction* (pp. 53–80), New York: Garland Publishing Co.

Friedrichs, D. O. (2010) 'On Resisting State Crime: Conceptual and Contextual Issues', *Social Justice*, 36, 4–27.

Githongo, J. (2011) 'When Wealth Breeds Rage', *New York Times*, 24 July, week 6–7.

Goldberg, J. (2011) 'Danger Falling Tyrants', *The Atlantic*, June, 46–54.

Hagan, J. (2003) *Justice in the Balkans: Prosecuting War Criminals in the Hague Tribunal*, Chicago: University of Chicago Press.

Hagan, J. (2010) *Who Are the Criminals?* Princeton: Princeton University Press.

Hagan, J. and Kaiser, J. (2011) 'The Displaced and Dispossessed of Darfur: Explaining the Sources of a Continuing State-led Genocide', *The British Journal of Sociology*, 62, 1–25.

Hagan, J. and Rymond-Richmond, W. (2009) *Darfur and the Crime of Genocide*, New York: Cambridge University Press.

Hoyle, C. and Bosworth, M. (2011) 'Mapping the Borders of Criminology: Concluding Thoughts', in M. Bosworth and C. Hoyle (eds), *What is Criminology?* (pp. 530–42), Oxford, UK: Oxford University Press.

Kirkpatrick, D. D. (2011) 'Ousted Tunisian President and His Wife Found Guilty of Taking State Funds', *New York Times*, 21 June, A4.

Knepper, P. (2010) *The Invention of International Crime: A Global Issue in the Making, 1881–1914*, Hampshire, UK: Palgrave MacMillan.

Lenning, E. and Brightman, S. (2009) 'Oil, Rape and State Crime in Nigeria', *Critical Criminology*, 17, 35–48.

Levy, C. J. (2011) 'The Lands Autocracy Won't Quit', *New York Times*, 27 February, available at http://www.nytimes.com/2011/02/27/weekinreview/27tyrants.html?_r=1&pagewanted=all.

Mullins, C. W. (2009) 'We Are Going To Rape You and Taste Tutsi Women', *British Journal of Criminology*, 49, 719–35.

Mullins, C. W. and Rothe, D. L. (2008) *Blood, Power, and Bedlam: Violations of International Criminal Law in Post-Colonial Africa*, New York: Peter Lang.

Parmentier, S. (2011) 'The Missing Link: Criminological Perspectives on Transitional Justice and International Crimes,' in M. Bosworth and C. Hoyle (eds), *What is Criminology?* Oxford, UK: Oxford University Press.

Proal, L. (1898; 1973) *Political Crime*, Montclair, NJ: Patterson Smith.

Rodenbeck, M. (2011) 'Volcano of Rage', *The New York Review of Books*, 24 March, 4–7.

Ross, J. I. (ed.) (1995) *Controlling State Crime: An Introduction*, New York: Garland Publishing Inc.

Ross, J. I. (ed.) (2000) *Varieties of State Crime and Its Control*, Monsey, NY: Criminal Justice Press.

Rothe, D. L. (2009) *State Criminality: The Crime of All Crimes*, Lanham, MD: Lexington Books.

Rothe, D. L. and Mullins, C. W. (eds) (2011) *State Crime: Current Perspectives*, New Brunswick, NJ: Rutgers University Press.

Sagarin, E. (1973) 'Introduction to the Reprint Edition', in L. Proal, *Political Crime* (pp. v–xvi), Montclair, NJ: Patterson Smith.

Salkie, R. (1990) *The Chomsky Update: Linguistics and Politics*, London: Unwin Hyman.

Savelsberg, J. J. (2010) *Crime and Human Rights: Criminology of Genocide and Atrocities*, Los Angeles: Sage.

Schabas, W. A. (2011) 'Criminology, Accountability, and International Justice', in M. Bosworth and C. Hoyle (eds), *What is Criminology?* Oxford, UK: Oxford University Press.

Schwartz, M. D. and DeKeseredy, W. S. (1997) *Sexual Assault on the College Campus: The Role of Male Peer Support*, Thousand Oaks, CA: Sage.

Simons, M. (2011) 'Charges of War Crimes Brought against Qaddafi', *New York Times*, 28 June, A11.

Smeulers, A. L. and Haveman, R. (2008). *Supranational Criminology: Towards a Criminology of International Crimes*, Antwerp: Intersentia Publishers.

Wachtel, J. (2006) 'John Braithwaite: Peacebuilder, Social Scientist and Restorative Justice Activist', available at http://canada.iirp.edu/articles.html?articleId=534.

Wells, H. G. (1898) *The War of the Worlds*, London: William Heinemann.

Wolin, R. (2011) 'A Fourth Wave Gathers Strength in the Middle East', *The Chronicle Review*, 18 February, B6–B8.

3 Civil society, resistance and state crime

Penny Green and Tony Ward

This chapter sets out to clarify the conceptual relationship between the three terms used in its title and, in so doing, to refine and advance one of the main arguments of our previous work (Green and Ward 2004). It also gives an account of our current work and that of our colleagues in the International State Crime Initiative (ISCI) and raises some questions to be addressed in a three-year research project, which, at the time of writing, we have just begun under the title 'State Crime and Resistance: A Comparative Study of Civil Society'.[1]

Insofar as our book on state crime (Green and Ward 2004) had a single unifying argument, it was that civil society is both the most important counterweight to state crime and one of the most important sources of the norms that define state crime. While this idea has also been taken up by other scholars, such as Faust and Carlson (2011), Grewcock (2010), Lasslett (2010a, 2010b) and Pickering (2005), no major comparative studies have been conducted within this framework. The extensive body of literature on civil society has focused mainly on developed or middle-income countries, although there has also been considerable debate on the nature of civil society in Africa (see, for example, Bayart 1986; Comaroff and Comaroff 1999; Adekson 2004), which has afforded evidence that civil society has played a significant role in peacebuilding and democratic transition in several West African states (Adebajo 2002).

Within state crime research, an important debate exists over whether 'crime' is essentially a legal construct – something defined and punished by domestic and international courts – or whether it is better understood as a violation of social norms that may or may not reflect legal definitions (Green and Ward 2004; Kramer and Kauzlarich 2005). On the latter view – which we advocate – 'crime' is not a rigid legal category but a fluid and contested construct. Moreover, endemic and systematic state crime must be seen as a process – involving, for example, the early marginalization and dehumanization of certain groups – rather than understood simply as a series of discrete criminal events. The law is ill-equipped to respond to these diffuse, complex and subtle processes. Yet civil society potentially affords an authentic force for resistance and change.

Following Adamson's (1987/8: 320) exegesis of Gramsci, we have taken the concept of civil society to refer to 'the space between large-scale bureaucratic structures of state and economy on the one hand and the private sphere of family, friendship, personality and intimacy on the other'. This space is occupied by associations such as pressure groups, voluntary associations, religious bodies and those of media outlets and academic institutions that enjoy a degree of independence from the state. Among other activities, these associations 'generate opinions and goals with which they seek not only to influence public opinions and policies within existing structures and rules, but sometimes also to alter the structures and rules themselves' (Adamson 1987–8: 320–1). Gramsci was concerned to distinguish civil society not only from the institutionalized coercive apparatus of the state but also from the economic structures and institutions of society (Gramsci 1957, 1971). Given the growth in the hegemonic role of global economic power centres such as the World Bank, the International Monetary Fund and the World Trade Organization (Cox 1993), Gramsci's distinction contributes clarity to our understanding of the political limitations he saw in economism. On this view, civil society is not confined merely to promulgating an ideology that reflects the 'natural order' of relations under capitalism – it has the capacity to understand and yet stand outside the hegemonic nature of economic institutions, and in some instances to challenge them. Accepting the economic parameters of social order gravely limits the possibility of the subjugated 'ever becoming dominant, or ... developing beyond the economic-corporate stage and rising to the phase of ethical-political hegemony in civil society, and domination of the state' (Gramsci 1971: 125). The Occupy movement of late 2011, which, as we write, is spreading globally, represents a form of civil society engagement that has the potential to fundamentally challenge economic hegemonic processes.

Our argument for the importance of civil society in defining and controlling state crime draws on two strands of the broader argument, or rather the broader complex of interwoven arguments, which Foley and Edwards (1996) distinguish as 'Civil Society I' and 'Civil Society II'. Civil Society I, associated with the work of de Tocqueville and, more recently, Robert Putnam (1993), portrays civil society as fostering habits of civility, trust and civic engagement which are conducive to legitimate democratic government. Gramsci's analysis is, at least in part, a more critical version of the same argument. One of the features of civil society which Putnam celebrates – its ability to cut across major social divides to foster a sense of common interest – is, for Gramsci, an aspect of the hegemonic rule that obscures the real divisions and oppressive social relations that characterize capitalism. Hardt (1995: 33–4) further contributes to our understanding of the ambiguity of civil society by warning of its disciplinary character:

> While Gramsci highlights the democratic potentials of the institutions of civil society, Foucault makes clear that civil society is a society founded on discipline and that the education it offers is a diffuse network of normalization. From this perspective, Gramsci and Foucault highlight the two contrasting faces of Hegel's civil society. And in all of this what is primary is the way our labor or our social practice is organized and recuperated in social institutions and educated in the general interest of political society.

What Putnam plays down in his celebration of civil society (although de Tocqueville, at least on Foley and Edwards' reading, was well aware of it) is that civil society can also foment major social divisions. Yet for Gramsci this could, in some circumstances, be grounds for hope.

'Civil Society II', on the other hand, is the argument popularized by various Eastern European intellectuals and their Western allies in the closing years of the Cold War, which 'lays special emphasis on civil society as a sphere of action that is independent of the state and that is capable – precisely for this reason – of energizing resistance to a tyrannical regime' (Foley and Edwards 1996: 39). In a nutshell, the first line of argument sees civil society as strengthening the democratic state, whereas the second argument sees it as resisting the authoritarian state.

Applied to state crime, the first argument suggests that a strong civil society is conducive to a relatively non-repressive, non-corrupt or, in other words, non-criminal type of state. One reason for this is that there is relatively little motivation for state agencies to engage in criminal violence under conditions of hegemonic rule; it is more efficient, and more conducive to political and social stability, to rule by a blend of consent and that degree of coercion which most of the population will accept as legitimate. Conversely, the costs of illegitimate behaviour will be high, given the combination of a vigilant civil society (civil liberties groups, trade unions, lawyers associations and so forth) and a democratic political settlement that gives them scope to publicize their criticisms of government excesses.

Another implication of Civil Society I is that a strong civil society tends to foster conditions in which citizens expect and trust officials to act in accordance with publicly promulgated rules and consensual definitions of the 'public interest'. The converse of this situation is a state based on clientelism, where the only officials citizens can trust are those with whom they have direct or indirect personal ties based on an exchange of favours – a relationship which can easily shade into outright corruption (Roniger 1994; Green and Ward 2004: Ch. 2).

The criminological version of Civil Society II posits, of course, that civil society plays a crucial part in resisting state crime: in defying criminal regimes, in organizing protests in the teeth of violent repression and in transmitting information about repression to the outside world. Such resistance does not, in the short term, necessarily reduce state crime; it may well provoke it, as we see all too clearly, at the time of writing, in the news from Syria and Yemen. Yet the hope, illustrated again by the 'Arab Spring', is that the mobilization of civil society will eventually bring about a change of regime.

These two versions of the 'civil society argument' (Walzer 1992) are not incompatible but rather, in our view, reflect two aspects of a dialectical process (Green and Ward 2012).

Resistance and engagement

We begin the illustration of our approach with two defining examples[2] from British political life. The first example is taken from the period of the 1980s in the United Kingdom (UK) – a critical moment in the development of civil society's response to state violence. Britain at the time was defined by key think-ers as an increasingly 'authoritarian state' (Sim *et al.* 1987), tilting towards the 'pole of coercion' (Hall 1980). Our example concerns the Broadwater Farm riot of 1985: as violent and 'uncivil' an act of resistance as any in recent English history, sparked by the death of a woman during a police search of her home and involving extensive damage to property and the notoriously brutal murder of Police Constable Keith Blakelock. Broadwater Farm, a housing estate in North London, was described by the Metropolitan Police (1986: para 2.3) as a place with 'an unenviable reputation, [where] normal policing methods are resisted by a vociferous and ill-disposed minority'. Yet in the aftermath of the riot, the most 'vociferous' spokespersons of this 'ill-disposed minority', the Broadwater Farm Youth Association, were clearly expressing their support for something like the 'community policing' espoused by the liberal local commander of the Metropol-itan Police but which had been thwarted, in the Association's view, by the behaviour of officers on the ground: 'Everyone agrees that the police need to be kept in the community as we rely on them for help in many ways. BUT they must be prepared to become a part of the community, not act against it' (*Broad-water Review*, December 1985, quoted by Ward 1986: 65).

Alongside more 'respectable' manifestations of civil society, such as the UK's National Council for Civil Liberties (now Liberty) and progressive fac-tions within the state (such as the public inquiry set up by the local authority, chaired by a left-wing peer), this combination of militant resistance and civic engagement was probably quite effective in countering the grosser manifesta-tions of police racism in the 1980s.

For a more recent example, we consider WikiLeaks, whose illicit publication of confidential government documents has been a bonanza for scholars of state crime (Green forthcoming 2013). WikiLeaks came to prominence in 2009 with its release of Afghan and Iraq War Logs, followed in June 2010 by 251,287 leaked US Embassy diplomatic cables. Its website claimed that these were 'the largest set of confidential documents ever to be released into the public domain' (WikiLeaks, http://wikileaks.org/cablegate.html). The publication of this data was a manifestation of one of the most important forms of resistance to author-itarian and democratic states alike: resistance to state secrecy (Lasslett 2012). While WikiLeaks itself operates outside the bounds of what is legally and politi-cally acceptable to democratic governments, it clearly intends to contribute to the processes by which civil society holds governments accountable for their actions.

In its raw state, this vast mass of documentation can contribute little to most citizens' understanding of their governments' activities, but it does add greatly to the data sources at the disposal of those interested in the nuanced deliberations of states and their representatives. The analysis of this mass of material is one way in which scholars, including critical criminologists, can contribute some-thing of value to transnational civil society. The formerly secret Embassy cables provide researchers with data that lay bare the organizational goals and decision-making processes underpinning the sometimes criminal practices delivered by

US foreign policy, as well as the insights of US officials into the workings of criminal regimes, such as Muammar Gaddafi's Libya (Peachey 2011). Julian Assange, the enigmatic founder of WikiLeaks, expressed surprise in an interview with John Pilger at the general lack of academic and journalistic interest in the leaked data. The reasons for this disinterest are complex and encompass both political and methodological dimensions. We have yet to see the impact of the controversial publication of the whole cache of diplomatic cables in August 2011, but a more systematic approach to the study of this information is now likely.[3] Assange's overriding credo that 'the goal is justice, the method is transparency' (www.johnpilger.com/videos/julian-assange-in-conversation-with-john-pilger) is a clear directive for those analysing the cables and the other source material released by the organization. The method is thus valuable in as much as it provides a pedagogic tool for exposing state malpractice, thereby contributing to the knowledge base upon which civil society can build resistance and change.

Hegemony and resistance

The alliance between resistance by civil society in authoritarian states and organizations espousing human rights in the advanced democracies is central to the 'spiral model' developed in international relations scholarship by Risse *et al.* (1999), which was a major influence on our earlier formulation of the role of civil society in defining, controlling and resisting state crime. The civil society organizations that resist authoritarian rule can cooperate with the established human rights organizations based in democratic states, which can, in turn, reflect criticism of such states' repressive practices back to them in a way that seriously damages their international image. To the extent that even (some) authoritarian rulers care about their international image, this can lead to their making tactical concessions to the critics, with the result that human rights norms gradually become embedded in the political discourse of the state in question, which simultaneously comes under increasing pressure to conform to them.

The political ambiguity of this process is evident. What, from one perspective, is effective resistance to an authoritarian regime is, from another perspective, the imposition of hegemonic Western norms. The imposition of such norms is now seen to be reinforced by the clear threat of military force, as in the case of Libya (Traynor 2011). The process that Risse *et al.* (1999) celebrate is seen in a very different light by Hardt and Negri (2000: 36), who portray non-government organizations (NGOs) such as Amnesty International, Oxfam and Médicins Sans Frontières as:

> in effect (even if this is contrary to the intentions of their participants) some of the most powerful pacific weapons of the new world order – the charitable campaigns and the mendicant orders of Empire. These NGOs conduct 'just wars' without arms, without borders.... [M]oral intervention has become a frontline force of imperial intervention.

In their paradoxical and exaggerated fashion, Hardt and Negri raise an important point on which scholars of state crime need to reflect (Johnstone and Ward 2010: 185–8). The language of 'state crime' carries the risk of being seen as a call for global policing, and using the language of resistance carries a risk of romanticizing the harbingers of global policing. Conversely, we certainly do not want to romanticize Muammar Gaddafi as a hero of resistance to the North Atlantic Treaty Organization!

One symptom of this political ambiguity is the growing volume of literature that describes, and sometimes celebrates, the contribution of civil society to 'global governance'. Arts (2006: 181) observes:

> Most conceptions of global governance include the (potential) relevance of so-called non-state actors [NSAs] – NGOs, firms, epistemic communities, etc. – for governing global issues. Even more so, most approaches consider NSAs as being *internal*, not external to the global governance system.... [F]ormally as well as informally, NSAs are ever more part of, and giving shape to, international networks of governance.

Tallberg and Jönson (2010: 1) provide some examples of this phenomenon:

> The World Bank, for instance, draws on the expertise of NGOs in the formulation of country reports, engages in operational collaboration with civil society actors in the field, and conducts policy dialogue through the NGO–World Bank Committee. Whereas only 21 percent of all World Bank funded projects involved civil society participation in 1990, this figure had risen to 72 percent in 2006 (World Bank 2009). The United Nations Environmental Programme (UNEP) provides another example, engaging transnational actors by offering NGOs accreditation to its meetings, operating a Global Civil Society Forum, and drawing on civil society in the implementation of its programs. At the 2008 Global Civil Society Forum, about 190 representatives of civil society organizations from 42 countries participated (UNEP 2009: 23).

In relation to some forms of state–corporate crime, it may well make sense to describe civil society organizations (CSOs) as a form of 'alternative regulation' (Omorogbe 2006). In states where corporations are largely immune from governmental regulation, CSOs can be much more effective in pressurizing corporations to conform to international environmental norms (or to the CSOs' own interpretation of such norms). It could perhaps be said that human rights NGOs are attempting to 'govern' or 'regulate' state agencies that are similarly free from effective regulation by their governments, but their efforts at governance are necessarily restrained by the issue-based nature of human rights NGOs. Indeed, there are important differences between regulating a corporation and regulating an agency that is part of the state with the dominant resources of organized coercion in its territory (though the two overlap when the corporation has the state's coercive resources at its disposal: see Lasslett 2010a). If one shares Hardt and

Negri's taste for colourful metaphors, one can certainly describe such NGOs as the 'mendicant orders' of a global Empire; but to suggest that they govern the states whose repression they oppose seems to us to be taking the paradox of non-state governance too far.

Civil society as a continuum

If we are going to use 'civil society' as a broad term for a range of NSAs that are capable of resisting or challenging the illegitimate practices of any kind of state, then the term must embrace associations that display very different degrees of 'civility'. Clearly, outright armed struggle, whatever its degree of popular support or legitimacy, is something different from civil society, though civil society may foment armed struggle and armed struggle may (as we hope may be the case in Libya) afford conditions for the flourishing of a more civil society. However, as Adekson (2004) argues in his study of Nigeria, it can make sense to include, within the concept of civil society, organizations whose relations with the state and with other groups are marked by extremely 'uncivil' rhetoric and occasional serious violence. Such groups may contribute to ethnic divisions and vigilantism but also operate as checks on state and corporate power. Civil society can be thought of as lying on a continuum between militant resistance to and complete incorporation within a hegemonic system of government, and also on a continuum between 'civil' engagement in orthodox political discourse and more aggressive or confrontational forms of resistance. Militancy should not, however, be conflated with incivility. The Occupy movement, for example, in its highly public protest outside St Paul's Cathedral, London, has been at pains to conform to the requirements placed on it by Cathedral officials, with whom the organizers have maintained a cordial relationship (Kingsley 2011).

We have argued thus far that: (1) civil society in democratic states embraces forms of resistance as well as civic engagement, and the two are intricately connected; (2) the hegemonic civil society of Western democracies is closely connected (with politically ambiguous consequences) to the civil society that resists authoritarian rule; and (3) both 'civic' and militantly oppositional forms of civil society form a continuum, with organizations moving between these two poles as political conditions change.

Where more research is now needed is in understanding how far these arguments apply to non-democratic states, formally democratic but highly repressive states, and fledgling democracies emerging from conflict. The 'State Crime and Civil Society' project mentioned at the start of this chapter will do precisely this. Implicit in this research is an understanding that scholars engaged in examining state crime and resistance rarely do so from a position of detachment. Engagement with civil society in efforts to understand both state crime and resistance to such crime inevitably raises questions about praxis and the role of intellectuals within civil society. Karl Marx's injunction to change the world is less likely to be ignored by those scholars who are committed to exposing the crimes of the powerful through a rigorous attention to the victims of state criminality.

Resistance through research

The present authors have attempted to connect critical scholarship to the global network of resistance to state crime through work with ISCI and its website (www.statecrime.org). ISCI, launched in June 2010, embodies an international community of leading scholars working to further our understanding of state crime. It is an interdisciplinary forum for research, reportage and debate, and through empirical and theoretical enquiry its concern is to connect rigorous research with emancipatory activism. Many scholars working on state violence, corruption and civil society's attempts to combat these crimes themselves engage in resistance struggles or at the very least engage politically with those activists who lead and define those struggles. ISCI provides an opportunity for both researchers and activists to combine the pedagogical with the emancipatory. One of our primary tasks is to encourage rigorous empirical research so that we may develop the strongest possible evidence base. Understanding and knowledge are fundamental requirements of resistance strategies (Marx (1969 [1845]); Foucault 1977), which is why we are launching a major research investigation, funded by the UK Economic and Social Research Council, into the development of organizational resistance to state and insurgent violence and corruption.

In recent years, considerable attention has been given to the creation of formal legal processes in order to respond to violations of international criminal law (see, for example, Hagan 2003). By contrast, and for the reasons stated above, our concern is to explore the potential of informal, non-legal censure employed by civil society rather than censures employed by formal legal institutions.

As we have argued above, civil society organizations are directly involved in exposing, labelling and informally sanctioning state crime. We need to understand much more about how they do this, particularly outside the context of Western democracies. We need to identify where their information comes from, how they understand the boundaries of legitimate state action, how they see and use the law, and what strategies and tactics they find effective in resisting state violence and corruption. We aim to explore how far civil society organizations articulate consistent definitions of legitimate or criminal state conduct and how far these definitions reflect or differ from legal norms.

Risse *et al.*'s (1999) spiral model discussed above provides a framework for understanding the impact of domestic and transnational civil society on compliance with human rights norms. The ability of domestic groups to relay information to large international civil society organizations (CSOs) enables them to put sufficient pressure on states to induce them to make concessions that are initially tactical but which can eventually lead to lasting change. While the main focus of the spiral model is on the state's response to the exposure and censure of its crimes, our research seeks to understand this process from the standpoint of victims and the organizations that (purportedly) represent them.

At the core of our research will be the construction of a series of 'organizational life histories' of local CSOs in the range of post-conflict countries under study (Cambodia, Colombia, Papua New Guinea, Sierra Leone, Tunisia and

Turkey). The project draws on the life histories of individuals in which their own narrative accounts are employed to make sense of the past and current values, projects and achievements (Dearey 2009). An organizational life history is a similar narrative that is shared (or is perhaps current in several overlapping versions) among members of a group. It may well be interwoven with individual life histories in the way that Higginbotham (2008: 165) found among members of social movements in Colombia: his interviewees trod 'a shifting line between individual biography and group experience', expressing 'a strong sense of group memory and identity'. Such accounts of group experience are, of course, likely to be selective, but they afford insight into how civil society organizations understand state crime and their own role in combating it. These organizations, with their individual memories, embody a particular institutional 'history' of state crime, which offers a potentially rich knowledge base for researchers.

In exploring both the structural and the socio-cultural processes involved in the formation of civil society resistance within a number of transitional post-conflict states, we hope to assess whether, in societies traumatized by state and other forms of related internal violence, there is a dialectical relationship between state violence, the cooperative efforts of individuals within victim communities and the development of a fully articulated civil society.

Comparative analysis is central to the study of state crime. In our recent work, we have learned much from the research into collective violence and civil conflict carried out by Charles Tilly (2003) and Stathis Kalyvas (2006). Their work suggests that there is a 'logic' or 'deep structure' of violence that can be identified among diverse cultures and historical periods. In very simple terms, collective violence serves as a means of heightening social divisions and breaking down trust, thus facilitating increased violence; and it also creates opportunity structures which some individuals are able to turn to their own advantage. What is missing from these analyses is an account of the countervailing process by which people try to maintain or rebuild relationships of trust and cooperation, such as those Carolyn Nordstrom discussed in her study of Mozambique, *A Different Kind of War Story* (1997). We hypothesize that such processes will occur in many, if not all, cases of civil conflict and state violence, and that they create an embryonic civil society which is able to develop into a more organized form as the violence diminishes.

Our previous work suggests civil society (over and above international law) as the strongest candidate for resisting and transforming state violence. Violent society, however, is not conducive to civil society and, as our recent research on Iraq indicates, a breakdown in the monopoly of force exercised by violent states can lead to a dispersal of violence and the emergence of competing power blocs, which themselves provide further terrain for the emergence (and inhibition) of civil resistance (Green and Ward 2009). Specifically we are interested in exploring the underlying conditions that foster the emergence of civil society in the context of widespread state violence and corruption. How do nascent peacebuilding and justice-driven organizations develop and grow under conditions of widespread repression, and is there an underlying logic to their emergence similar to that which is understood for state violence? That the study covers both corruption and violence is important because the two are often closely linked (Green and Ward 2004). In states characterized by patrimonial and clientelist relations, forms of clandestine exchange not only encourage state violence but also are integral to it. We wish to study how CSOs perceive those links, and also the extent to which CSOs themselves are involved in corruption. Thomas MacManus's (2011) work on the Ivory Coast, for example, reveals civil society to be fertile ground for organized crime in a context where the potential for lucrative compensation claims arising from toxic waste dumping gave rise to a 'commodification of victimhood'.

The countries selected for our research afford a wide range of patterns of conflict in diverse political and cultural contexts. Cambodia represents the most extreme example of political violence, out of which has emerged, apparently, a particularly vibrant civil society (Downie and Kingsbury 2001). Colombia differs in the degree to which the major insurgent groups succeeded in establishing what were effectively their own states with a narcotics-based economy (Higginbotham 2008). Papua New Guinea (specifically Bougainville) underwent a civil war that originated in the breakdown of relations between a section of civil society and the state's corporate allies (Lasslett 2009). Sierra Leone is in the process of reconstructing a failed state; the conflict there was understood as egregiously barbarous and anarchic (Richards 1996) and occurred in a society where governance exemplified the 'criminalization of the state' (Bayart *et al.* 1999) and civil society was severely underdeveloped (Reno 1995). Turkey is a classic case of ethnically based insurgency countered by state terror in a relatively developed economy and polity (Yildiz and Breau 2010), while Tunisia's emergence from decades of repression under Ben Ali's police state instigated one of the most powerful resistance movements witnessed since the 1960s.

Our central hypothesis is that, even under the most adverse conditions of state repression and corruption, CSOs dedicated to challenging and resisting state criminality will emerge and develop, and that some of them are capable of instigating effective and fundamental change. The extent to which each CSO flourishes, however, will depend on its own organizational history, the normative frameworks it employs, its power to define and label state criminality, and the political and legal strategies it adopts for change. We also hypothesize that the process of communicating human rights norms is more complex than is suggested in the literature on transnational advocacy networks and that local CSOs will be engaged in their own selective and creative means of norm adaptation that best articulate local grievances.

Conclusion

Civil society is a notoriously ambiguous and elastic concept. It is distinct from, while being closely entangled with, the institutions of the economy and the state. Gramsci's clear articulation of the complex dualities embodied in civil society reveal it primarily to be a site of contest. It is both a complement to state power, educating and disciplining responsible citizens within a hegemonic order, and a potential source of opposition, capable of educating and disciplining the state itself. Yet in this latter, oppositional role it may also serve as an adjunct of a globally hegemonic order, a means of 'alternative regulation' for states that cannot be relied upon to regulate themselves in accordance with international norms. Ultimately these factors may compromise or constrain civil society's power to challenge tyranny.

Patterns of association that are identifiable as civil society can be discerned in almost every state, just as behaviour that is identifiable as state crime is ubiquitous. We have postulated that state crime and civil society are always related, and that it is largely through civil society that state crime is identified, labelled and resisted. This broad generalization can serve as a starting point for a detailed study of what are likely to be extremely varied, complex and subtle processes.

Notes

1 The authors gratefully acknowledge the support of the ESRC (ESRC Grant Reference ES/I030816/1 *Resisting State Crime: A Comparative Study of Civil Society*).
2 One of which, the Broadwater Farm riot, was something of a formative experience for at least one of us.
3 Up until that point in time, the cables had appeared in tranches of between one and 20 or so, depending on the country of origin, which, while manageable for researchers engaging in long-term systematic analysis, was inevitably constraining for those with restricted deadlines.

References

Adamson, W. L. (1987/8) 'Gramsci and the Politics of Civil Society', *Praxis International*, 7, 320–9.

Adebajo, A. (2002) *Building Peace in West Africa: Liberia, Sierra Leone and Guinea-Bissau*, Boulder: Lynne Rienner.

Adekson, A. O. (2004) *The 'Civil Society' Problématique: Deconstructing Civil Society and Southern Nigeria's Ethnic Radicalization*, London: Routledge.

Arts, B. (2006) 'Non-state Actors in the Global Environmental Governance: New Arrangements Beyond the State', in M. Koenig-Archibugi and M. Zürn (eds), *New Modes of Governance in the Global System*, Basingstoke: Palgrave Macmillan.

Bayart, J.-F. (1986) 'Civil Society in Africa', in P. Chabal (ed.), *Political Domination in Africa*, Cambridge: Cambridge University Press.

Bayart, J.-F., Ellis, S. and Hibou, B. (1999) *The Criminalization of the State in Africa*, Oxford: James Currey.

Comaroff, J. L. and Comaroff, J. (eds) (1999) *Civil Society and Political Imagination in Africa: Critical Perspectives*, Chicago: University of Chicago Press.

Cox, R. W. (1993) 'Gramsci, Hegemony and International Relations', in S. Gill (ed.), *Gramsci, Historical Materialism and International Relations*, Cambridge: Cambridge University Press.

Dearey, M. (2009) *Radicalization: The Life Writings of Political Prisoners*, London: Routledge Cavendish.

Downie, S. and Kingsbury, D. (2001) 'Political Development and the Re-emergence of Civil Society in Cambodia', *Contemporary Southeast Asia*, 23(1), 43–64.

Faust, K. L. and Carlson, S. M. (2011) 'Devastation in the Aftermath of Hurricane Katrina as a State Crime: Social Audience Reactions', *Crime, Law and Social Change*, 55, 33–51.

Foley, M. W. and Edwards, B. (1996) 'The Paradox of Civil Society', *Journal of Democracy*, 7, 38–52.

Foucault, M. (1977) *Discipline and Punish*, New York: Vintage Press.

Gramsci, A. (1957) *The Modern Prince and Other Writings*, New York: International Publishers.

Gramsci, A. (1971) *Selections from the Prison Notebooks*, London: Lawrence & Wishart.

Green, P. (forthcoming 2013) 'State Crime and US Imperialism in Turkey: What the Diplomatic Cables Reveal', *State Crime*, 2(1).

Green, P. and Ward, T. (2004) *State Crime: Governments, Violence and Corruption*, London: Pluto Press.

Green, P. and Ward, T. (2009) 'The Transformation of Violence in Iraq', *British Journal of Criminology*, 49(5), 609–27.

Green, P. and Ward, T. (2012) 'State Crime: A Dialectical View', in M. Maguire, R. Morgan and R. Reiner (eds), *The Oxford Handbook of Criminology* (5th edition), Oxford: Oxford University Press.

Grewcock, M. (2010) *Border Crimes: Australia's War on Illicit Migrants*, Sydney: Institute of Criminology.

Hagan, J. (2003) *Justice in the Balkans: Prosecuting War Crimes in the Hague Tribunal*, Chicago: University of Chicago Press.

Hall, S. (1980) *Drifting into a Law and Order Society*, London: Cobden Trust.

Hardt, M. (1995) 'The Withering of Civil Society', *Social Text*, 45(Winter), 27–44.

Hardt, M. and Negri, A. (2000) *Empire*, Cambridge, MA: Harvard University Press.

Higginbotham, A. (2008) 'Solidarity Action Research Methodology: The Crimes of the Powerful in Columbia', *Latin American Perspectives*, 35, 158–70.

Johnstone, G. and Ward, T. (2010) *Law and Crime*, London: Sage.

Kalyvas, S. (2006) *The Logic of Violence in Civil Wars*, Cambridge: Cambridge University Press.

Kingsley, P. (2011) 'Occupy London: My Nights with the St Paul's Protesters', *Guardian*, 20 October, available at www.guardian.co.uk/uk/2011/oct/20/occupy-london-st-pauls-protesters.

Kramer, R. and Kauzlarich, D. (2005) 'War, Aggression and State Crime: A Criminological Analysis of the Invasion and Occupation of Iraq', *British Journal of Criminology*, 45, 446–9.

Lasslett, K. (2009) 'Winning Hearts and Mines: The Bougainville Crisis, 1988–90', in S. Poynting, R. Jackson and E. Murphy (eds), *Contemporary State Terrorism: Theory and Practice*, London: Routledge.

Lasslett, K. (2010a) 'Crime or Social Harm? A Dialectical Perspective', *Crime, Law & Social Change*, 54(1), 1–19.

Lasslett, K. (2010b) 'Scientific Method and the Crimes of the Powerful', *Critical Criminology*, 18, 211–28.

Lasslett, K. (2012) 'Strategic State Crime Research: A Theoretical Model and Empirical Case Study', *State Crime*, 1(1), 126–48.

MacManus, T. (2011) *State–Corporate Crime and Civil Society: Impunity, Resistance and the Commodification of Victimhood in Ivory Coast*, unpublished Ph.D. thesis, submitted King's College, London, December 2011.

Marx, K. (1969 [1845]) 'Theses on Feuerbach' (Thesis XI), in *Marx/Engels Selected Works: Vol. I*, Moscow: Progress Publishers.

Metropolitan Police (1986) *Public Order Review: Civil Disturbances, 1981–84*, London: Metropolitan Police Office.

Nordstrom, C. (1997) *A Different Kind of War Story*, Philadelphia: University of Pennsylvania Press.

Omorogbe, Y. O. (2006) 'Alternative Regulation and Governance Reform in Resource-rich Developing Countries of Africa', in B. Barton, A. Lucas, L. Barrera-Hernández and A. Rønne (eds), *Regulating Energy and Natural Resources*, Oxford: Oxford University Press.

Peachey, P. (2011) 'Leaked Cables Reveal Gadaffi's Iron Grip on Corrupt Regime', *The Independent*, 24 February.

Pickering, S. (2005) *Refugees and State Crime*, Annandale, NSW: Federation Press.

Putnam, R. (1993) *Making Democracy Work: Civic Traditions in Modern Italy*, Princeton: Princeton University Press.

Reno, W. (1995) *Corruption and State Politics in Sierra Leone*, Cambridge: Cambridge University Press.

Richards, P. (1996) *Fighting for the Rain Forest: War, Youth and Resources in Sierra Leone*, Oxford: James Currey.

Risse, T., Ropp, S. C. and Sikkink, K. (eds) (1999) *The Power of Human Rights*, Cambridge: Cambridge University Press.

Roniger, L. (1994) 'The Comparative Study of Clientelism and the Changing Nature of Civil Society in the Contemporary World', in L. Roniger and A. Günes-Ayata (eds), *Democracy, Clientelism and Civil Society*, Boulder, CO: Lynne Rienner.

Sim, J., Scraton, P. and Gordon, P. (1987) 'Introduction: Crime, the State and Critical Analysis', in *Law, Order and the Authoritarian State*, Milton Keynes: Open University Press.

Tallberg, J. and Jönson, C. (2010) 'Transnational Actor Participation in International Institutions: Where, Why, and with What Consequences?' in C. Jönson and J Tallberg (eds), *Transnational Actors in Global Governance*, Basingstoke: Palgrave.

Tilly, C. (2003) *The Politics of Collective Violence*, Cambridge: Cambridge University Press.

Traynor, I. (2011) 'Libya: NATO Bombing of Gaddafi Forces "Relying on Information from Rebels"', *Guardian*, 19 May, available at www.guardian.co.uk/world/2011/may/18/libya-nato-bombing-benghazi-rebel-leaders.

UNEP (2009) *Natural Allies: Engaging Civil Society in UNEP's Work*, Nairobi: United Nations Foundation.

Walzer, M. (1992) 'The Civil Society Argument', in C. Mouffe (ed.), *Dimensions of Radical Democracy: Pluralism, Citizenship, Community*, London: Verso.

Ward, T. (1986) *Death and Disorder: Three Case Studies of Public Order and Policing in London*, London: INQUEST.

World Bank (2009) *Civil Society – Background*, World Bank online, available at http://web.worldbank.org/WBSITE/EXTERNAL/TOPICS/CSO/0,,pagePK:220469~theSiteP K:228717,00.html.

Yildiz, K. and Breau, S. (2010) *The Kurdish Conflict: International Humanitarian Law and Post-conflict: International Humanitarian Law and Post-conflict Mechanisms*, London: Routledge.

4 Public criminology and the responsibility to speak in the prophetic voice concerning global warming

Ronald C. Kramer

The theme of this volume, state crime and resistance, suggests the following question: do criminologists have a professional responsibility to assist in the identification, analysis and prevention of state (and corporate) actions that have the potential to cause great physical harm to the biosphere and enormous social harm to large numbers of people around the world, even if those actions are not illegal? This chapter takes the position that criminologists do in fact have such a responsibility, particularly with regard to the existential threat of anthropogenic global warming that is causing catastrophic climate change. I argue that criminologists have a professional obligation to engage in a *public criminology* on this issue, speaking in the prophetic voice and participating in social and political actions concerning this potentially devastating form of state–corporate crime (Michalowski and Kramer 2006; Kramer and Michalowski 2012).

Public criminology and the prophetic voice

According to Michael Burawoy (2007: 28), '[p]ublic sociology brings sociology into a conversation with publics, understood as people who are themselves involved in a conversation'. Following this conceptualization, Kramer *et al.* (2010) argue that a public criminology of state crime would seek out extra-academic audiences and enter into dialectical conversations with various publics, such as the victims of state crimes, the international political community, non-government organizations (NGOs), state agents, media organizations and other more generalized, amorphous 'publics'. The content of these conversations would be quite varied, but would take the form of some kind of dialogue about the moral and political implications of criminological research findings and theoretical explanations concerning state crime.

A public criminology of state crime can take several forms. Again, following Burawoy (2007), Kramer *et al.* (2010) distinguish between *traditional* public criminology and *organic* public criminology. Traditional public criminology attempts to initiate a conversation, instigate a debate or provoke a critical questioning within or between publics through the publication of books and articles addressed to audiences outside the academy or opinion pieces in national or international newspapers that identify and analyse state crimes or comment on important public issues related to such crimes. Organic public criminology, on the other hand, involves criminologists working directly with specific groups, organizations, movements or state officials, engaging in a dialogue or a process of mutual education that may or may not lead to specific political actions related to the prevention or control of state crime.

This chapter expands on these conceptions of public criminology using a slightly different language and focusing on the potentially apocalyptic state–corporate crime of catastrophic climate change due to global warming. I argue that criminologists, as part of their professional role, can and should assume two important responsibilities in the larger struggle to resist this and other state–corporate crimes, and the serious harms they cause. First, criminologists should take seriously the responsibility to *speak in the prophetic voice* concerning state and corporate crimes (traditional public criminology); and second, where they can, they should assume the responsibility to *engage in social and political actions* to reduce or prevent these harms (organic public criminology). The language here borrows from Robert Jensen's *All My Bones Shake: Seeking a Progressive Path to the Prophetic Voice*. As Jensen (2009: 162–3) argues, given the 'cascading crises' humanity now faces, '[i]t is time to recognize that we all must strive to be prophets now. It is time for each of us to take responsibility for speaking in the prophetic voice.'

'Prophecy' in this sense does not mean predicting the future. To speak prophetically with regard to state and corporate crime is to identify or name the harms committed by the corporate state as 'criminal', call out the social injustices that states and corporations produce or tolerate, confront the abuses of powerful officials and analyse how political and economic systems cause destruction, devastation and untold suffering. By speaking in the prophetic voice, criminologists can attempt to break through the denial and normalization of state and corporate crimes, critique the structural and organizational forces that give rise to them and create political or 'deliberative frames' (Wilson 2009: 139) that can reorient the debate on these issues. Thus, to speak in the prophetic voice carries a responsibility to act in the political arena. To engage in progressive political action involves, among other things, organizing or participating in peace, environmental or transitional justice movements, challenging empire, contesting the power of the corporate state, working to reinvigorate democratic governance and enhancing the power and control of international political and legal institutions. By engaging in such 'political' actions, criminologists can raise awareness of the obstacles to and possibilities for progressive social change and perhaps contribute to the construction of collective solutions to state–corporate criminality.

Speaking in the prophetic voice about global warming

Criminologists can assist the effort to resist state–corporate crime by speaking in the prophetic voice to publicly identify, sociologically analyse and politically frame major forms of these crimes. In my judgement, one of the most significant crimes we face today involves state and corporate actions that contribute to global warming. These corporate and state actions are potentially apocalyptic events in that they could result in the destruction of the biosphere and the annihilation of most forms of life on earth. Speaking in the prophetic voice would require criminologists to identify and describe these state and corporate actions as criminal and then to explain the structural and cultural forces that give rise to them. By adopting the prophetic voice in discussing these issues, criminologists may then be able to assist in the construction of a deliberative frame that can galvanize public debate and political action on global warming and the associated environmental and social harms resulting from climate change.

Although concerns about the possible harms associated with anthropogenic global warming have existed since at least the 1970s, Lynch and Stretesky (2010: 62) point out that '[c]riminologists have been slow to consider climate change as a relevant issue'. More recently, however, the development of what some term a 'green criminological perspective' (Lynch and Stretesky 2003, 2010; Beirne and South 2006, 2007), and others an 'eco-global criminology' (White 2008, 2010, 2011), has led some to begin considering the criminological import of global warming and climate change. This requires blending criminological insights with existing environmental science. This science has provided clear evidence of the crisis, the extreme urgency of the situation and the grave crime that is unfolding. As James Hansen (2009: ix), director of the National Aeronautics and Space Administration (NASA) Goddard Space Studies Center, points out: 'The startling conclusion is that continued exploitation of all fossil fuels on Earth threatens not only the other millions of species on the planet but also the survival of humanity itself – and the timetable is shorter than we thought.'

Currently, there is no established body of international or domestic law that offers a legal framework for criminologists concerned with global warming and the environmental and social harms flowing from this phenomenon. However, there are some efforts underway to change this situation. Polly Higgins (2010), for instance, has proposed that 'ecocide' be recognized by the United Nations as an international crime along with genocide, crimes against humanity, war crimes and crimes of aggression. Higgins (2010: 63) defines ecocide as: 'The extensive destruction, damage to or loss of ecosystem(s) of a given territory, whether by human agency or by other causes, to such an extent that peaceful enjoyment by the inhabitants of that territory has been severely diminished.' If adopted, ecocide would constitute a legal definition under which global warming and climate change would become not only an environmental problem, but also an international crime. Another effort to include the emission of harmful greenhouse gases within a legal framework is the ongoing lawsuit brought by six American states (New York, California, Connecticut, Iowa, Rhode Island and Vermont) against the five largest American utilities (American Electrical Power, Southern Company, Xcel Energy, Cinergy Corporation and the Tennessee Valley Authority) in an effort to have their emissions defined as a 'public nuisance'. If successful, this suit could force the United States (US) government to impose more stringent regulations on the fossil fuel industry (BusinessGreen 2011).

Despite these legal efforts, however, the emission of carbon dioxide and other greenhouse gases is not defined as a crime under any current legislation. With regard to global warming, there is nothing comparable to the Montreal Protocol, which was adopted in 1987 to eliminate aerosols and other chemicals that were responsible for a growing hole in the Earth's protective ozone layer. This protocol has been so successful in eliminating the hydrofluorocarbons that damage the ozone layer that some policy experts have suggested that we should curb global warming by including greenhouse gases under this existing and demonstrably successful treaty (Broder 2010).

To date, the Kyoto Protocol of 1997 is the only major international accord aimed at regulating and reducing greenhouse gas emissions. Unfortunately, this treaty, 'an unambitious little thing', as Dyer (2010: 142) calls it, is fatally flawed and has done next to nothing to reduce carbon emissions. In the first place, the reductions in greenhouse gases mandated by the treaty were too small and applied to only a few countries. Second, climate scientists failed to anticipate that extreme weather events and climatic changes due to global warming would increase as dramatically or quickly as they have. Third, most governments resisted calls for larger reductions, and fast-emerging nations such as China and India won agreements that exempted them from any obligation to curb their emissions. The biggest failure of the Kyoto Protocol, however, was that the largest emitter of greenhouse gases, the US, failed to ratify the treaty. As NASA scientist James Hansen points out: 'The US sabotaged the effectiveness of the Kyoto Protocol by not signing on. Without the biggest polluter by far, and without the biggest economy, Kyoto could not be very effective' (quoted in Dyer 2010: 143).

The lack of a legal framework that criminologists can use as a juridical warrant to address anthropogenic global warming as a state–corporate crime should not be seen as a barrier to this inquiry. Instead, criminologists concerned with this issue can and should utilize concepts such as 'social injury/harm' (Michalowski 1985, 2010; Pemberton 2007; Tift and Sullivan 2001) or 'state crimes of omission' (Barak 1991; Kauzlarich et al. 2003) as the starting point for their work. As White (2011: 21) asserts: 'A basic premise of green criminology is that we need to take environmental harm seriously, and in order to do this we need a conceptualization of harm that goes beyond conventional understandings of crime.' Lynch and Stretesky (2010: 71) argue that, insofar as 'scientists are continually discovering new ways in which global warming produces harm, it is important for green criminologists to stay abreast of this literature in order to address the varieties of victimization and emerging crimes and harms science identifies'.

Recent overviews of the scientific research on global warming and climate change do indeed demonstrate the catastrophic nature of the harms that are being inflicted on the ecosystem (Dyer 2010; Hamilton 2010; Hansen 2009; McKibben 2010), harms that are more severe and occurring at a faster pace than predicted in the report of the 2007 Intergovernmental Panel on Climate Change. The burning of fossil fuels has already raised the temperature of the planet by almost one degree Celsius over the pre-industrial average and some scientists estimate that it could rise as high as an extremely alarming five or six degrees (Dyer 2010; Hamilton 2010). The concentration of carbon dioxide in the atmosphere has increased from 275 parts per million at the dawn of the industrial age to close to 400 parts per million currently, and it appears to be headed for 550 or 650 (McKibben 2010: 14–18). James Hansen (2009: 288) argues that the only safe level – that is, one that would not risk catastrophic global warming – is 350 parts per million. Unfortunately, even if we could return to that level in the near future, great damage has already been done. Again, the research provides clear evidence of this damage: the melting of the polar ice caps, the Greenland ice sheet and the Himalayan glaciers that will trigger a rise in sea levels; extreme weather events, such as an increase in global rainfall in some areas with intractable droughts in others, more severe heat waves and more frequent and stronger hurricanes; increasing deforestation, particularly in the Amazon rainforest, and the expansion of the tropics, which in turn extends the reach of dry subtropics; and the acidification of the oceans, with a corrosive effect on shellfish and coral reefs (Hansen 2009; McKibben 2010).

Hansen (2009) also points out that, as global warming continues, positive feedback effects will occur that will trigger runaway heating that is essentially uncontrollable and irreversible. These positive feedback tipping points, which will dramatically accelerate the heating of the planet, include the Arctic albedo effect, whereby dark open water in the Arctic absorbs more solar radiation, the release of huge quantities of methane from the melting permafrost and the die-back of the Amazon rainforest. Moreover, Hamilton (2010: 25) argues that '[t]he lag between emissions and their effects on climate and the irreversibility of those effects makes global warming a uniquely dangerous and intractable problem for humanity'. Unfortunately, the lag between cause and effect also makes it uniquely difficult to mobilize political will to address the problem, even though as McKibben (2010: 27) notes, '[t]he planet on which our civilization evolved no longer exists.... The Earth that we knew – the only earth that we ever knew – is gone.'

Furthermore, the environmental damage caused by global warming will result in a wide range of social, economic and political harms for human communities and the social systems on which they depend (Dyer 2010). For example, the rise in sea levels, extreme heat and chronic droughts will lead to drastic reductions in the food supply, increasing famine, and mass migrations. The large movement of people across borders seeking food and an escape from the heat will fuel violent conflicts, genocides and other crimes (Alvarez 2009; Parenti 2011). These movements have already led to the heightened militarization and securitization of borders in the Global North as neoliberal policies intersect with climate change to produce declines in agricultural and pastoral economies in the Global South, fuelling an increasing mobility among irregular migrants seeking a minimum of food and physical security (Parenti 2011). Massive social upheavals, class conflict and pandemics caused by climate change will stress social institutions, create ideological turmoil and generate political crises (Dyer 2010). The number of failed and failing states will increase as their incapacity to adapt to climate change heightens poverty and violence around the world, particularly in those parts of the Global South that Parenti (2011) terms 'the tropic of chaos'. Resource wars and other forms of international conflict will increase. As Dyer (2010: xii) bluntly states: 'There is a probability of wars, including even nuclear wars, if temperatures rise 2 to 3 degrees Celsius.' Increased warfare would also sabotage the planetary cooperation needed to reduce further global warming. It should also be noted that the social and political consequences of climate change and ecosystem damage will occur first in those geographic areas and countries that have contributed the least to the problem (Lynch and Stretesky 2010). The northern industrial nations have, in the words of Foster (2009: 243), accumulated a huge 'ecological debt' towards Third World countries due to resource plundering and the infliction of environmental harms.

Given these catastrophic scenarios, I argue that speaking in the prophetic voice means that criminologists should treat the grave harms, both present and future, resulting from global warming and climate change as serious crimes warranting criminological analysis. As White (2011: 36) points out: 'Climate change is arguably the most important issue, problem and trend in the world today and a key area of interest to eco-global criminology.' Based on the scientific evidence of the harm it causes, criminologists should identify the continually increasing production of carbon dioxide by corporations in the fossil fuel industry as a crime of corporate violence. Indeed, James Hansen describes how '[t]he trains carrying coal to power plants are death trains. Coal-fired power plants are factories of death' (quoted in Foster 2009: 21). The state is also involved in this form of crime. In particular, the imperial US military presence is a major contributor to this criminal violence. As Sanders (2009: 22) argues: 'The military – that voracious vampire – produces enough greenhouse gases, by itself, to place the entire globe, with all its inhabitants large and small, in the most immanent danger of extinction.'

That the actual emission of greenhouse gases beyond levels scientifically determined to be low enough to avoid or slow global warming should be illegal is non-controversial for most green criminologists. However, we need to take this one step further. The failure to reduce or mitigate the production of greenhouse gases and decarbonize the economy should also be understood as a form of state–corporate crime. The failure of state officials to take effective and immediate actions to compel both the private sector and government institutions to reduce the emission of greenhouse gases is, arguably, a state crime of omission. For example, the George W. Bush administration has been accused of 'crimes against nature' (Kennedy 2004) for its denial of and inaction on a whole range of environmental issues, including global warming. As Lynch *et al.* (2010) document, eight critical years were lost in the battle against global warming due to the stonewalling and negligence of an administration that had extraordinary ties to the main culprits in the coal and gas industry.

The US is not alone in its foot-dragging on the matter of global warming. Other states, and the international political system in general, have similarly failed to take aggressive action. The Copenhagen Conference in December 2009 may have been the last, best opportunity for the governments of the world to act forcefully to prevent catastrophic climate change. Yet the administration of Barack Obama and the entire international political community utterly failed to take any strong actions that might avert the impending ecocide. As John Sauven, Executive Director of Greenpeace UK, bluntly stated after the failure of this conference: 'The city of Copenhagen is a crime scene tonight, with the guilty men and women fleeing to the airport. There are no targets for carbon cuts and no agreement on a legally binding treaty' (quoted in Dyer 2010: 208).

The orchestrated denial of global warming and climate change, despite the extensive evidence to the contrary, can also be labelled a state–corporate crime. It is a deliberate attempt to thwart efforts to respond in an effective and just way to the emerging problems resulting from the heating of the planet. The global warming denial movement is funded for the most part by money from the fossil fuel industry (Greenpeace 2011; Hoggan 2009; Oreskes and Conway 2010). It consists largely of corporate propaganda built around lies and deceptions masquerading as science, which is then disseminated by ideological and political forces in conservative think tanks, industry trade associations, the corporate media and some government officials (Friel 2010; Gelbspan 1998, 2004; Greenpeace 2011; Hamilton 2010; Hoggan 2009; Jacques 2009; McCright and Dunlap 2000, 2003; Oreskes and Conway 2010). The intent of the climate change denialists is to cast doubt on the scientific evidence of anthropogenic global warming and thus impede governmental actions that would force the fossil fuel industry to make changes that would reduce emissions. Some environmental scientists contend that corporate and/or government-sponsored climate science disinformation and denial should be labelled as crime. As climate scientist Donald Brown (2010: 2) states: 'We may not have a word for this type of crime yet, but the international community should find a way of classifying extraordinarily irresponsible scientific claims that could lead to mass suffering as some type of crime against humanity.'

State–corporate crimes that result in catastrophic climate change are rooted in broader structural and cultural forces. The continued 'criminal' emission of greenhouse gases throughout much of the world arises from the global dominance of a mostly unfettered predatory corporate capitalist economic system and the popular desires it stimulates, protected by imperial military actions that promote and protect that system from any challenges. In this regard, Foster (2009: 46) asserts that:

> [c]apital by its very logic imposes what is in effect a scorched earth strategy. The planetary ecological crisis is increasingly all-encompassing, a product of the destructive uncontrollability of a rapidly globalizing capitalist economy, which knows no law other than its own drive to expand.

The globalized political economy of predatory capitalism also gives rise to two broad cultural factors that, in turn, reinforce the economic relationships and forces that facilitate global warming. These two factors are 'growth fetishism' (Hamilton 2010) and state-supported cultures of consumption and production (Lynch and Stretesky 2010). The pathological promotion and pursuit of endless economic growth on a planet with finite resources, such as fossil fuels, is unsustainable in the long run. It also produces a kind of 'tunnel vision', which prevents people from considering any solution to global warming other than a technological one (Hamilton 2010). Insofar as '[t]he more an individual or culture consumes, the more that person or culture contributes to climate change' (Lynch and Stretesky 2010: 64), the only path away from continued global warming is to reduce levels of consumption – a politically difficult task.

Engaging in political action concerning global warming and climate change

Those criminologists who do speak in the prophetic voice about global warming and climate change have a responsibility to act in the public arena. This section briefly describes three potential approaches to engaging in progressive political action on these issues.

The first approach is to break through the denial and normalization that usually covers state–corporate crimes related to global warming. Most harmful state actions are enmeshed in a 'culture of denial' (Cohen 2001) and a socio-historical process that results in their 'normalization' (Kramer 2010). One of the most important things criminologists can do by speaking in the prophetic voice is to challenge this denial and normalization. Unless we disrupt the denial and negate the normalization of the crimes related to global warming and climate change, none of the necessary public conversations or political actions concerning the prevention and control of these crimes is likely to take place.

Cohen (2001) has demonstrated how individuals, organizations, publics, political cultures and governments, whether victims, perpetrators or observers, frequently incorporate statements of denial into their social definitions, beliefs, knowledge and practices in such a way that atrocities and suffering, such as those related to state crimes, are not acknowledged or acted upon. According to Cohen (2001: 51), denial 'refers to the maintenance of social worlds in which an undesirable situation (event, condition, phenomenon) is unrecognized, ignored or made to seem normal'. He identifies three categories of denial: literal, interpretive and implicatory. A literal denial is 'the assertion that something did not happen or is not true'. In the case of interpretive denial, the basic facts are not denied, yet 'they are given a different meaning from what seems apparent to others' (Cohen 2001: 7). Interpretive denial probably occurs more often than literal denial. Here, the event or the harm is socially and morally framed in such a way as to deny the state's responsibility or culpability. Finally, the notion of implicatory denial 'covers the multitude of vocabularies – justifications, rationalizations, evasions – that we use to deal with our awareness of so many images of unmitigated suffering'. Thus, 'knowledge itself is not an issue. The genuine challenge is doing the "right" thing with this knowledge' (Cohen 2001: 7–9).

The global warming denial counter-movement has been able to create doubts about climate science and block policies that would seek to reduce greenhouse gas emissions and create clean energy alternatives. This movement started with literal denials about global warming. When the evidence made literal denials an unsustainable position, the movement shifted to adopting interpretive denial, claiming that, even if the planet were experiencing global warming, it was not caused by human activity but by natural forces. This denial has become an article of faith among right-wing politicians in the US, and almost every candidate for the 2012 Republican presidential nomination was a global warming denialist. Even more troubling is the fact that many of those who do accept the evidence of global warming and are aware of the unfolding tragedy remain apathetic and take no social actions to mitigate the problem, as Norgaard (2011) has demonstrated in her powerful analysis of implicatory denial around climate change. As long as these three forms of denial continue to operate, there appears to be little chance to prevent global catastrophe.

Criminologists who speak in the prophetic voice by presenting research evidence that documents state crimes concerning global warming, and dispute literal denials of these crimes, or who challenge the narratives of interpretive or implicatory denial with empirically grounded theoretical counter-narratives, are engaging in an important form of public criminology. They are entering into a conversation with various publics that may impact on whether or not these crimes will be socially defined as 'crimes' that can then become suitable targets for prevention and control efforts. It should be clear that, when critical scholars disrupt denials or negate normalization in their role as public criminologists, they are participating as 'claims-makers' in a process of the social construction of crime as a social problem to be addressed by society (Blumer 1971; Spector and Kitsuse 1977). There are problems and pitfalls inherent to this form of engagement (Kramer *et al.* 2010), yet it is vital for critical scholars to speak in the prophetic voice and take on the roles and responsibilities of the public criminologist. Whether we act as traditional public criminologists or work directly with social movements, we can use our knowledge and intellectual skills to undermine denial and normalization, and help define global warming as a state–corporate crime and a legitimate target for social control efforts.

Once criminologists have spoken in the prophetic voice, and these crimes become 'problematized', denial might begin to recede. Environmental protection organizations, along with other progressive social movements working to contest the power of the responsible corporate state, may be energized and their political efforts may be enhanced. Therefore, a second strategy for public criminologists is to assist various progressive movements in their efforts to challenge the corporate state and change policies related to the release of massive quantities of carbon dioxide into the atmosphere. In general, these movements seek to prevent transnational corporations that form the military-industrial complex and the fossil fuel industry from completely capturing the state and continuing their criminality. As Coleman and his colleagues (2009: 15) point out:

> Those who have adopted a neo-Marxist analysis of the state have ... not only consistently emphasized the contradictory nature of its institutional power base, but also its place as a site of struggle, which has been, and can be, mobilized by powerless groups to subvert policy proposals and challenge social injustice.

The state is, indeed, a site of struggle. Zinn (1980) demonstrated that, throughout American history, powerless groups and people's movements have repeatedly challenged social injustices, fought against corporate domination, resisted imperialism and contested state power, frequently winning important victories. From the progressive era at the turn of the twentieth century (Nugent 2010) to President Franklin Delano Roosevelt's 'New Deal', social movements and radical agitation has forced the US Congress to enact many important social and economic programmes (Zinn 1980). During the 'long Sixties', a broad array of movements and counter-cultures arose to challenge the 'Machiavellians' who represented the US corporate state (Hayden 2009). The civil rights and anti-Vietnam War movements both played a central role in contesting state power during this era.

Although the progressive movements of the long Sixties won some important civil rights victories, ended the imperial war against Vietnam and produced some significant social and cultural changes in American society, an extremely well-funded and well-organized conservative counter-movement developed in the 1970s to seek to overcome progressive people's movements and to protect corporate interests. The election of Ronald Reagan in 1980 represented a significant victory for this counter-movement. Increasingly, corporate power 'holds the government hostage' (Hedges 2009: 143) and corporate interests have the ability to subvert democracy in the US – a phenomenon that Wolin (2008) calls 'inverted totalitarianism'.

The grip of the corporate forces that control the state are indeed strong, and Hedges (2010) argues that the 'liberal class' that once provided a minimal level of opposition to such private tyranny is now dead. Still, the power of the corporate state and the imperial and ecological violence it inflicts must be contested. By speaking in the prophetic voice, by producing theory and research on state crimes related to global warming and climate change, criminologists, acting as both traditional and organic public intellectuals, can attempt to contest the corporate state and reinvigorate democratic governance.

As Rothe and Kauzlarich (2010: 183) have noted, '[c]ontrol over state crime is strongest at the international level'. Ultimately, the problems posed by global warming will require action by the international political community. The only hope to limit catastrophic climate change will be an international agreement that drastically cuts greenhouse gas emissions around the world and promotes the global development of alternative energy sources and conservation efforts. Such a treaty must not only cut emissions in all countries, including China and other developing countries, but also require a massive transfer of financial resources and other forms of assistance from the developed Global North that created the problem to the countries of the underdeveloped Global South, which have contributed little to the problem but which will be the first to suffer from climate change. As the Copenhagen Conference of 2009 demonstrated, neither the US nor any of the other developed countries have the political will to create such an agreement at this time. Breaking through the denial and normalization of the threat of global warming, contesting the power of the corporate state through progressive social movements and developing international agreements to mitigate carbon emissions appear to be impossible political tasks at this point in global history. However, as Max Weber (1946: 128) once observed, 'historical experience confirms the truth – that man would not have attained the possible unless time and again he had reached out for the impossible'. By speaking in the prophetic voice about the state and corporate crimes relating to global warming, and by engaging in political action concerning this critical issue, criminologists can help create a public discourse that makes it more likely that the impossible becomes possible and the global community can avoid the most catastrophic forms of climate change.

References

Alvarez, A. (2009) *Genocidal Crimes*, London: Routledge.

Barak, G. (ed.) (1991) *Crimes by the Capitalist State: An Introduction to State Criminality*, Albany: State University of New York Press.

Beirne, P. and South, N. (eds) (2006) *Green Criminology*, Aldershot: Ashgate.

Beirne, P. and South, N. (eds) (2007) *Issues in Green Criminology: Confronting Harms against Environments, Other Animals and Humanity*, Cullompton: Willan Publishing.

Blumer, H. (1971) 'Social Problems as Collective Behavior', *Social Problems*, 18, 298–306.

Broder, J. (2010) 'A Novel Tactic in Climate Fight Gains Some Traction', *New York Times*, 8 November, available at www.nytimes.com.

Brown, D. (2010) 'Is Climate Science Disinformation a Crime against Humanity?', *Commondreams*, 3 November, available at www.commondreams.org.

Burawoy, M. (2007) 'For Public Sociology', in D. Clawson, R. Zussman, J. Misra, N. Gerstel, R. Stokes, D. Anderton and M. Burawoy (eds), *Public Sociology: Fifteen Eminent Sociologists Debate Politics and the Profession in the Twenty-first Century* (pp. 23–64), Berkeley: University of California Press.

BusinessGreen (2011) 'US States Accuse Polluting Power Stations of "Public nuisance"', *BusinessGreen*, available at www.businessgreen.com/bg/news/2034401/accuse-polluting-power-stations-public-nuisance.

Cohen, S. (2001) *States of Denial: Knowing about Atrocities and Suffering*, Cambridge, UK: Polity Press.

Coleman, R., Sim, J., Tombs, S. and Whyte, D. (eds) (2009) *State, Power, Crime*, London: Sage.

Dyer, G. (2010) *Climate Wars: The Fight for Survival as the World Overheats*, Oxford, England: Oneworld Publications.

Foster, J. B. (2009) *The Ecological Revolution: Making Peace with the Planet*, New York: Monthly Review Press.

Friel, H. (2010) *The Lomborg Deception: Setting the Record Straight about Global Warming*, New Haven: Yale University Press.

Gelbspan, R. (1998) *The Heat Is On: The Climate Crisis, the Cover-up, the Prescription* (updated edition), Reading, MA: Perseus Books.

Gelbspan, R. (2004) *Boiling Point: How Politicians, Big Oil and Coal, Journalists, and Activists Are Fueling the Climate Crisis – and What We Can Do to Avert Disaster*, New York: Basic Books.

Greenpeace (2011) *Who's Holding Us Back? How Carbon Intensive Industry is Preventing Effective Climate Legislation*, Amsterdam: Greenpeace International.

Hamilton, C. (2010) *Requiem for a Species: Why We Resist the Truth about Climate Change*, London: Earthscan.

Hansen, J. (2009) *Storms of My Grandchildren: The Truth about the Coming Climate Catastrophe and Our Last Chance to Save Humanity*, New York: Bloomsbury.

Hayden, T. (2009) *The Long Sixties: From 1960 to Barack Obama*, Boulder, CO: Paradigm Publishers.

Hedges, C. (2009) *Empire of Illusion: The End of Literacy and the Triumph of Spectacle*, New York: Nation Books.

Hedges, C. (2010) *Death of the Liberal Class*, New York: Nation Books.

Higgins, P. (2010) *Eradicating Ecocide: Exposing the Corporate and Political Practices Destroying the Planet and Proposing the Laws Needed to Eradicate Ecocide*, London: Shepheard-Walwyn Publishers.

Hoggan, J. (2009) *Climate Cover-up*, Vancouver: Greystone Books.

Jacques, P. (2009) *Environmental Skepticism: Ecology, Power and Public Life*, Farnham: Ashgate.

Jensen, R. (2009) *All My Bones Shake: Seeking a Progressive Path to the Prophetic Voice*, Berkeley: Soft Skull Press.

Kauzlarich, D., Mullins, C. and Matthews, R. (2003) 'A Complicity Continuum of State Crime', *Contemporary Justice Review*, 6, 241–54.

Kennedy, R. F. (2004) *Crimes against Nature*, New York: HarperCollins.

Kramer, R. (2010) 'From Guernica to Hiroshima to Baghdad: The Normalization of the Terror Bombing of Civilian Populations', in W. Chambliss, R. Michalowski and R. Kramer (eds), *State Crime in the Global Age* (pp. 118–33), Cullompton: Willan Publishing.

Kramer, R. and Michalowski, R. (2012) 'Is Global Warming a State–Corporate Crime?', in R. White (ed.), *Climate Change from a Criminological Perspective*, New York: Springer.

Kramer, R., Michalowski, R. and Chambliss, W. (2010) 'Epilogue: Toward a Public Criminology of State Crime', in W. Chambliss, R. Michalowski and R. Kramer (eds), *State Crime in the Global Age* (pp. 247–61), Cullompton: Willan Publishing.

Lynch, M. and Stretesky, P. (2003) 'The Meaning of Green: Contrasting Criminological Perspectives', *Theoretical Criminology*, 7, 217–38.

Lynch, M. and Stretesky, P. (2010) 'Global Warming, Global Crime: A Green Criminological Perspective', in R. White (ed.), *Global Environmental Harm: Criminological Perspectives* (pp. 62–84), Cullompton: Willan Publishing.

Lynch, M., Burns, R. and Stretesky, P. (2010) 'Global Warming and State-Corporate Crime: The Politicalization of Global Warming under the Bush Administration', *Crime, Law and Social Change*, 54, 213–39.

McCright, A. and Dunlap, R. (2000) 'Challenging Global Warming as a Social Problem: An Analysis of the Conservative Movement's Counter-Claims', *Social Problems*, 47, 499–522.

McCright, A. and Dunlap, R. (2003) 'Defeating Kyoto: The Conservative Movement's Impact on U.S. Climate Change Policy', *Social Problems*, 50, 348–73.

McKibben, B. (2010) *Eaarth: Making Life on a Tough New Planet*, New York: Times Books.

Michalowski, R. (1985) *Order, Law and Crime*, New York: Random House.

Michalowski, R. (2010) 'In Search of "State and Crime" in State Crime Studies', in W. Chambliss, R. Michalowski and R. Kramer (eds), *State Crime in the Global Age* (pp. 13–30), Cullompton: Willan Publishing.

Michalowski, R. and Kramer, R. (2006) *State-Corporate Crime: Wrongdoing at the Intersection of Business and Government*, New Brunswick, NJ: Rutgers University Press.

Norgaard, K. M. (2011) *Living in Denial: Climate Change, Emotions, and Everyday Life*, Cambridge: The MIT Press.

Nugent, W. (2010) *Progressivism: A Very Short Introduction*, New York: Oxford University Press.

Oreskes, N. and Conway, E. (2010) *Merchants of Doubt: How a Handful of Scientists Obscured the Truth on Issues from Tobacco to Global Warming*, New York: Bloomsbury Press.

Parenti, C. (2011) *Tropic of Chaos: Climate Change and the New Geography of Violence*, New York: Nation Books.

Pemberton, S. (2007) 'Social Harm Future(s): Exploring the Potential of the Social Harm Approach', *Crime, Law and Social Change*, 48(1–2), 27–41.

Rothe, D. and Kauzlarich, D. (2010) 'State Crime Theory and Control', in H. Barlow and S. Decker (eds), *Criminology and Public Policy* (pp. 166–87), Philadelphia: Temple University Press.

Sanders, B. (2009) *The Green Zone: The Environmental Costs of Militarism*, Oakland: AK Press.

Spector, M. and Kitsuse, J. (1977) *Constructing Social Problems*, Menlo Park, CA: Cummings.

Tift, L. and Sullivan, D. (2001) 'A Needs-based, Social Harms Approach to Defining Crime', in S. Henry and M. Lanier (eds), *What is Crime? Controversies Over the Nature of Crime and What to Do About It* (pp. 259–77), Lanham, MD: Rowman & Littlefield.

Weber, M. (1946) 'Politics as a Vocation', in H. Gerth and C. W. Mills (eds), *From Max Weber: Essays in Sociology* (pp. 77–128), New York: Oxford University Press.

White, R. (2008) *Crimes against Nature: Environmental Criminology and Ecological Justice*, Cullompton: Willan Publishing.

White, R. (ed.) (2010) *Global Environmental Harm: Criminological Perspectives*, Cullompton: Willan Publishing.

White, R. (2011) *Transnational Environmental Crime: Toward an Eco-Global Criminology*, London: Routledge.

Wilson, W. J. (2009) *More than Just Race: Being Black and Poor in the Inner City*, New York: W. W. Norton.

Wolin, S. (2008) *Democracy Incorporated: Managed Democracy and the Specter of Inverted Totalitarianism*, Princeton: Princeton University Press.

Zinn, H. (1980) *A People's History of the United States: 1492–Present*, New York: HarperCollins.

5 The great escape

Refugees, detention and resistance

Michael Grewcock[1]

Introduction

In March 2002, approximately 1000 protesters converged on the remote (now closed) Woomera immigration detention centre in South Australia. Their intention was to demonstrate their opposition to Australia's mandatory detention policies and to show solidarity with the detained asylum seekers who were protesting inside the centre. As has been memorably recorded on film,[2] the protesters unexpectedly broke through the perimeter fence to come face to face with the detainees. With all parties clearly taken by surprise, sections of the security fence were prised open and about 50 detainees managed to break out. Given the spontaneous nature of the escape and the lack of any obvious place of refuge in the open desert, most either surrendered or were recaptured immediately. However, 12 remained at large for over three years.[3] In 2005, two Iranian escapees were arrested in Melbourne and re-detained, although both subsequently had their claims for refugee status accepted. This triggered a series of surrenders by the remaining escapees during 2006. Eventually all of the 12 were accepted as refugees and were granted permanent residence. At least one now has citizenship.

While the protester involvement made the March 2002 escape relatively unique, the events at Woomera were not isolated. Between January 1999 and July 2008, there were 373 recorded escapes from immigration detention in Australia (O'Neill 2008: 103). This figure does not reflect accurately the numbers engaged in mass escapes as a form of protest, given that, on 8 June 2000, approximately 400 detainees broke through the fence at Woomera and marched into the nearby town where they peacefully protested until they returned to the centre the following day (Mann 2003: 2). Similarly, in Western Australia on 9 June 2000, approximately 100 detainees escaped from the Port Hedland detention centre and 150 from the Curtin detention centre (Department of Immigration and Citizenship 2011). Ten years later, this pattern re-emerged when approximately 80 detainees broke through the perimeter fence and sat down outside the Darwin immigration detention centre in September 2010 and 400 detainees engaged in two separate breakouts during sustained protests at the Christmas Island detention centre in March 2011.[4]

As will be discussed below, the levels of planning of and individual motivations for the escapes have varied, but in general escapes from immigration detention are best understood as a form of resistance to Australia's policy of the mandatory detention of unlawful non-citizens. Since 1992, this policy has been central to the Australian state's response to illicit migration, especially refugees seeking to enter Australia by boat without a visa. In that time, Australia's immigration detention complex has evolved into a network of mainland detention centres predominantly situated in remote locations, including offshore centres on Nauru and New Guinea between 2001 and 2007, and since 2008, a purpose-built high-security centre on the Australian territory of Christmas Island. Both Sharon Pickering (2005) and I (Grewcock 2009) have argued that mandatory detention and other aspects of the Australian government's border policing policies constitute a form of state crime as defined by Green and Ward (2004: 2): 'state organisational deviance involving the violation of human rights'. This chapter seeks to locate resistance to detention within that state crime framework and, in the process, to explore some of the conceptual issues arising from criminological definitions of state crime.

A state crime framework

Australia's border policing practices evidence the reasons why criminologists should adopt a state crime paradigm that includes more than state officials committing unlawful acts. As successive Australian governments have repeatedly argued in response to their critics, indefinite administrative detention of 'unlawful non-citizens' is lawful. It complies with a narrow reading of the Refugee Convention and international humanitarian law and operates in accordance with specific domestic legislation that has been confirmed as constitutional by the High Court of Australia.[5] It has also operated with the support of a high level of institutional legitimacy and political bipartisanship, although at the time of writing, the parliamentary consensus has broken over the government's plans to forcibly return asylum seekers to Malaysia following the High Court's finding that aspects of the plan contravene Australia's obligations under international law (see Pickering and Weber, this volume). Nevertheless, the tradition of bipartisanship has allowed successive governments to evade responsibility for the systemic and extensively documented abuse within detention centres by employing elaborate techniques of denial or blaming errant individuals in some of the most egregious cases.[6]

I have therefore used Green and Ward's (2004: 2) definition of state crime as a starting point but have developed it in two ways. The first is to emphasize the state's use of force as an indicator of its deviant and damaging behaviour (Grewcock 2008). This is significant because, while the monopoly of the legitimate use of physical force is considered a defining characteristic of the modern state (Weber 1994), the legitimacy of the use of such force is not fixed. Rather, it is contingent upon there being, within the wider civil society, a degree of 'willing compliance', 'passive acquiescence' and 'ingrained dependence' (Draper 1977: 251), which, in

Gramscian terms, are produced through processes of hegemony that neutralize the inherent tensions within society (Gramsci 1971). Moreover, while the mechanisms for implementing state force 'consist not merely of armed men, but also of material appendages, prisons and coercive institutions of all kinds' (Engels 2010), the visibly abusive and deviant consequences of state force (death, detention, torture and deportation, to name but a few) mean that hegemonic explanations such as 'defending law and order' or 'policing borders' will invariably be contested. Indeed, sections of civil society, including the victims of state-sanctioned violence, are routinely driven to reject the legitimacy of that state's actions and to resist the use of state force.

The second development in this conceptualization of state crime is to focus on three dimensions that are relevant to border policing – the *alienation, criminalization* and *abuse* of unauthorized migrants (Grewcock 2009). Each of these elements has shaped the forms of resistance that have developed in response to Australian government policy and practice in this area, and each is discussed in turn below.

The *alienation* of detainees operates through their lack of lawful status and their legal construction as aliens (Grewcock 2009: 250–9); their restricted access to legal redress, in particular through the use of excision to exclude the islands off the Australian mainland from Australia's migration zone (Grewcock 2009: 169–70); their physical separation from civil society; and their ideological construction as potentially dangerous outsiders, often by playing on historic fears of 'invasion' from Asia and Islamophobia (Grewcock 2009: 260–72; Poynting *et al.* 2004). For the government, the alienation of refugees is an important mechanism for enabling it to ignore or minimize its obligations under international law and to subjugate human rights to what the government determines is in the national interest. Thus, refugees who are resettled by the Australian state according to a predetermined quota are considered legitimate, while those who seek protection independently of this process are met with large-scale mobilizations of state force. In this context, resistance represents a claim to legitimacy by refugees whose authenticity is systematically denied or challenged. It underlines the need for internationalist conceptions of humanity, emphasizes the universal nature of human rights and reinforces the legitimate expectations of forced migrants to be able to access free movement, safety and stability.

The *criminalization* of detainees derives from their construction as 'illegal'; their association with illicit migration agents ('people smugglers'), whose activities can now draw sanctions as severe as those imposed on the most serious violent offenders[7]; and their incarceration in prison-like institutions. The elemental cry of the detainee filmed at Woomera[8] – 'we are not criminal' – not only reflected the detainees' self-perception of being criminalized but also exposed the cruel sophistry of technical distinctions between administrative and punitive detention.[9] The highly regulated and oppressive conditions of detention necessarily shape the nature of resistance, which despite the profound power imbalances operating within a detention environment has proven to be remarkably enduring. Resistance by detainees can range from individual acts of survival and creativity to overt forms of collective protest that are likely to elicit further exercises of state force, such as physical confrontation, segregation, forced transfers, criminal charges and other measures that reinforce the cycle of criminalization. In this sense, detainee resistance bears similarities to prisoner resistance (Carlton 2007), although I will argue that escapes from immigration detention should be conceptualized differently from escapes from prisons, not least because most immigration detainees involved in these actions have been refugees and have received a degree of community support, particularly as they do not deserve to be punished simply because of their mode of entry into the country.

The *abuse* of detainees can be measured in part by the physical and psychological impacts of detention. The extensive evidence of depression and mental illness being triggered or exacerbated by detention helps explain the high levels of self-harming, self-destructive and suicidal behaviours among detainees.[10] However, these can also represent desperate acts of individual protest in circumstances in which all other avenues of complaint and redress appear to have been exhausted. Moreover, the abusive impact of detention can be measured against a range of social norms established through international human rights conventions, domestic medical and welfare standards, and community expectations about the decent treatment of people by state agencies. The disclosures of abuse in immigration detention have played a pivotal role in shaping opposition to the government's detention policies, particularly in relation to detained children. In a criminological sense, the systemic abuses arising from detention not only establish state deviance but also legitimize resistance to it.

Resistance and escapes

While the detention policy has involved the systematic abuse or removal of rights of detainees, this has not resulted in the total destruction of the capacity to resist or the complete denial of agency among detainees. There has been significant resistance by detainees, much of which has not been reported, and has been largely misconstrued when it has.

Since the inception of the mandatory detention policy in Australia, detainees have engaged in multiple, often overlapping, forms of resistance at both a collective and an individual level. These have ranged from low-level non-compliance to full-scale riots, and include strikes by detainees employed to work in the detention centres; political protests and sit-ins; hunger strikes; acts of self-harm, including stitching up one's lips, carving words such as 'freedom' onto one's limbs and jumping into razor wire; inter-detainee violence, usually triggered by perceived advantages being given to a particular group; and physical confrontations with staff, including responses to verbal and physical assaults by staff or institutional displays of force, such as lockdowns (Grewcock 2009: 196–241).

Within this broad pattern of resistance, it is also possible to identify various types of individual and group escape.

First, there have been escapes undertaken as a form of protest. These include the breakouts at Woomera detention centre in June 2000 and Darwin in September 2010, which seemed intended as collective short-term actions designed to highlight the plight of detainees by entering the neighbouring community, rather than attempts to flee detention.

Second, there have been escapes that have resulted spontaneously from protests, such as occurred at Woomera in March 2002. In such instances, the circumstances leading to a return to detention have been more variable, although only a minority have remained at large for any length of time.

Third, there have been escapes that have been planned or initiated from the outside. For example, in June 2002, a group of activists prised open the fence at Woomera detention centre, enabling about 35 detainees to escape. Although there appeared to be no clear strategy on what to do with the detainees, and 25 were caught within a few days (O'Neill 2008: 104–10), the group included two brothers, Alamdar and Muntazar Bakhtiyari, aged 13 and 11, whose arrest three weeks later following a failed attempt to claim asylum at the British Consulate in Melbourne focused attention on the human impact of the government's policy.

Fourth, there have been escapes carefully planned by detainees as a final act of desperation. In July 2001, 23 people tunnelled out of the Villawood immigration detention centre along sewerage drains, followed by another 23, who cut a hole in the fence a few days later. 'Z', a detainee who managed to escape at this time, but who has since settled in Australia, explained his reasons for joining the group after he was told about the plan:

> I was really scared of going back to my country. I knew I couldn't go, especially given the journey I had. I just couldn't cope with it ... I knew this was my only opportunity. This was just about saving myself. I was under lots of pressure personally. I felt so powerless, unsupported. It was the only course to get out.[11]

While the actions of 'Z' and others can be seen as legitimate responses to state-inflicted harm, many such resisters have faced disciplinary sanctions, including prolonged segregation within the detention centres and transfers to prisons, and in some cases, criminal prosecutions and prison sentences,[12] accompanied by threats that refugees engaged in such actions will be refused protection.[13] Such responses reinforce the alienation, criminalization and abuse of refugees, and the deviance vested in detainees by virtue of their detention can be used to legitimize the generally punitive government response to unauthorized migrants. However, despite the official hostility to detainee resistance, many of the refugees who have escaped detention managed to negotiate surrender and obtain residency status. In this context, escaping from detention ought to be understood as an aspect of a forced migration experience that necessitates that desperate measures be taken to protect the personal and collective safety of those seeking protection.

The courts and the right to escape

While escapes from custody have inspired a rich genre within literature and film[14] that celebrates the ingenuity if not heroism of escapees, the legal consequences are usually severe. In New South Wales, for example, escaping from prison custody carries a maximum sentence of ten years.[15] In Australia, the common law defence of necessity offers the only legal justification for convicted prisoners escaping from custody. Australian courts have construed this very narrowly and will only countenance the defence in life-threatening situations, where the acts of the prisoner are proportionate to the acts faced – for example, a prisoner escaping from the immediate vicinity of a fire.[16] The position is a little more flexible in the United States, where access to the defence has been extended to include avoiding intolerable conditions (Brown *et al.* 2011: 622–3).

The rigid legal approach to prison escapes derives from the nature of the prison sentence as a court-sanctioned punitive deprivation of liberty. However, immigration detainees are not serving a specific sentence imposed by a criminal court. Instead, they are formally detained for administrative reasons in circumstances in which their liberty is not denied for reasons of punishment. This is clearly of little consolation to detainees facing years of detention, but legal attempts to justify escapes on the grounds that detainees are subjected to systemic human rights abuses have not been successful.

In August 2004, the High Court of Australia handed down its decision in the case of Mehran Behrooz,[17] an Iranian refugee who escaped from Woomera detention centre with five others in November 2001, only to be arrested a few hours later. Behrooz, who was charged with escaping from immigration detention, sought to obtain in the Magistrates Court evidence detailing the conditions at the centre, in order to argue that these conditions were so harsh that they fell outside the definition of detention in the *Migration Act 1958*. It followed that, if he was not lawfully detained, a charge of escape could not be made. The High Court rejected these propositions by a 6–1 majority. It found that immigration detention for administrative purposes was a lawful exercise of Commonwealth power and that the conditions of detention were irrelevant to determining its validity. Chief Justice Gleeson summed up the decision by declaring:

> Harsh conditions of detention may violate the civil rights of an alien. An alien does not stand outside the protection of the civil and criminal law.... But the assault, or the negligence, does not alter the nature of the detention.... The detention is not for a punitive purpose.... And the detainee does not cease to be in immigration detention within the meaning of the Act.[18]

The decision in *Behrooz* played its part in legitimizing the use of detention. The narrow legal distinctions between administrative and punitive detention have facilitated official denial of the impact of detention on detainees in circumstances that reinforce their alien status. Moreover, escaping such conditions reinforces the deviance of detainees, who are already being de-legitimized through their labelling by the government and the media as 'queue jumpers' and 'illegals' (Lygo 2004: 94–106). This has applied particularly to young adult men from the Middle East, who apart from being the main embodiment of the 'threatening asylum seeker' (Lygo 2004; Poynting *et al.* 2004) have tended to be the refugees charged and brought before the courts.[19]

While Mehran Behrooz was the target of an ideological offensive conducted at the highest levels of the state, he and other escapees ultimately did not face extensive additional criminal sanctions. In October 2004, Behrooz pleaded guilty in the Magistrates Court to the original escape charge. Previously, in October 2003, following several suicide attempts, he had been admitted to a psychiatric hospital in Adelaide as a result of 'serious suicidal intent and behaviours and symptoms suggestive of major depression'.[20] He remained in hospital until July 2004, when he was released into community detention, although still diagnosed as 'suffering from a major depressive disorder'.[21] In December 2004, given this history, the Chief Magistrate discharged Behrooz without recording a conviction, requiring him only to enter into a two-year good behaviour bond. In accordance with departmental policy, the Crown appealed against this and a number of similar sentences for escapees. In a series of related judgements,[22] the South Australian Supreme Court rejected the appeals on the basis that leniency should apply 'under the doctrine of mercy'.[23] This ensured that good behaviour bonds became the norm in subsequent escape cases before South Australian magistrates.[24]

The Supreme Court's reasoning was clearly influenced by the individual suffering of the escapees, and its implicit censure of what had occurred at Woomera could be interpreted as a partial recognition of the state's deviant exercise of force. Despite the High Court's unwillingness to allow evidence of the conditions at Woomera detention centre, there seems little doubt that the environment within the centre was profoundly abusive. In particular, the Human Rights and Equal Opportunity Commission's report into children in detention (HREOC 2004) provided a devastating catalogue of abuse at Woomera. To quote just one example, a psychologist who worked there in 2002 recalled:

> The self-harming was so prevalent and so pervasive that no child would have avoided seeing adults self-harming.... There was very visible self-harm, constant talk of it. The children, for example, when I arrived would have seen people in graves.... Some of the children – it was their parents or people they knew. They knew why the parents were doing this. They knew that the parents were talking about possibly dying. They were on a hunger strike. There was visible self-harming on the razor wire. People were taken to the medical centre at regular intervals having slashed. People taken to hospital. There were attempted hangings that these children would have seen.
>
> (Quoted in HREOC 2004: 405)

I have detailed elsewhere how such descriptions illuminate the systemic patterns of abuse operating within Australia's immigration detention centres (Grewcock

2009: 196–241). In addition to providing legitimate reasons for why people like Mehran Behrooz would want to escape, such descriptions also give insight into the scale of desperate, high-risk, self-injurious resistance. At the time, much of this was dismissed by the government as manipulative behaviour; but within the wider community, the revelations about Woomera contributed to a growing hostility towards the government's policy (particularly in relation to children).

As confronting and damaging as these acts of self-harm might have been, they nevertheless provided a mechanism for the plight of the detainees to be recognized. Combined with more orthodox protests and escapes, they demonstrated that the detainees were prepared and able to act on their own behalf. This raises important conceptual issues for theorists of state crime regarding the levels of abuse required to satisfy definitions of state crime and the role of resistance in constructing a social audience capable of rejecting and resisting state policy.

Detention, social agency and resistance

One of the enduring debates about state crime concerns the extent of the social injury required to satisfy a criminologically sound definition (Green and Ward 2000a, 2000b). Narrow paradigms of state crime that require indisputable or egregious breaches of international law do not have to engage much with this if, as suggested by Cohen (1993: 98), the focus is limited to 'gross violations of human rights – genocide, mass political killings, state terrorism, torture, disappearances'. Such state actions would satisfy any definition of state crime because of their unambiguous criminality and level of impact on the victim. Again, for reasons I have outlined elsewhere (Grewcock 2008, 2009: 12–20), such frameworks risk overlooking or excluding the continuum of abuses inflicted upon unauthorized refugees, especially in circumstances where the state can claim compliance with the law and neutralize the extent of the injury.

A further question arising in considering definitions of state crime that focus on gross human rights violations is: to what extent are the victims of state crime deprived of agency? Clearly, the severity of state crime, especially when injury or death is being inflicted by overwhelming state force, has some bearing on the victim's capacity to resist. For example, unarmed victims of massacres and violent assaults, isolated individuals subjected to torture and those detained in concentration camps and other highly controlled prison environments may have few opportunities to openly resist. Nevertheless, situations where there is a total deprivation of agency, where victims are reduced to a condition that makes any resistance impossible or futile and where they must rely solely on the responses of others to resist the state's deviant behaviour are relatively rare. Rather, while highly oppressive situations may ensure resistance is unlikely to succeed without solidarity within the wider community, resistance should be seen as the norm. Moreover, we should be wary of taking too prescriptive an approach to defining resistance. For an isolated individual, survival itself may constitute resistance, especially if the victim is sufficiently alienated from the wider community to be stripped legitimately of all rights as a result of being defined by the state as outside the 'universe of obligation' (Fein 1979: 33).

In contrast to the above scenario, however, incarceration within Australia's immigration detention complex represents state criminality that is not predicated on the reduction of its victims to an absolute state of rightlessness or powerlessness. As dismal as the Woomera detention centre might have been, it was not Auschwitz; and this is more than simply a rhetorical comparison. The death camps of Nazism represented an extreme dystopia, where state-organized violence literally did reduce many of its victims to the barest social existence as part of a wider government programme of extermination. Thus, Sofsky describes the concentration camp as a site of 'absolute power' of a 'distinctive and singular kind', that was incapable of being 'integrated into the history of despotism, slavery or modern discipline', and that could not 'be mapped onto a continuum of domination'. In this environment, 'the causal nexus between action and survival' was destroyed (Sofsky 1999: 16–27). 'The ultimate fate of prisoners did not depend on their own actions. Only a minute fraction managed to escape. The others survived only because the Gestapo released them or the liberators arrived in time' (Sofsky 1999: 25).

In his extraordinary testament of survival in Auschwitz, Primo Levi (1987: 93–106) distinguished two types of detainee – the 'saved' and the 'drowned':

> This division is much less evident in ordinary life; for there it rarely happens that man loses himself...
>
> But in the Lager, things are different: here the struggle to survive is without respite, because everyone is desperately and ferociously alone. If some Null Achtzehn [literally, 'zero 18'] vacillates, he will find no-one to extend a helping hand; on the contrary someone will knock him aside, because it is in no-one's interest that there will be one more 'musselman' [literally, 'Muslim'[25]] dragging himself to work every day...
>
> All the musselmans who finished in the gas chambers had the same story, or more exactly have no story; they followed the slope down to the bottom, like streams that run down to the sea.... Their life is short but their number is endless; they, the *muselmänner*, the drowned, form the backbone of the camp, an anonymous mass, continually renewed and always identical, of non-men who march and labour in silence, the divine spark dead within them, already too empty to really suffer. One hesitates to call them living: one hesitates to call their death death, in the face of which they have no fear, as they are too tired to understand.

For the *muselmann*, resistance, escape or even a claim to identity was beyond their social capacity. As Giorgio Agamben (2008) describes, the existential desire of survivors like Levi to bear witness contrasted with the almost total denial of the existence of the *muselmann*, even within historical accounts of the Holocaust. Here was a population not only reduced to a barely recognizable social state but also almost beyond any retrospective designation of victimhood. Yet even in these circumstances, it is important to recognize that there was some resistance within the camps, particularly among those with histories of political activity (Bailey 2009). Lore Shelley's remarkable compilation of survivor testimonies (including drawings) of the Auschwitz Munition Factory highlights multiple forms of resistance, including theft of food, sabotage and the smuggling of gun powder by women to men who set fire to the Auschwitz crematoria in October 1944 (Shelley 1996). The retribution was savage – 300 men were shot and four women were hanged. Even so, while the *muselmann* should be remembered as a product of some of the worst manifestations of state crime, it should also be remembered that there were those who fought being reduced to that status, despite knowing that their chances of being killed were high (Shelley 1996: 103–42). Their courage should remain inspirational.

Liminality, deviance and the social audience

For theorists of state crime, looking back on the period of the Holocaust allows us to generalize about the grotesque consequences of the enforced separation of designated alien groups. Even though some of the descriptions of life in Australia's immigration detention centres do conjure images of the living dead, and while the abuse is systemic and the degree of psychological damage often permanent and severe (Grewcock 2009: 217–29), it is important to recognize the relative degree of agency that contemporary detainees retain in the Australian context. Despite the Australian government's deliberate strategy of physically isolating refugees in desert camps or offshore islands, the social isolation is not total and the detainees' humanity is not completely destroyed. The restrictions imposed by the Australian state have not rendered impossible all communication between detainees and civil society: lawyers, non-government organizations and politicians can visit these centres; and family members, friends, political activists and occasionally journalists can maintain communication through visits, letters, emails and phone calls. There has also been extensive illicit contact between detainees and their supporters in the community.

Such links between the detainee and civil society are tenuous, imperfect and often conditioned by restrictive state practices. Yet combined with the actions of the detainees themselves, they enable detainees to have a contemporary voice. For these reasons, detainees ought not to be viewed as the modern day *muselmann*. Instead, they are more appropriately understood as being in a liminal state, in which they have a limited but fluid degree of agency and some capacity to engage with civil society. From this miasmic zone of the social order, detainees' attempts to assert their legal rights, their determination to resist, and on some occasions escape, and their persistent claims to legitimacy have important implications for the way we construct a paradigm of state crime.

Within a state crime framework, recognition of the liminal state and potential agency of the immigration detainee is important for both practical and conceptual reasons.

From a practical perspective, resistance renders detainees visible; it can highlight the contemporary reality of state-organized abuse; it encourages a sense of social solidarity by appealing to a common humanity; and it gives a sense of urgency to the need to change state policy and practice. In short, it helps opposition to the state cohere within civil society. Thus, the escapes and protests that became a feature of the domestic political debate about immigration detention in the early 2000s in turn became a central concern for an 'emerging refugee movement' described by O'Neill as a 'gangly, amorphous group numbering, by some counts, at least 15,000', and including 'top medical specialists, middle class housewives, rural workers, leading lawyers and radical students' (O'Neill 2008: 103). And while there are sharp divisions among activists over the value of escapes,[26] cases like the Bakhtiyari boys highlighted the plight not only of their family but also of the vulnerability of refugees more generally. Moreover, while there is no formal sanctuary movement that houses and protects escaped refugees, it is clear that there are significant numbers of individuals willing to help those escapees being sought by the Australian authorities.

Conceptually, state crime is a more dynamic and nuanced criminological concept when it incorporates a level of victim agency and can be based on a deviance identified and formulated from below (Grewcock 2008). In a criminological sense, detainees form part of and help construct the social audience that is capable of challenging the deviance of the state. As part of this process, detainee resistance challenges the static and conditional nature of human rights selectively bestowed by the state and subjugated to overriding ideologies of sovereignty. It challenges carefully crafted mechanisms of denial, such as the High Court's distinction between punitive and administrative detention. It lays claim to an authenticity and legitimacy denied to detainees by the state. It enables various forms of political solidarity to develop and it helps de-legitimize the systematic alienation, criminalization and abuse of unauthorized migrants.

Conclusion

Criminological understandings of state crime are not absolutely dependent upon victim or survivor resistance. As the experience of the Holocaust demonstrated, there are forms of state crime that can substantially undermine the capacity of victims to resist, although not necessarily the ability of sections of civil society to intervene. However, while an absence of resistance does not negate the concept of state crime, I would suggest that resistance is possible – indeed likely – more often than not, and that the fundamental challenge for criminology is how to recognize and conceptualize it. A failure to do this leaves us with conceptions of state crime that render state crime incapable of challenge or solution, contribute to a sense of pessimism or powerlessness on the part of victims or those who reject the state's actions and deny criminology a role in public discourse beyond critique.

Escaping from immigration detention is formally criminal and may be tactically counterproductive. There was certainly hostility to the escapes from some quarters (O'Neill 2008: 102–3), but the actions of Mehran Behrooz and his fellow escapees also posed questions about the legitimacy and nature of the immigration detention regime. In doing so, they also demonstrated that they were not helpless victims. Instead, they provided an opportunity for us to focus on the legitimate expectations and rights of forced migrants – rather than the determinations of courts, state agencies and non-government organizations – as a baseline measure of state deviance.

Notes

1 I am grateful to Richard Bailey for his helpful comments on an earlier version of this draft based on the paper delivered at the Victoria University of Wellington symposium on 18 January 2010, and to Ian Rintoul and Claire O'Connor for providing information as noted.

2 The film *The Woomera Break-Out* was made by activists involved in the protests; a copy is in the author's possession. An edited version of the film under the title *Through the Wire* was produced in 2006. See www.engagemedia.org/Members/pipstarr/videos/through-the-wire-10.mov/view. See also O'Neill (2008: 83–103).

3 The information regarding the 12 who remained at large and their subsequent surrender is drawn from a personal communication with Ian Rintoul, Refugee Action Coalition, 2 October 2009.

4 At the time of writing, the 2010 escapes are the subject of a wider inquiry into immigration detention being conducted by an Australian Parliamentary Joint Select Committee. See www.aph.gov.au/Parliamentary_Business/Committees/Senate_Committees? url=immigration_detention_ctte/immigration_detention/report/index.htm. The Christmas Island events are the subject of a separate inquiry. See www.minister.immi.gov.au/media/cb/2011/cb162787.htm.

5 For a discussion of the key High Court cases, see Grewcock (2009: 250–9).

6 For a discussion of the abusive impacts of Australian immigration detention up until 2007, see Grewcock (2009: 196–241).

7 For a brief discussion of Australia's anti-people smuggling regime, see Grewcock (2010).

8 See note 2 above.

9 See note 5 above.

10 See, for example, Human Rights and Equal Opportunity Commission (HREOC) (2004) and Senate Legal and Constitutional References Committee (SLCRC) (2006). At the time of writing, the Joint Select Committee on Australia's Immigration Detention Network, established by the Australian parliament in June 2011 (see note 4 above), has heard extensive evidence of ongoing abuses. In July 2011, following revelations of extensive self-harm at the Christmas Island Immigration Detention Centre, the Commonwealth Ombudsman announced he was establishing an inquiry to examine suicide and self-harm in immigration detention. See www.ombudsman.gov. au/media-releases/show/189. See also note 6 above.

11 Interview conducted with author, 30 June 2011.

12 At the time of writing, a number of detainees involved in protests at the Christmas Island and Villawood immigration detention centres were facing criminal charges, although some of these cases have been withdrawn or dismissed (Guest and Taylor 2011).

13 The maximum penalty for escaping from immigration detention was increased to five years in 2001. See *Migration Legislation Amendment (Immigration Detainees) Act 2001.* In 2011, the *Migration Act 1958* was further amended to enable a protection visa to be refused to a person convicted of a criminal offence while in immigration detention. See *Migration Amendment (Strengthening the Character Test and Other Provisions) Act 2011.*

14 Compare, for example, the characterization of the escapees in the 1963 film *The Great Escape*, which tells the story of an escape by 76 allied airmen from a German Prisoner of War camp in 1944; the 1973 film *Papillon*, based on an autobiographical account of an escape from the French Penal Colony on Devil's Island; and the 1994 film *Shawshank Redemption*, based on a fictional account of an escape from a US maximum security prison. Interestingly, one of the best-selling books in Australia in the past decade has been Gregory David Roberts' *Shantaram: A Novel*, based loosely on his experiences on the run, having escaped from Pentridge Prison in Melbourne in 1980 and remaining at large (mainly in India but punctuated by several other escapes in New Zealand, Italy and Switzerland) for ten years.

15 S. 310D *Crimes Act 1900*.

16 See, for example, *R* v. *Loughnan* [1981] VR 443; *R* v. *Rogers* (1996) 86 A Crim R 542.

17 *Behrooz* v. *Secretary, Department of Immigration and Multicultural and Indigenous Affairs (DIMIA)* (2004) 219 CLR 486.

18 *Behrooz* v. *Secretary, DIMIA*, as cited, at para 21.

19 Personal communication with Adelaide barrister Claire O'Connor, 11 December 2009.

20 Quoted in *Morrison* v. *Behrooz* [2005] SASC 142, at para 8.

21 *Morrison* v. *Behrooz*, as cited, at para 11.

22 See *Shillabeer* v. *Hussain* [2005] SASC 198; *Police* v. *Kakar; Elder* v. *Kakar* [2005] SASC 222; *Boonstoppel* v. *Hamidi* [2005] SASC 248; *Elder* v. *Shojaee* [2005] SASC 285; *Elder* v. *Said* [2005] SASC 286; *Bridle* v. *Gomravi* [2005] SASC 295. My thanks to Adelaide barrister Claire O'Connor for alerting me to these cases and providing me with background information.

23 *Morrison* v. *Behrooz*, as cited, at para 46.

24 According to O'Neill (2008: 103), of the 373 escapees, 'two were gaoled, 183 were re-captured and deported, and 13 left Australia voluntarily'.

25 For a discussion of the origin of the term's use in this context, see Agamben (2008: 44–8).

26 A view confirmed through numerous discussions between the author and Ian Rintoul of the Refugee Action Coalition.

References

Agamben, G. (2008) *Remnants of Auschwitz: The Witness and the Archive* (trans. Daniel Heller-Roazen), Brooklyn, NY: Zone Books.

Bailey, R. (2009) 'Up against the Wall: Bare Life and Resistance in the Camp', *Law and Critique*, 20(2), 113–32.

Brown, D., Farrier, D., Egger, S., McNamara, M., Steel, S., Grewcock, M. and Spears, D. (2011) *Criminal Laws* (5th edition), Sydney: The Federation Press.

Carlton, B. (2007) *Imprisoning Resistance: Life and Death in an Australian Supermax*, Sydney: Institute of Criminology Press.

Cohen, S. (1993) 'Human Rights and Crimes of the State: The Culture of Denial', *Australian and New Zealand Journal of Criminology*, 26, 97–115.

Department of Immigration and Citizenship (2011) *Submission (number 32 supplementary) to the Joint Select Committee on Australia's Immigration Detention Network, September*, available at www.aph.gov.au/Parliamentary_Business/Committees/Senate_Committees?url=immigration_detention_ctte/immigration_detention/submissions.htm, accessed 10 July 2012.

Draper, H. (1977) *Karl Marx's Theory of Revolution, Volume 1: State and Bureaucracy*, New York: Monthly Review Press.

Engels, F. (2010) *The Origins of the Family, Private Property and the State* (1884), available online at Marxist Internet Archive, www.marxists.org/archive/marx/works/1884/origin-family/ch09.htm, accessed 23 November 2011.

Fein, H. (1979) *Accounting for Genocide*, New York: Free Press.

Gramsci, A. (1971) *Selections from the Prison Notebooks*, in Q. Hoare and G. Nowell-Smith (eds), London: Lawrence and Wishart.

Green, P. and Ward, T. (2000a) 'State Crime, Human Rights and the Limits of Criminology', *Social Justice*, 27(1), 101–15.

Green, P. and Ward, T. (2000b) 'Legitimacy, Civil Society and State Crime', *Social Justice*, 27(4), 76–93.

Green, P. and Ward, T. (2004) *State Crime: Governments, Violence and Corruption*, London: Pluto Press.

Grewcock, M. (2008) 'State Crime: Some Conceptual Issues', in T. Anthony and C. Cunneen (eds), *The Critical Criminology Companion*, Sydney: Hawkins Press.

Grewcock, M. (2009) *Border Crimes: Australia's War on Illicit Migrants*, Sydney: Institute of Criminology Press.

Grewcock, M. (2010) ' "Scum of the Earth"? People Smuggling, Criminalisation and Refugees', *Human Rights Defender*, 19(3), 14–16.

Guest, D. and Taylor, P. (2011) 'Riot "Ringleaders" Escape Charges and Awarded Visas', *The Australian*, 28 June, available at www.theaustralian.com.au/national-affairs/riot-ringleaders-escape-charges-awarded-visas/story-fn59niix-1226083058222, accessed 27 June 2012.

HREOC (Human Rights and Equal Opportunities Commission) (2004) *A Last Resort? National Inquiry into Children in Immigration Detention*, Sydney: HREOC.

Levi, P. (1987) *If This is a Man* (trans. Stuart Woolf), London: Abacus.

Lygo, I. (2004) *News Overboard: The Tabloid Media, Race Politics and Islam*, Geelong: Southerly Change Media.

Mann, T. (2003) *Desert Sorrow: Asylum Seekers at Woomera*, Kent Town: Wakefield Press.

O'Neill, M. (2008) *Blind Conscience*, Sydney: New South.

Pickering, S. (2005) *Refugees and State Crime*, Sydney: The Federation Press.

Poynting, S., Noble, G., Tabar, P. and Collins, J. (2004) *Bin Laden in the Suburbs: Criminalising the Arab Other*, Sydney: Institute of Criminology Press.

Shelley, L. (1996) *The Union Kommando in Auschwitz*, Lanham and London: University Press of America.

SLCRC (Senate Legal and Constitutional References Committee) (2006) *Administration and Operation of the Migration Act 1958*, Canberra: Senate Printing Unit.

Sofsky, W. (1999) *The Order of Terror: The Concentration Camp* (trans. William Templer), Princeton, NJ: Princeton University Press.

Weber, M. (1994) 'Politics as a Vocation' (1919), in *Political Writings*, Cambridge: Cambridge University Press.

6 The politics of state crime and resistance

Self-determination in Sri Lanka

Suthaharan Nadarajah and Victoria Sentas

Where there is power, there is resistance.

(Foucault 1976/1978: 95)

I was once asked: 'You say Tamil Eelam, but where are the boundaries of this Tamil Eelam that you talk about? Show me.' I was taken aback by the directness of the question. I thought for a while. Then I replied: 'Take a map of the island. Take a paint brush and paint all the areas where Sri Lanka has bombed and launched artillery attacks during these past several years. When you have finished, the painted area that you see – that is Tamil Eelam.'

(LTTE Colonel Kittu, cited in Satyendra 1993)

Introduction

Sri Lanka's three-decade-old civil war ended in May 2009 with the military defeat of the Liberation Tigers of Tamil Eelam (LTTE) by the Sinhala-dominated armed forces. The state's military campaign, although conducted under close international scrutiny, was characterized by mass killings and draconian blockades preventing food and medicine from reaching trapped civilians. The final months of the war were especially bloody. From January to May 2009, the Sri Lankan armed forces conducted widespread and large-scale military bombardment of civilians in 'safe zones', hospitals and humanitarian centres, despite repeated protests by Western states, human rights groups and others (Human Rights Watch 2009, 2010; International Crisis Group 2010b; Amnesty International 2010). A United Nations (UN) panel of experts stated that the Sri Lankan military campaign, during which over 40,000 people perished, 'constituted persecution of the [Tamil] population' (UN 2011: ii, 69). The state's declaration of victory over the LTTE was followed by the internment of hundreds of thousands of Tamils for months in crowded militarized camps, amid persistent reports of rape, 'disappearances' and torture (Freedom from Torture 2011; UN 2011: 41–7).

Three years after the fighting ended, while the Sri Lankan state now claims that 'peace' has been established and a post-war economic boom is imminent,

Tamils on the island and abroad argue that a state-orchestrated genocide is continuing (British Tamil Forum 2011; Tamil National Alliance 2009). Despite international pressure, rather than resettlement and rehabilitation of the war-shattered Tamil areas, the state has prioritized 'national development'. This has translated into massive infrastructure projects, primarily in the south, and a multifaceted militarized effort to order national life according to homogenized and Sinhala-dominated terms (International Crisis Group 2011). At the same time, despite international pressure pushing for the Sri Lankan government to negotiate a political solution to the long-running ethno-political conflict with elected Tamil representatives, the state has declared the 'problem' ended by the defeat of the LTTE. Moreover, the state has further centralized and militarized the governance of Tamil areas, where it continues to violently suppress dissent (Hogg 2011).

Sri Lanka's international relations, meanwhile, are increasingly being defined by the question of its accountability for the mass killings and atrocities of 2009. Sri Lanka has become the focus of sustained campaigns to this end among international human rights groups, Western states and Tamil Diaspora organizations. Since the end of the war, such efforts have converged on establishing an independent international investigation into the war crimes, crimes against humanity and, as Tamils claim, acts of genocide. Denying any wrongdoing, the Sri Lankan state has responded by mobilizing its diplomatic and political machinery to thwart such an investigation and to demonize its advocates (Manor 2011). Three years after the war's end, avoiding an international investigation has arguably become the prime foreign policy goal of the Sri Lankan government.

Amid all of this, the hitherto central plank of Tamil resistance – the right to self-determination of the Tamil nation – appears, at first glance, to have faded from the main field of contestation. However, a closer look at the interrelated action and counteraction between the Sri Lankan state and the Tamils reveals that self-determination (fundamentally meaning the recognition of a Tamil nation and its homeland in the island's north-east) remains the primary fault line. The state denounces demands for war crimes accountability, demilitarization of the north-east and a negotiated political solution as part of the LTTE's continuing 'separatist agenda'. Political actors in the Diaspora are characterized as the 'LTTE rump', and Western critics of the Colombo regime as its agents (Ladduwahetty 2011). Conversely, Diaspora actors denounce the government's economic, development and military strategies in the Tamil areas as the continuation of genocide in the service of Sinhala supremacy. They also strive to identify the Diaspora as equally integral to the Tamil nation as the 'homeland Tamils', in contrast to the perception of Diaspora Tamils as outsiders to post-war Sri Lanka, as the state and some others insist (e.g. RAND 2001).

The central argument of this chapter is that neither state crime nor resistance to it can be fully understood through reference to the acts of violence themselves (that is, as violations of international or domestic law, on the one hand, or demands for justice or accountability, on the other), or to the self-evident identities of the perpetrators and victims (in our case, the Sinhala armed forces and

Tamils, respectively). Instead, paraphrasing Clausewitz's (1976) famous neologism, state crime and resistance constitute the continuation of politics by other means. By this, we do not refer to the possible motivations of the perpetrators (for example, racism) or of those who resist (such as survival), although these are often clearly discernible dynamics. We are concerned with the content of the subjectivities and social relations that engender state crime and resistance, armed or otherwise, as self-evidently necessary and rightful acts. Moreover, state crime and resistance to it cannot be understood merely as cause and effect, but as mutually bound and intimate relations of action and counteraction. These relations not only result in destruction, in terms of lives and property, but they are also productive, in the Foucauldian sense of the word, creating new and sometimes hybrid subjectivities that, in turn, engender resistance and counter-resistance anew.

We support our argument through an empirical study of the struggle between the Sri Lankan state and the Tamils, particularly the Diaspora, using a Foucauldian reading of the power relations and subjectivities that constitute this struggle and, conversely, the impact of the latter on the former. We begin with a discussion of power and resistance in order to explain state crime and resistance to it. We then briefly outline the historic antecedents to contemporary power–resistance dynamics between the Sri Lankan state and the Tamil Diaspora. In the third and fourth sections, we outline how current contestations over the accountability for Sri Lankan state crime depend, for both the state and Tamils, on the largely submerged question of Tamil self-determination.

State crime, power and resistance

While Foucault's conception of power has often been criticized for supposedly foreclosing the possibility of resistance, this reading of his work has been convincingly challenged by others (Heller 1996; Pickett 1996). Foucault himself was at pains to stress, against such criticisms, that resistance is immanent to power, with both functioning in a co-extensive, even mutually constitutive, relation: 'where there is power, there is resistance, and yet, or rather consequently, this resistance is never in a position of exteriority in relation to power' (Foucault 1976/1978: 95). Insofar as resistance is the response to the state violence against which it struggles, and state violence is the response to defiance to state rule ('resistance'), the conditions for resistance are immanent to the power it opposes.

Crucially for our argument, resistance to power coalesces through and against the same field of social relations that give rise to state power, instead of being exterior to it. Rather than being unidirectionally linked, Sri Lankan state crime and Tamil resistance are imbricated, bound in intimate circular relations of action and counteraction that are manifestations of the same field of contested social relations that comprises 'Sri Lanka'. If we are to make sense of what follows from the Sri Lankan state's repression of the Tamil people, the processual dynamic of resistance allows us to call into consideration its productive and generative effects. The inherent unpredictability of the contestations inherent to the field of social relations is also why, as we demonstrate here, annihilatory violence is not guaranteed to produce acquiescence and docility, but may instead intensify resistance.

For Foucault, resistance is itself a form of power. Conversely, what appears as power may itself be resistance to other forms of power. In other words, genocide and oppression may constitute resistance to the exercise of power that posits specific subjectivities as existential threats to a given order (consider the implications of the terms *counter*-insurgency/terror). This is not to suggest an equivalency between state power and the power wielded by those who are repressed by it. Rather, conceiving of resistance as a form of power highlights the interaction between state crime and opposition to it. The Sri Lankan state's efforts since the war's end to obliterate the sites of alleged war crimes, maintain draconian security laws and revoke even the limited devolution of powers to the provinces cannot be separated from the mounting international pressure in the same period for war crimes investigations, demilitarization and (territorial) power-sharing negotiations with the Tamils.

According to Foucault's categories, sovereign power – the arbitrary power to kill or let die – functions alongside more diffused forms of power, circulating and (re)constructing the strategies, subjectivities, actors and meanings of oppression and resistance. These circulating forms of power include discipline (Foucault 1975–7) and governmentality (Foucault 2007, 2008). Discerning the specificities of the operations of power, therefore, can begin by asking: what is the rationality that informs them? Moreover, to fully understand state conduct, Foucault exhorts us 'to cut off the king's head' (1980: 121). In other words, rather than starting with the state as a self-evident reality, we must consider the state – and its actions – as a manifestation and product of circulating power. Without such an analysis of social relations, an examination of state crime attributes to the state a total autonomy of action that it does not possess. In Sri Lanka, the hierarchical ethnic and social order we term 'Sinhala-Buddhist' is not only embedded and manifest in the state, it emerges through, and is sustained by, the routine practices of a much wider set of actors – political parties, civil society organizations, trade unions, the Buddhist clergy, corporate actors, individual citizens and so on.

In relation to state crime, therefore, mass atrocities cannot be seen as merely acts of sovereign power; they are informed by a specific circulating rationality which registers what is to be defended, what is to be destroyed, by whom and to what end. For the Sri Lankan state, fighting 'terrorism' is synonymous with fighting 'separatism', and vice versa (Bartholomeusz 2002). The enemies of the Sri Lankan state are therefore not only those who take up arms against it but, equally, those who challenge the ideal of Sinhala rule over a homogenized and unitary territorial space, as we explain below. It is in this way, for example, that some Sinhalese – such as left-wing advocates of Tamil self-determination and even liberals who reject Sinhala ethnocracy – also become 'traitors' and existential threats who must be destroyed in the pursuit of a stable order.

Power organizes meanings and socially constructs subjects. A power that is repressive, negative and constraining can simultaneously produce and construct – including in ways that resource resistance to such domination. Foucault (1982: 212) conceptualized resisting subjects as not merely oppressed but as brought into being as an *effect* of subjection:

> This form of power applies itself to immediate everyday life which categorizes the individual, marks him by his own individuality, attaches him to his own identity, imposes a law of truth on him which he must recognize and which others have to recognize in him. It is a form of power which makes individuals subjects. There are two meanings of the word *subject*: subject to someone else by control or dependence, and tied to his own identity by a conscience or self-knowledge. Both meanings suggest a form of power which subjugates and makes subject to.

Rather than power being simply wielded by, or over, subjects, the subject is constituted by social power, the manifestation of which includes, but is not limited to, state crimes. This does not mean that the subject is absolutely determined by power. Instead, the conditions for acting are both impeded and made possible by the social relations which produce these conditions (see Butler 1997). Holistic interpretations of Foucault's entire work consider the subject to be both constituted and 'self-constituting'; that is, while power produces subjects, the subject may simultaneously resist and remake the powers that constitute it (see Armstrong 2008). The Tamil Diaspora, for example, has been constituted as a *foreign* enemy of the state, a role it actively embraces now through its resistance to state crime, while at the same time rejecting its supposed externality to the island's 'internal affairs' – a dynamic we discuss below.

In sum, we argue that state crime and resistance to it are deeply structured by the entire field of social relations that has come to constitute post-independence Sri Lanka. The ethnic strife that has escalated since 1948, the armed conflict that erupted in 1983, the cataclysmic violence that marked its end and the state violence since the war's end are all manifestations of the contestations inherent to this field. State violence has an enduring, routine presence in politics – a dynamic that obscures the material conditions of its violence (Poynting and Whyte 2012). In Sri Lanka, the mass killings of 2009 and what has followed since should not therefore be understood simply as unlawful aberrations to the otherwise legitimate endeavours of the state (aimed at defeating terrorism). Rather, these should be seen as the inevitable consequences of a social field in which a majoritarian order seeks to propagate and defend itself against perceived existential challenges – represented first and foremost by the Tamil demand for self-rule.

The content of state crime

In this section, we consider how the project of state-led social transformation in post-independence Sri Lanka (previously Ceylon) led to two interwoven phenomena: first, to the consolidation and polarization of ethnicity as a political force; and second, to the concomitant emergence of oppression, conflict and escalating state crime, as well as coeval Tamil resistance, both political and militant. As Camilla Orjuela (2003: 198 see also Krishna 1999: 31) puts it:

> Sri Lanka could be seen as a textbook example of an ethnic conflict, where economic, political and cultural deprivation and grievances of a minority have provoked a violent rebellion against a state that has come to be seen as representative of only the majority ethnic group.

Discrimination against the Tamils by the post-independence Sinhala-dominated state has been discussed in numerous scholarly works and policy studies and need not be elaborated further here (see, for example, Balasingham 2004; Bartholomeusz 2002; Bose 1994; De Votta 2004; Krishna 1999; Wilson 1994; Winslow and Woost 2004; and discussion in Nadarajah and Vimalarajah 2008: 16–32). Inexorable 'Sinhalization' of the post-colonial state has resulted in a bureaucracy, judiciary, police and military with an entrenched majoritarian ethos. Even by the mid-1970s, well before the armed conflict began, Sri Lanka was perceived as having 'regressed to an illiberal, ethnocentric regime bent on Sinhala superordination and Tamil subjugation' (De Votta 2004: 6). What is of importance for our purposes is how the all-pervasive discourse and state practices of Sinhala nationalism came to establish an antagonistic dichotomy between the island's Tamil and Sinhala collectives, one that quickly replaced the promise of the singular collective – 'Ceylonese' – to which the departing colonial power believed it had transferred power.

While at independence Tamil and Sinhala were already politicized ethnic identities (Orjuela 2010: 15), the post-independence majoritarian state-building project transformed these into *essentially* antagonistic ones, turning on competing conceptions of territorial belonging (Krishna 1999; Stokke 1998). First, the demographic distribution of power immediately provided the Sinhala majority with an unassailable domination of parliament, which enabled effective capture of the machinery of state. Second, whereas until the end of centuries of colonial rule in 1948, the Tamils had lived predominantly in the north-east and the Sinhalese in the south, after independence the notion that the island belonged to the Sinhala, and that the Tamils were latecomers or vestiges of past invasions from India, informed a grand attempt at territorial and demographic reorganization by the state. This comprised both constitutional redrawing of electoral boundaries and state-sponsored 'internal' colonization by the Sinhalese of historically Tamil areas (Wilson 1994).

These processes precipitated a specific form of Tamil resistance: self-recognition as a Tamil nation with rights equal to the Sinhala nation's and a political project to protect the integrity of the (north-eastern) Tamil homeland through territorialized rule (Krishna 1999: 68–9). This resistance flowed from power's forceful ordering of the population into the valued 'Sinhala' and threatening 'Tamil' categories; but while embracing this divide, this resistance rejected an inherent hierarchy between them and instead pursued parity between the two 'nations' (TULF 1976). It is in this way that demands for Tamil self-determination and, in particular, territorial autonomy emerged as a direct reaction to an increasingly violent Sinhala state-building project.

The clearest early manifestation of this resistance was the formation in 1947 of the Federal Party (FP), which, advocating federal self-rule for the Tamil homeland as a response to Sinhala colonization, repeatedly won elections in the north-east for the next two decades (Wilson 1994; Krishna 1999: 68–77). Indeed, Tamil parties advocating self-rule of the Tamil homeland have consistently received popular backing in the north-east in post-independence Sri Lanka. Amid the intensification of processes of state exclusion, repression and violence that the FP's success spurred, the demand for federalism made way in the mid-1970s for calls for outright independence of Tamil Eelam, first articulated in 1976 by the Tamil United Liberation Party (TULF) that was formed by the merger of the FP and other Tamil parties. These contestations over self-determination reveal how the Tamil homeland became reified in Sri Lanka's social relations; Tamil resistance turned on the defence of this territorial space, and Sinhala domination on its denial and dismantling.

Tamil resistance to the Sinhala project manifested itself not only in repeated electoral endorsement of the FP, but also in widespread participation across the homeland in the party's civil disobedience and protest campaigns (Wilson 1994). The state responded to these agitations with greater repression (alongside episodic anti-Tamil rioting); accelerated colonization; and legal, constitutional and bureaucratic changes that further favoured the majority (ibid.). In 1972, the British-supplied constitution was discarded and, despite vehement Tamil objections, was replaced with one that explicitly held Sri Lanka (the country's new Sinhala name) to be a Sinhala-Buddhist state. The Tamil response, as enunciated by the TULF (1976) in the landmark Vaddukoddai Resolution, was to declare further efforts at cohabitation futile and outright independence for Tamil Eelam as the central Tamil demand (Wilson 1994: 113–32).

The demonstrable futility of Tamil peaceful agitation had by then already stirred the first moments of militancy. The state responded to these sporadic acts of sabotage and assassination with military repression and a massive (World Bank-funded) expansion in colonization after 1978. Following the state-backed anti-Tamil pogrom in July 1983, a full-scale armed struggle erupted for Tamil Eelam (Balasingham 2004). From the outset, the conflict was characterized by state crime – massacres and other atrocities, as well as humanitarian blockades of Tamil areas (see, for example, Paust 1998). Crucially, the state's conflation of fighting 'terrorism' with fighting (Tamil) 'separatism' became explicit (Bartholomeusz 2002). For example, alongside its first major military operations, the state also passed the sixth amendment to the Constitution, outlawing the advocacy of secession (Nadarajah and Vimalarajah 2008: 29–30).

In sum, since independence, the constitution and consolidation of 'Tamils' and 'Sinhalese' as self-evidently antagonistic collectives has informed, and has in turn been reinforced by, drastic changes in state policy, constitutional arrangements and security practices. These practices have produced specific forms of Tamil resistance, the intensification of which has led to the intensification of the former, and vice versa. As the armed conflict progressed, state crime – in which tens of thousands of Tamils were massacred, summarily executed or 'disappeared' – fuelled Tamil support for armed struggle (Bose 1994; Balasingham 2004). Conversely, the expanding Tamil armed resistance – which soon led to the internationalization of the Tamil question – spurred ever more violent efforts by the state not only to crush the armed challenge, but also to deny and destroy the territorial bases for Tamil autonomy (through intensified colonization, militarization and the redrawing of electoral boundaries). At the same time, the state has rejected international involvement in the recognition and resolution of the ethnopolitical crisis (articulated most often in the language of 'internal affairs' or as 'defending sovereignty').

To restate our argument, neither the logic of state crime, which soon reached genocidal intensity, nor that of Tamil resistance can be understood in isolation from the contested social field that has been post-independence Sri Lanka. Moreover, the struggle for autonomy of the Tamil homeland constitutes a specific response to Sri Lankan state crime. State crime is in turn a response (resistance) to the self-constitution of Tamils as a self-governing nation and the existential threat this poses to the ideal of the island as a bastion for Sinhala-Buddhism.

Accountability and foreign enemies

These same dynamics now inform the heavily internationalized contestations over the question of accountability for the mass atrocities of 2009. The findings of the UN panel of experts (2011) and international human rights groups (Amnesty International 2010; Human Rights Watch 2009, 2010; International Crisis Group 2010b) support the conclusion that Sri Lanka's conduct in the final months of the war unambiguously constitutes state crime. However, this is not so in Sinhala-Buddhist terms, whereby actions undertaken in defeating terrorism and separatism – a paramount and cardinal duty of the state – are seen to be beyond reproach. This is why the increasingly forceful demands by the international community that Sri Lanka pursue accountability for the 2009 atrocities, and the associated charge that large numbers of Sri Lankan *citizens* were massacred, have not produced alarm or disquiet among the Sinhala polity and media. Instead, these demands have provoked outrage, anger and a strident assertion of state sovereignty and independence, discursively framed in calls to arms against Western 'neocolonialism' (see, for example, Peiris 2010).

Conversely, Tamil demands for accountability, now led primarily by Diaspora actors (Vimalarajah and Cheran 2010), overlap with those of the international community. Crucially, these two projects have very different contents and rationalities, a difference that is reflected best in how victims and state crimes are understood. For international actors, the victims are primarily human beings or, if viewed politically, citizens of Sri Lanka. However, for the Tamils, victims are first and foremost members of the Tamil nation. This difference is exemplified by Tamils' reference to the atrocities as self-evident genocide (see British Tamil Forum 2011; Tamils Against Genocide 2011). In contrast, the international community prefers the language of war crimes and crimes against humanity (see Amnesty International 2010; Human Rights Watch 2010; International Crisis Group 2010b; UN 2011). We consider the significance of this later.

In Sinhala-Buddhist terms, however, these subtleties matter little. As such, the largely West-based Tamil Diaspora, international human rights organizations and Western states have come to be lumped together (see International Crisis Group 2010b: 31) as a nefarious coalition of *foreign* enemies intent on both thwarting the hard-won victory against terrorism and dividing the country. This discourse has been reinforced by another key demand by the international community: that Sri Lanka pursue a political – that is, power-sharing – solution to 'Tamil grievances' through negotiations with the main Tamil party, the Tamil National Alliance (Blake 2011).

What is important for our study of the productive nature of power is how state crime has worked to generate the Diaspora as Sri Lanka's nemesis. There are two dimensions to this constitution: as a human collective and as a political entity. First, while Tamil emigration began in the 1970s amid discrimination and repression, it was after the armed conflict erupted in the early 1980s that state massacres and other atrocities triggered wave upon wave of refugee flight to the West. Over three decades, these overseas destinations became home to a large and cohesive Tamil community, which not only prospered, albeit with great difficulty amid vicious anti-immigration regimes and local hostility and racism, but also continued to cherish its ties to the homeland (Vimalarajah and Cheran 2010). The Tamil Diaspora now represents a heterogeneous global community that shares multiple, hybrid identifications: the Diaspora are Western citizens with deep roots in their 'host countries', but are also members of the Tamil nation, who maintain strong familial, social, cultural, economic and political ties to Sri Lanka's north-east.

Second, while expatriate Tamils were always part of Sri Lanka's social field, in social, political and humanitarian terms it was only in the last years of the armed conflict that the Diaspora manifested as a distinct (singular) entity on this terrain. Amid the overarching discursive frame imposed on the Sri Lankan conflict – that is, as a war between the state and the LTTE – expatriate Tamils were given little consideration, being seen merely as an adjunct of the island's Tamil community. From 2007, the Tamil Diaspora not only became an object (singular) of scholarly and international policy and security studies (Vimalarajah and Cheran 2010; Sentas 2012), but also one attributed with specific characteristics, mentality and agency. As Sri Lanka's offensive against the LTTE expanded after 2006, and mass civilian casualties mounted rapidly, expatriate Tamil activity (such as mass protests and rallies, or advocacy targeting international governments and human rights groups) intensified. This mobilization reached a crescendo in the final months of the conflict, with tens – sometimes hundreds – of thousands marching through Western capitals (see Vimalarajah and Cheran 2010). Diaspora campaigns sought international action to initially stop, and then to seek justice for, the slaughter *of their people, in their homeland*, the details of which were being reported hourly through Tamil websites and satellite television.

Thus, it was through its resistance to Sri Lankan state crime that 'the Diaspora' emerged on the international stage as a distinct entity with autonomous agency. Prior to this, despite decades of demonstrations and campaigns in support of Tamil self-determination, its members were understood only in relation to the LTTE – either as its recalcitrant supporters (RAND 2001) or its hapless victims (Human Rights Watch 2006). In other words, Diaspora campaigns against Sri Lankan state crime are a form of self-constitution as a legitimate actor, alongside Tamils on the island, within the internationalized contestation over Sri Lanka's future.

It is the destruction of the LTTE, in particular, that has served to foreground the Diaspora as a distinct, forceful and consequential element of the internationalized politics of Sri Lanka's conflict. First, the ongoing military repression within Sri Lanka has largely silenced domestic Tamil agitation. Despite episodic Tamil outbursts – spontaneous demonstrations, the occasional riot and, perhaps inevitably, robust electoral endorsement of the Tamil National Alliance – the oppressive security presence in the north-east, replete with paramilitary and extra-judicial violence, has all but smothered organized Tamil political resistance (International Crisis Group 2011; Hogg 2011). Diaspora actors, despite manifest rivalry and discord, have – at least for the moment – become the de facto vanguard of the Tamil liberation project, thus replacing the LTTE in the state's view as its primary Tamil threat.

Second, and consequently, the Diaspora has become a key actor in the discourses on 'Sri Lanka' engaged in by the international community, the state and, crucially, the Tamils themselves, both on the island and abroad. To the international community, the Diaspora has appeared as a 'hard-line', albeit heterogeneous, Tamil bloc, but also an unavoidable one given its persistent political agitation in Western capitals (International Crisis Group 2010a, but see Vimalarajah and Cheran 2010). For the Tamil self-determination struggle, the Diaspora became an indispensable vehicle – including as an important source of material support for Tamils on the island. Crucially, in taking up the issue of accountability, Diaspora actors are potentially powerful allies. However, they are also unpredictable ones, remaining beyond the authority and reach of the Tamil political party leadership.

The meaning of accountability

It is its pursuit of accountability that has led, most of all, to the Diaspora being represented by the Sri Lankan state/Sinhala discourse as a dangerous enemy that has taken up the 'separatist' project of the LTTE. The state and mainstream (Sinhala-owned) media swing between denouncing the Diaspora as a singular entity and claiming those attacking Sri Lanka to be a minority among Tamils abroad (see Peiris 2010). In either case, it is the Diaspora's machinations in the

West – rather than objective concern over alleged state crimes – that are blamed for the international community's post-war hostility to the Sri Lankan state. Western politicians are said to be in hock with Tamil voters and Western media to be in the pay of the Tamil expatriates or LTTE agents sitting on the organization's cash piles (Pennels and Probyn 2011). Alternatively, the West is seen as having sinister designs on Sri Lanka, in which the Tamils are complicit (Reuters 2011).

Whatever the ascribed logic, according to this discourse, the Tamil Diaspora is routinely merged with the West as a composite existential threat to the state. This conflation was already developing amid the mobilization of the Diaspora during the final phase of the conflict, most visible in the mass protests against the war, alongside repeated calls by the United States, United Kingdom and other states for Sri Lanka to cease its shelling of safe zones and hospitals and to respect international humanitarian law. In other words, calls for humanitarian ceasefire or restraint were primarily understood as a shared *foreign* effort to thwart the state from defeating terrorism or, equivalently, as self-evident support for 'dividing' the country – a belief reinforced by growing international calls for a power-sharing/devolution 'solution' to address 'Tamil grievances'.

Sri Lanka's construction of the Diaspora as a composite threat with the West prevails in spite of the existence of some friction between Diaspora and international and state actors, such as criticism of the UN's inaction during the final stages of the war. More importantly, Diasporic subject positions reflect the fundamentally different political stakes for Tamils from those of international actors, in seeking accountability from the Sri Lankan government. Diaspora actors campaigning against state crime during and after the conflict have foregrounded the Tamil identity in their work – conceptualizing themselves as part of the Tamil nation/people, agitating against state persecution of Tamils (as opposed to 'Sri Lankans') and interpreting state repression through the territorial frame of the Tamil homeland (see, for example, British Tamil Forum 2011). Thus, as noted earlier, in contrast to international claims of war crimes and crimes against humanity in seeking accountability, Diaspora groups foreground genocide.[1] In reference to a 'solution', the Diaspora seeks the exercise of self-determination (for example, calling for a referendum on independence among homeland Tamils), rather than the pursuit of 'reconciliation', as the international community urges.

'Diaspora' therefore reflects contingent processes of subjects' self-constitution – a collective process that has resourced a renewed drive for self-determination since the war's end. Resistance generates strategic or affective attachments to collective identities through oppression and hardship suffered, both in Sri Lanka and abroad. Consequently, Tamil advocacy operates within a discourse whereby state crime is integral to a wider state campaign to extinguish the Tamil challenge to Sinhala majoritarian rule. Thus, while conducting advocacy through the rubric of international humanitarian law, human rights or press freedoms, Diaspora campaigns turn on the rights of *Tamils*, rather than these universalist principles per se. In contrast, international efforts on accountability notably avoid the question of genocide and centre on upholding international humanitarian law or human rights, without reference to the specific identities of the victims. These differences have also led to strident criticism by some international actors of the Diaspora as 'hard-line' and its activities as an impediment to 'reconciliation' and 'peace' (see, for example, International Crisis Group 2010a).

At the same time, Sri Lankan state/Sinhala resistance to the notion of accountability or a negotiated solution is based on the view that Diaspora activities are part of a Tamil campaign against a rightful majoritarian rule. International actors are understood to share this goal (a conflation reinforced by persistent Western pressure for a political solution as well as criticism and demands for state reform along liberal democratic lines). As such, the state has increasingly pursued efforts targeting the Diaspora, such as overt and intimidating surveillance and videotaping of expatriate protests and meetings (Vimalarajah and Cheran 2010: 26). Sri Lanka has also promulgated laws to seize monies or land in the northeast belonging to expatriates, and sometimes detained and tortured individuals when they return to the island (Freedom from Torture 2011).

In seeking to maintain majoritarian domestic order, Sri Lanka has increasingly concentrated its machinery against external threats. The state therefore fiercely resists an independent, especially international, investigation of the 2009 mass atrocities; negotiations with Tamil leaders; as well as demilitarization and international/Diaspora-led rejuvenation of the war-shattered north-east. However, in doing so, it also *constitutes* these external threats: it is by resisting these supposedly Diaspora-inspired international demands that Sri Lanka has come to alienate itself from its closest allies in the West. These action, counteraction dynamics are increasingly producing 'Sri Lanka' as a problematic state in the global liberal landscape (see, for example, Manor 2011), in contrast to the long-standing and widely held view that Sri Lanka was one of this predominant world order's most promising new members, albeit one that was being held back by 'terrorism'.

Conclusion

To return to our argument, today's post-war antagonisms around Sri Lanka's accountability for state crimes reflect a struggle between subjectifying power and resistance to it. The latter is manifest as the Diaspora and its campaigns for accountability, the former in practices of state defiance to such demands. This relation, in turn, is the product of a concomitant struggle between subjectifying power and resistance. The former is manifest as the 'Sinhalized' state and its practices, including state crime, since independence; and the latter by the self-constitution of the Diaspora as an exiled part of the Tamil nation. Thus, both state crime and the drive for accountability are deeply conditioned by the contested social field that constitutes 'Sri Lanka'. In this regard, the ongoing struggle over accountability for state crime, just like the mass atrocities of 2009, are rooted in the longer and deeper contestations that have been played out since

1948: that is, between power that seeks to reify a Sinhala majoritarian domestic order and resistance that seeks a different order, one that ensures Tamil freedom from this power embedded in the post-independence Sri Lankan state.

Self-determination, rather than being a demand of the LTTE that has been annihilated along with the organization, is a diffuse and circulating ambition that has been reformulated through subjectivities such as the Diaspora and thus deeply embedded in routine Tamil practices. In short, the struggle for accountability for Sri Lankan state crimes is underpinned by Tamil claims for self-determination, even if these are not explicitly articulated. It is thus unsurprising that the struggle over who has the right to make political claims vis-à-vis Sri Lanka, and the content of these claims, overlaps with the question of accountability for state crime and constitutes the central site of the power–resistance dynamic since the war's end.

While the state's defiance of its accountability for war crimes has served to constitute the Diaspora as an existential foreign threat, the Diaspora's concomitant self-constitution as an integral part of the Tamil nation has been advanced through its pursuit of accountability. Transnational campaigns seeking recognition of, and justice for, the genocide against the Tamil nation generate new sites and practices of Tamil self-governance (alongside political agitation and civil disobedience in the Tamil homeland); it is on behalf of the Tamil people, and not 'just' individuals, that justice is sought. State crime and resistance against it cannot then be understood simply by reference to abstracted acts of violence and demands for accountability. If we are to contest the rationality of the genocidal practices enacted against Tamils, then state crime can never be separated from the subjectivities and social relations that form their normative basis.

Note

1 Unlike war crimes, which are violations of International Humanitarian Law by individuals, both crimes against humanity and genocide occur where governments or de facto authorities perpetrate or tolerate systemic attacks against civilians. Only the crime of genocide, however, requires that a government *intends* to destroy a national, ethnic, racial or religious group.

References

Amnesty International (2010) *International Inquiry Needed to Address Alleged War Crimes in Sri Lanka*, 14 October.

Armstrong, A. (2008) 'Beyond Resistance: A Response to Žižek's Critique of Foucault's Subject of Freedom', *Parrhesia*, 5, 19–31.

Balasingham, A. S. (2004) *War and Peace: Armed Struggle and Peace Efforts of Liberation Tigers*, London: Fairmax Publishing.

Bartholomeusz, T. J. (2002) *In Defense of Dharma: Just-War Ideology in Buddhist Sri Lanka*, Richmond: Curzon.

Blake, R. (2011) *Press Conference by United States Assistant Secretary of State Robert Blake in Colombo, Sri Lanka*, 4 May, available at http://srilanka.usembassy.gov/tr-5may11.html, accessed 11 November 2011.

Bose, S. (1994) *States, Nations, Sovereignty: Sri Lanka, India, and the Tamil Eelam Movement*, California: Sage Publications.

British Tamil Forum (2011) *Justice and Accountability Cannot Be Bartered for Reconstruction and Rehabilitation*, London, 14 August, available at http://tamilsforum.co.uk/2011/08/justice-and-accountability-cannot-be-bartered-for-reconstruction-and-rehabilitation/, accessed 11 November 2011.

Butler, J. (1997) *The Psychic Life of Power*, Stanford: Stanford University Press.

Clausewitz, Carl von (1976) *On War* (ed./trans. Michael Howard and Peter Paret), Princeton: Princeton University Press, revised 1984.

DeVotta, N. (2004) *Blowback: Linguistic Nationalism, Institutional Decay, and Ethnic Conflict in Sri Lanka* (Contemporary Issues in Asia & the Pacific), Stanford: Stanford University Press.

Foucault, M. (1975/1977) *Discipline and Punish: The Birth of the Prison* (trans. A. Sheridan), Harmondsworth: Peregrine.

Foucault, M. (1976/1978) *The History of Sexuality, Volume 1: An Introduction* (trans. R. Hurley), London: Penguin Books.

Foucault, M. (1980) *Power/Knowledge: Selected Interviews and Other Writings 1972–1977*, (ed. C. Gordon), New York and London: The Harvester Press.

Foucault, M. (1982) 'The Subject and Power', in H. Dreyfus and P. Rabinow (eds), *Michel Foucault: Beyond Structuralism and Hermeneutics*, Chicago: Chicago University Press.

Foucault, M. (2007) *Security, Territory, Population: Lectures at the Collège de France, 1977–78*, Basingstoke, New York: Palgrave Macmillan.

Foucault, M. (2008) *The Birth of Biopolitics: Lectures at the College de France, 1978–1979*, Basingstoke: Palgrave Macmillan.

Freedom From Torture (2011) *Out of the Silence: New Evidence of Ongoing Torture in Sri Lanka 2009–2011*, available at www.freedomfromtorture.org/sites/default/files/documents/Sri%20Lanka%20Ongoing%20Torture_Freedom%20from%20Torture_Final%20Nov_07_2011.pdf, accessed 10 July 2012.

Heller, K. J. (1996) 'Power, Subjectification and Resistance in Foucault', *SubStance*, 25, 78–110.

Hogg, C. L. (2011) *Sri Lanka: Prospects for Reform and Reconciliation*, Chatham House Asia Programme Paper ASP PP 2011/06, October, available at www.chathamhouse.org/sites/default/files/1011pp_srilanka_0.pdf, accessed 11 November 2011.

Human Rights Watch (2006) *Funding the 'Final War': LTTE Intimidation and Extortion in the Tamil Diaspora*, available at www.hrw.org/sites/default/files/reports/ltte0306webwcover.pdf, accessed 10 July 2012.

Human Rights Watch (2009) *Sri Lanka: Repeated Shelling of Hospitals Evidence of War Crimes*, 8 May, available at www.hrw.org/news/2009/05/08/sri-lanka-repeated-shelling-hospitals-evidence-war-crimes, accessed 11 November 2011.

Human Rights Watch (2010) *Sri Lanka: New Evidence of Wartime Abuses*, 20 May, available at www.hrw.org/news/2010/05/20/sri-lanka-new-evidence-wartime-abuses, accessed 30 September 2011.

International Crisis Group (2010a) *The Sri Lankan Tamil Diaspora After the LTTE*, Asia Report No. 186, 23 February, available at www.crisisgroup.org/en/regions/asia/south-asia/sri-lanka/186-the-sri-lankan-tamil-diaspora-after-the-ltte.aspx, accessed 11 November 2011.

International Crisis Group (2010b) *War Crimes in Sri Lanka*, Asia Report No. 191, 17 May, available at www.crisisgroup.org/en/regions/asia/south-asia/sri-lanka/191-war-crimes-in-sri-lanka.aspx, accessed 11 November 2011.

International Crisis Group (2011) *Reconciliation in Sri Lanka: Harder than Ever*, Asia Report No. 209, 18 July, available at www.crisisgroup.org/en/regions/asia/south-asia/sri-lanka/209-reconciliation-in-sri-lanka-harder-than-ever.aspx, accessed 11 November 2011.

Krishna, S. (1999) *Postcolonial Insecurities: India, Sri Lanka, and the Question of Nationhood*, Minneapolis: University of Minnesota Press.

Ladduwahetty, R. (2011) 'Ingredients of LTTE rump in UN report: Media Minister', *Daily News*, 23 April, available at www.dailynews.lk/2011/04/23/pol01.asp, accessed 11 November 2011.

Manor, J. (2011) *To Sustain the Commonwealth Commitment to Human Dignity: Reconsider the Award of the 2013 CHOGM to Sri Lanka*, October, London: Commonwealth Advisory Bureau.

Nadarajah, S. and Vimalarajah, L. (2008) *The Politics of Transformation: The LTTE and the 2002–2006 Peace Process in Sri Lanka*, Berghof Transitions Series No. 4, Berlin: Berghof Research Center for Constructive Conflict Management.

Orjuela, C. (2003) 'Building Peace in Sri Lanka: A Role for Civil Society?', *Journal of Peace Research*, 40(2), 195–212.

Orjuela, C. (ed.) (2010) *Power and Politics in the Shadow of Sri Lanka's Armed Conflict*, Sida Studies No. 25.

Paust, J. J. (1998) 'The Human Rights to Food, Medicine and Medical Supplies, and Freedom from Arbitrary and Inhumane Detention and Controls in Sri Lanka', *Vanderbilt Journal of Transnational Law*, 31, 617–42.

Peiris, G. L. (2010) *Keynote Address*, 1st International Institute for Strategic Studies – Sri Lanka Foreign Ministry Dialogue, 19 October, available at www.iiss.org/programmes/south-asia/conferences-and-seminars/iiss-sri-lanka-foreign-ministry-dialogue/gl-peiris-address, accessed 11 November 2011.

Pennells, S. and Probyn, A. (2011) 'Embattled Sri Lankan Leader on the Attack', *The West Australian*, 27 October, available at http://au.news.yahoo.com/thewest/full-coverage/chogm-2011/a/-/article/10884295/embattled-sri-lankan-leader-on-the-attack/, accessed 11 November 2011.

Pickett, B. L. (1996) 'Foucault and the Politics of Resistance', *Polity*, 28(4), 445–66.

Poynting, S. and Whyte, D. (2012) 'The Political Violence of the State: Bringing the Political Content of "Terrorism" Back In', in S. Poynting and D. Whyte (eds), *Counter-Terrorism and State Political Violence*, London: Routledge, Critical Terrorism Studies Series.

RAND (2001) *Trends in Outside Support for Insurgent Movements*, authored by D. Byman, P. Chalk, B. Hoffman, W. Rosenau and D. Brannan, Santa Monica: National Security Research Division, RAND.

Reuters (2011) 'War Crimes Push Aimed at Ousting Sri Lanka Government, 18 August, available at http://af.reuters.com/article/worldNews/idAFTRE77H63920110818, accessed 11 November 2011.

Satyendra, N. (1993) 'The Boundaries of Tamil Eelam', available at http://tamilnation.co/saty/9314boundaries.htm, accessed 11 November 2011.

Sentas, V. (2012) 'One More Successful War? Tamil Diaspora and Counter-Terrorism after the LTTE', in S. Poynting and D. Whyte (eds), *Counter-Terrorism and State Political Violence*, London: Routledge, Critical Terrorism Studies Series.

Stokke, K. (1998) 'Sinhalese and Tamil Nationalism as Post-colonial Political Projects from "Above", 1948–1983', *Political Geography*, 17(1), 83–113.

Tamil National Alliance (2009) 'TNA: Tamils Subject to Genocide', Press Release,

12 April, available at www.sangam.org/2009/04/TNA_Release.php?uid=3413, accessed 11 November 2011.

Tamils Against Genocide (2011) *Press Release: The Report of the UN Panel of Experts Supports the Case for Genocide in Sri Lanka*, 1 May, available at www.prweb.com/releases/2011/5/prweb8353220.htm, accessed 11 November 2011.

TULF (1976) *Vaddukoddai Resolution*, 14 May, available at www.sangam.org/FB_HIST_DOCS/vaddukod.htm, accessed 11 November 2011.

United Nations (2011) *Report of the Secretary General's Panel of Experts on Account-ability in Sri Lanka*, 31 March, available at www.un.org/News/dh/infocus/Sri_Lanka/POE_Report_Full.pdf, accessed 11 November 2011.

Vimalarajah, L. and Cheran, R. (2010) *Empowering Diasporas: The Politics of Post-war Transnational Tamil Politics*, Berghof Peace Support, Occasional Paper No. 31, available at www.berghof-peacesupport.org/publications/SL_Empowering_Diasporas.pdf, accessed 11 November 2011.

Wilson, A. J. (1994) *S.J.V. Chelvanayagam and Crisis of Sri Lankan Tamil Nationalism, 1947–1977*, London: C. Hurst & Co.

Winslow, D. and Woost, M. (eds) (2004) *Economy, Culture, and Civil War in Sri Lanka*, Bloomington: Indiana University Press.

7 Resistance to state–corporate crimes in West Papua

Elizabeth Stanley[1]

West Papua, just 250 km north of Australia, is home to one of the most repressed and exploited peoples in the world. Over almost half a century, Papuans have suffered untold harms – mass killings, torture, 'disappearances', environmental destruction, resource pillage and the devastation of communities – at the hands of state and corporate officials. Yet, even in such bleak circumstances, Papuans have continually resisted such violations.[2]

This chapter outlines the nature of these crimes in West Papua and explores four key features of the ensuing resistance. First, in the face of significant terror as well as internal differences, Papuans have collectivized to sustain a coherent counter-discourse to the state–corporate denials of violation. Second, Papuans have challenged state and corporate impunity by questioning unjust laws and asserting international legal claims. Third, while some have employed violence, most Papuans have prioritized non-violent resistance in a bid to deepen support for their movement. And, fourth, Papuans have strategically engaged with international actors, to challenge the dominant discourse and to propel global action.

These ongoing practices of resistance demonstrate that, in the midst of suffering and repression, Papuans are building a radical hope of transformation in their country. Their resistant practices 'act against' Indonesian-led violence and repression while affirming Papuan ways of life. In this light, the chapter concludes with an evaluation of how resistance operates as a wider process of self-formation, extending beyond the scope of individual violations to encapsulate broader concerns of self-determination, power and culture.

The historical context of state terror in West Papua

Sharing an island and border with Papua New Guinea, West Papua has a diverse population, over 200 languages and a rich cultural heritage. Colonized by the Dutch from the early nineteenth century, West Papua began preparation for formal independence in 1961. Deemed by the Dutch to be 'racially, linguistically and culturally' different from their neighbours, Indonesia (Braithwaite *et al.* 2010: 57), Papuan people established a parliament, named the country 'West Papua' and adopted the Morning Star flag and an anthem (Tebay 2005).

Under the 1962 New York Agreement (drafted without consultation with West Papuans), the United Nations (UN) assumed administrative authority to ensure that Papuans had the right to self-determination in accordance with international human rights standards (Saltford 2006). However, the terms of this Agreement, ratified and signed by the Netherlands, Indonesia and the UN, were not fulfilled. In the face of Indonesia's campaigns to expand its political, strategic and economic territory, and with little commitment to providing adequate staffing for its own Temporary Administration, the UN transferred administration of West Papua to Indonesia on the proviso that local populations would be able to vote freely on their future (Drooglever 2011). This did not eventuate. Indonesian flags were raised over the new 'province' and a number of military operations were undertaken throughout the 1960s to quell sustained Papuan resistance (Tebay 2005). As one visiting United States (US) diplomat noted in 1968, 'The Indonesians have tried everything from bombing them with B26s, to shelling and mortaring them, but a continuous state of semi-rebellion persists' (Saltford 2011).

The final administrative clampdown came in 1969, with the so-called 'Act of Free Choice'. In the presence of UN observers, Indonesian officials chose 1026 male 'voting representatives' out of a West Papuan population of over 800,000. Intimidated over a period of weeks, these representatives voted unanimously to join Indonesia. Despite local protests, and challenges from numerous African states, the UN affirmed the outcome. The US, among other states, asserted that free elections would be inappropriate for such 'primitive' peoples (Bertrand 2007). Besides, the Indonesian state's control over the region would open up major economic opportunities for powerful external states and multinational companies. Thus, West Papua came to be widely accepted as the Indonesian province of 'Irian Jaya', establishing fertile ground in which state terror inevitably has been able to sustain state, military and corporate profit.

The nature of state–corporate crime

The current situation in West Papua cannot be understood without reference to the relationships between Indonesian powers and multinational corporations. West Papua has major reserves of forestry and natural gas, the latter of which has been exploited by BP; it also holds the world's largest gold deposits and the third-largest open-pit copper reserves. In terms of mining, the landscape is dominated by one multinational, Freeport (a joint venture between British/Australian company Rio Tinto and US-based Freeport-McMoRan). In 1967, even before the 'sham vote' for Indonesian rule, Indonesia contracted Freeport to gain access to West Papuan resources (Ballard 2002; Hedman 2007). Freeport, whose board included Henry Kissinger and a former CIA director, enjoyed the right to take control over land, without consultation, and resettle any populations (Braithwaite et al. 2010).

Indonesian power in West Papua has consistently reflected and reinforced multinational corporate interests, land appropriation and resource extraction.

Accordingly, many Indonesian state crimes – including the failure to establish a free vote for West Papuans, non-regulation of harmful corporate activities, corruption, repression of peaceful protesters, censorship, intimidation and impunity – have developed out of a state–corporate nexus.

For example, the Indonesian government has continually failed to halt or regulate the environmental destruction caused by mining and logging companies. Alongside the felling of significant areas of rainforest, it is estimated that Freeport discards 200–300,000 tonnes of riverine tailings every day (Braithwaite *et al.* 2010). This destructive practice, in which mine waste is dumped into valleys and lakes, has destroyed agricultural land and killed marine life across significant areas (West Papua Advocacy Team 2009). These 'eco-crimes' have generated extensive corporate and state profits. For example, one single mining area, Grasberg, holds deposits worth between US$54 billion and US$80 billion (Leith 2002). Freeport has enjoyed daily profits of more than a million dollars and the Indonesian state, which now holds a 9.36 per cent company stake, has long enjoyed healthy returns (Pilger 2009; Tapol 2009).

Profits have not filtered down to local populations and Papuans believe that, even with Freeport's contributions,[3] the company returns less than 1 per cent of the profits to the local economy (Braithwaite *et al.* 2010). Further, despite the recent input of 'special autonomy' funds,[4] in which Jakarta has returned some mining royalties to the region, extensive political corruption has ensured that most funds have been funnelled to individual military and police commanders, as well as regents and mayors (Braithwaite *et al.* 2010; Hernawan 2011; King 2010). Some estimate that, from 2002 to 2010, 'as much as Rp28 trillion' (approximately US$3.15 billion) of special autonomy funds have been 'embezzled' (West Papua Media 2011a). Corruption is also evident within the military-led forestry and logging industries. The Suharto family were, for many years, major shareholders in local forestry companies (Braithwaite *et al.* 2010). Most local logging is undertaken illegally and military officials enjoy 'hearty sources of corrupt income' by organizing the felling, and safe passage, of illegal logs (Braithwaite *et al.* 2010: 101; Chesterfield 2011a).

The 'prizes' of resource extraction and environmental destruction have either been funnelled offshore, to Jakarta and beyond,[5] or directed to migrants[6] who form the bulk of the Freeport workforce (Braithwaite *et al.* 2010; Leith 2002). While many migrants to West Papua enjoy the trappings of Western lives – running water, power, roads, medical support, schooling, telephone systems, shopping malls and hotels (Leith 2002) – over two-thirds of Papuans continue to live in the highlands that remain untouched by the mainstream economy, trades and services (Elmslie 2010). For the majority, general living standards and public services have deteriorated (Elmslie *et al.* 2010) and the region remains extremely poor on a whole range of measures, including life expectancy, maternal mortality, HIV/AIDS rates, literacy, access to schooling and household income (Braithwaite *et al.* 2010; Hernawan 2011; Rees *et al.* 2008; UNDP 2005).

The state and corporate takeover of West Papua; the profits enjoyed by corporate, governmental and military workers; the endemic socioeconomic disadvantages and environmental damages endured by Papuans; and the Indonesian refusal to accept demands for a vote on self-determination are all managed or supported through violence. With an estimated 200,000 Papuans killed under the regime, local populations have also faced systematic torture, assaults and ill-treatment (Banivanua-Mar 2008; Hernawan 2009; Human Rights Watch 2009). Freeport has funded the Indonesian military and police to quell protests[7] and to protect its mine (Chauvel 2007; Leith 2002). During 2010, senior police officers noted that Freeport provided Rp1,250,000 (approximately US$137) to 635 police officers each month, while, in 2011, an investigation exposed that the company had provided US$79.1 million to the police and military over the previous decade (Asian Human Rights Commission 2011). Security services continually exaggerate the levels of violent opposition in a bid to enhance their funding (Asian Human Rights Commission 2011).

Much military violence is openly undertaken in West Papua; for instance, torture, including sexual mutilation and rape, is regularly 'performed' in public spaces – on roads, in marketplaces or in communal areas around key logging or mining sites (Hernawan 2011). Numerous reports detail individuals being tortured to death and their mutilated bodies left 'on display filled with sticks, cabbages and leaves' (Banivanua-Mar 2008: 591; Ballard 2002; Hernawan 2009). This spectacle of state power creates widespread fear that no 'body' is exempt from state violence; anyone who works against state or corporate interests could be the next victim (Stanley 2012). Moreover, the landscape becomes a constant reminder of violence and the risks of acting against the state (Stanley 2012).

Restrictions on group gatherings, curfews, forcible displacements, house searches and everyday monitoring of Papuans are the norm (Hedman 2007). Kopassus (the elite Indonesian counter-insurgency force) have a significant presence and those indicted for crimes against humanity in Timor-Leste, including Colonel Burhannudin Siagian and Police Chief Timbul Silean, have found further work in West Papua (Human Rights Watch 2009; Asian Human Rights Commission 2010). Pursuing the same tactics as those used in Timor-Leste, the Indonesian military has increased the recruitment, arming and financing of militia forces in West Papua (Banivanua-Mar 2008). Following military instructions, militia members threaten and attack suspected enemies; they also intimidate political candidates and voters who might oppose the accepted military view (Braithwaite *et al.* 2010). In addition, Kopassus directs a 'small army' of agents who receive payment to inform on the activities and whereabouts of rebels (Asian Human Rights Commission 2010). This use of militias and informants undermines collective cohesion among West Papuans, creates an atmosphere of suspicion and terror, and rips apart the fabric of stable communities (Stanley 2012).

The denial and management of violations

Repression, intimidation, fear and violence have become normalized in West Papua, to facilitate state and corporate involvement in resource extraction, military expansionism and political domination (Stanley 2012). This situation has been largely neutralized or denied through a range of discursive strategies. First, Indonesian officials engage in overt denials of their involvement in state violence, even when the evidence for such is overwhelming. For example, in response to the 2010 killing of Papuan reporter Ardiansyah Matra'is – who was found naked, beaten and tethered to a tree – the local police claimed it was a case of suicide. Matra'is had braved months of threats from Kopassus for his reports on illegal logging, including messages telling him to 'be prepared for death' (Leaver 2010). Through their consistent denials of these events, Indonesian officials display their utter confidence that they can 'get away with anything'. Second, international journalists have been prevented from entering the region, while their local counterparts confront intimidation and death. Critical journalists endure threatening SMS messages and ransacked offices (Braithwaite *et al.* 2010); and four journalists died in suspicious circumstances in 2010 (Chesterfield 2011b). Third, the Indonesian government has banned many humanitarian organizations and international observers from gaining access to West Papua (Chesterfield 2011b). For example, in 2011, Peace Brigades International was forced out after being subjected to intense harassment by security officials. Similarly, human rights workers, health professionals and even international diplomats have been denied access to the region. Fourth, Indonesia has maintained an influential position within the global 'war on terror', such that powerful states and bodies have consolidated their economic and ideological support. For example, in 2010, the US government re-established its provision of military assistance to Kopassus, despite the organization's continuing involvement in violations; while, in 2011, Indonesia was re-elected onto the UN's Human Rights Council. Fifth, corporations have also used their powers to manage their own branding. For instance, James Moffett, the Chairman of Freeport McMoRan, advertises that he works to help others 'to be successful' and that *BusinessWeek* magazine has twice named his company the 'most philanthropic company in America' (Horatio Alger 2011). Taken together, these elements have ensured that state–corporate denials of violence within West Papua have dominated at both national and international levels.

The discursive management of state–corporate crime dovetails with a policy of impunity towards state perpetrators of gross human rights violations. The unwillingness of Indonesia to bring perpetrators to account is not seriously challenged by the UN. In a study of 74 political killings in West Papua during the period 1995–2005 (which recorded perpetrators from the military, the police, government employees and corporations), only five cases progressed to court (Braithwaite *et al.* 2010). Furthermore, even if cases do reach the courts, they are met with a state-supportive judiciary. It is not unusual for judges to make statements about how Papuans should be 'brought into line' if they misbehave (Braithwaite *et al.* 2010) and lenient sentences are common with convictions. For example, three of the soldiers who were videorecorded torturing civilians were – after much international pressure – brought to trial in 2010. Receiving less than a year's imprisonment, these soldiers were admonished by the judge for the shame they had brought upon their employer by filming the event (Chesterfield 2010).

Building resistance amid terror and repression

Papuans are dealing with numerous harms – political repression, physical viola-tions, state–corporate crimes and eco-crimes, among others. On a daily basis, Papuans are monitored, censored and turned against each other. In such circum-stances, it is difficult to see how resistance might flourish. Indeed, many people have submitted to Indonesian pressures, some are captured by the military,[8] others are disengaged, while some are incapacitated by terror. Yet these are not totalizing conditions. Terror, fear and disengagement do not 'orchestrate all the rhythms of daily life' (Margold 1999: 64). Resistance has emerged in multiple forms and has engaged a range of actors, including armed guerrillas, church leaders, students, tribal leaders and both local and international organizations. Moreover, as the state violence has continued, resistance has grown and solidi-fied among younger generations (Elmslie 2010). In this regard, four techniques of resistance are considered further: the challenge to denial through collectiviza-tion, the use of the law, the move from violence to non-violence, and interna-tional engagement.

Challenging denial through collectivization

When knowledge of violations is not widely shared, or socially acknowledged, state misrepresentations of 'how things are' are allowed to flourish. Yet, as Foucault (1981: 101) noted, 'discourse can be both an instrument and effect of power, but also a hindrance, a stumbling block, a point of resistance and a starting point for an opposing strategy'. Indeed, in West Papua, the dissonance between state–corporate denials of violations and the concentration of repression and vio-lence is such that resistance has intensified and thousands have mobilized.

This collectivization is illustrated in the regular mass public protests held in major towns across West Papua. With strength in numbers (many protests engage several thousand people and Papuans have established their own peace-keeping monitoring presence), Papuans routinely acknowledge the realities of state–corporate crime and call for change.

Mobilization has sometimes revolved around celebrated resistance leaders, such as Theys Eluay, who was assassinated by Kopassus in 2001 (MacLeod 2009). However, it has also emerged through a coordinated network of commu-nity groups that strategize together and widely distribute counter-narratives (MacLeod 2009). There are numerous coalitions[9] that promote dialogue, uphold human rights, demand truth, justice and compensation, pursue equitable condi-tions, mount strikes against poor conditions and pay, work towards self-determination and engage international audiences in their plight. These coalitions have a range of functions, in that: they engage multiple stakeholders (including, in some cases, Indonesian officials); they foster the diversity and dialogue required for democratic governance; and, given their decentralized structure, they make it more difficult for Indonesian authorities to target resistance 'leaders' (MacLeod 2009).

The use of the law

In West Papua, the Indonesian authorities use the law as a tool of repression: it protects perpetrators of gross violations and harshly punishes those Papuans who resist state authority. In 2012, for example, five Papuans faced trial on charges of treason for their involvement in peaceful protests, while the imprisonment of dozens of others continues for 'crimes' such as raising the Morning Star flag (in 2005, Filep Karma and Yusuk Pakage received 15 years and ten years imprisonment, respectively, for such an act) (Human Rights Watch 2009; WPAT 2012).

However, the law is also used to placate the population and to consolidate state power (Thompson 1975). For example, in 2001, the Indonesian-imposed Special Autonomy Law asserted Papuan autonomy over their economic, legal, social and political affairs. Promising a significant social shift, the law offered local economic control, a more equitable distribution of resources, political participation, a reduction in violence and reconciliatory processes. Yet for the most part, these outcomes have not materialized (Tebay 2010). While this new law temporarily masked Indonesian control, Papuans have come to recognize it as evidently unjust. In 2010, the Papuan People's Assembly – the official local body established by the law – symbolically 'returned' the illegitimate law to the Indonesian government (Tebay 2010). The local people, refusing to live a lie, rejected this central legislation in the midst of extensive supportive rallies.

The disconnection between established laws and practice remains a central focus of Papuan resistance. Yet Papuans also view the law as a source of protection. Local populations have not accepted the limits placed on justice. Drawing upon national as well as international legal standards, they have continued to campaign for the establishment of a human rights court, a truth and reconciliation commission and interventions from the International Court of Justice. In addition, local West Papuan groups have launched a number of (thus far, unsuccessful) international legal actions against violating corporations. The Amungme people, in particular, have pursued several actions against Freeport's occupation and destruction of their environment (Ballard 2002; Leith 2002). The latest, in March 2010, sought $32.5 billion in damages for the illegal acquisition of ancestral land (Andriyanto 2010). Through such continued legal action, Papuans have established evidence of the connections between governmental, military and corporate power, and detailed how economic expansion and resource capture has sustained violence against civilians. Even in defeated cases, legal processes have confronted the state–corporate management of events and identities. Moreover, these challenges have wider repercussions; for example, the BP Tangguh gas and liquid natural gas project has been criticized for its grievance procedures, employment record and lack of financial transparency, among other issues (Down to Earth 2011). Yet the company has also been credited for taking a different approach from that of Freeport by using local employees, considering human rights advocacy, taking a community security approach and distancing itself from the Indonesian military (Down to Earth 2011; Braithwaite et al. 2010). While legal cases may not appear to be successful, other 'wins' outside the courts have emerged over time.

From violence to non-violence

Relatively few people have been involved in organized violent resistance in West Papua. However, armed opposition has been employed by activists in the Free Papua Movement or *Organisasi Papua Merdeka* (OPM). The OPM emerged shortly after Indonesia assumed control over the region and, during the 1960s and 1970s in particular, members of the military wing engaged in 'bow and arrow' guerrilla violence against Indonesian opponents. Over the decades, the OPM has been hampered by limited weaponry, poor communications, an unclear strategy and a degree of factionalism among its (approximately 1500) members (MacLeod 2009). In recent times, the movement has been linked to events such as the abduction of international mine workers and the burning of police stations. Even so, the OPM retains broad symbolic appeal; many of those not directly linked with the organization still identify with its social and political agenda of *merdeka*, or freedom (Braithwaite *et al.* 2010).

Regarded as a central threat, the OPM is labelled an illegal separatist movement by the Indonesian authorities, who claim that they *themselves* are the victims in the region. Sustaining an ideological case for increased savagery against its opponents, the Indonesian state has undertaken numerous raids to quell or eradicate suspected separatists (Tebay 2005). However, sweeping operations and house-to-house searches on perceived OPM-related villages do not discriminate 'between ordinary villagers and OPM activists and supporters' (Chauvel 2007: 49; Hedman 2007). So state-led counter-resistance – involving intimidation, arbitrary arrest, torture, sexual violation and mutilation, execution-style killings, cluster bombings and aerial bombardment (Hernawan 2009) – targets all civilians. In a 2009 study of 393 cases of torture, victims were overwhelmingly found to be rural farmers, while only two cases involving OPM members were identified (Hernawan 2009).

OPM resistance is met with repressive state-led 'backfire' that affects all of the West Papuan Indigenous communities. For some Papuans, including some OPM members, there is a belief that Indonesia will eventually make the 'mistake' of massacring civilians in front of cameras or international observers (Braithwaite *et al.* 2010).[10] Such a situation could provoke a groundswell of support for self-determination processes. Certainly, the October 2010 video of Papuans being tortured attracted significant international condemnation of Indonesian practices and led to a rare criminal justice response (West Papua Media 2010a). The challenge to Indonesian denials, through the broadcasting of violations, might shift international loyalties; yet for many Papuans, this price of terror and death, as a consequence of resistance, is too high to pay.

The ascendancy of the OPM in the Indonesian state's imagination misrepresents the dominant forces of Papuan resistance. In reality, most resisters to the Indonesian regime are not 'rural guerrillas', but urbane, educated and astute Papuans from all walks of life (Chesterfield 2010). Moreover, they engage in civil forms of resistance. Papuans have largely fought for independence through non-violent means, such as rallies, symbolic flag-raisings, performing Papuan songs and dances, wearing traditional penis gourds, carrying out land occupations, preserving local languages, telling stories about national identity and resistance, restoring Indigenous names to the landscape, facilitating local and international alliances or by the voluntary exile of key campaigners (Leith 2002; Wainggai 2011; Webb-Gannon 2011). Local resistance is marked by non-violent struggle that emphasizes a shared national identity and cultural traditions.

In this respect, Papuan resistance is cultural as well as political and economic. They engage in formal and deliberate acts, but also pursue the everyday acts of 'being Papuan' to maintain and reshape their world. Besides, in line with Stephan and Chenoweth's (2008) analysis, these resisters are well aware that such non-violent resistance can be highly disruptive; will more readily engage local participants; will more likely secure international support and sympathy; will mean that violence against them would more likely be condemned; and will more likely result in a political openness to future negotiations.

International engagement

Despite their enforced isolation on the ground, Papuans have sought to internationalize their resistance strategies. Online media sites[11] present a constant counter-discourse to the official versions of events by providing testimonies, photographs and videos that expose state and corporate officials as violators. Tireless Papuans living in exile abroad engage in political campaigning to build support.[12] And Papuans have made themselves visible through theatrical political acts, seen, for example, in January 2006 when an organized group of 43 Papuans sought asylum in Australia. On arrival, they presented an unusual scene – they had travelled by outrigger canoes, with protest banners and the Morning Star flag – and thus became the subject of significant media attention.

These strategies have begun to gain increased traction. The claims of the asylum seekers were accepted by Australia and they were granted refugee status, much to Indonesia's expressed disappointment (Stanley 2012). In 2010, 50 US Congress members signed a letter to the US President stating their concerns over a 'slow-motion genocide' in West Papua (US Congressmen Faleomavaega and Payne 2010), while the British Prime Minister, his Deputy and the House of Lords have openly recognized the 'terrible situation' faced by the Papuan people (West Papua Media 2010b). In the same year, the Vanuatu parliament asserted its commitment to engage the UN and the International Court of Justice in the West Papuan situation (Elmslie et al. 2010). In 2011, this support was reiterated by a conglomeration of human rights and youth organizations from across the Pacific (West Papua Media 2011b).

This international recognition is valuable, and Papuans are well aware that they need to get international 'bystanders' on side, not least because resistance campaigns that 'receive external state support' are far more likely to 'succeed against a repressive opponent' (Stephan and Chenoweth 2008: 20). International condemnation, and the retraction of unconditional support, can 'go a long way' in challenging repressive states. However, such external support can lead to other problems – it can undermine the local focus, it can increase the dependency of the repressed people on outsiders (Stephan and Chenoweth 2008) and it can be used by violating states as proof that external powers are engaged in an 'insidious plot' to take over their country (Roberts 2009: 21). In addition, those who engage international attention can find themselves targeted. In November 2010, leaked Kopassus reports indicated that church leaders, journalists, lawyers, students and members of Indigenous political groups became Kopassus targets because they engaged the 'outside world' with their arguments for freedom and human rights (Asian Human Rights Commission 2010). Thus, involving the 'outside world' can have dangerous consequences.

Pre-empting these arguments and negative outcomes, West Papuan campaigners have adopted a cautious approach to their involvement with internationals. In particular, they provide legitimacy to international resistance efforts through real-time protests. A number of recent events – including the 2010 meeting of International Parliamentarians and Lawyers for West Papua at the European Union, the 2011 Road to Freedom Conference in Oxford and the 2011 Washington seminars of the Torture Abolition and Survivors Support Coalition – have been accompanied by simultaneous rallies in West Papua that show local support for international actions (Chesterfield and Kareni 2011; Makur 2010; PMC News Desk 2011). These local protests mark and mirror international resistance, usurp Indonesian claims that international actors are engaged in colonizing practices and legitimize international challenges to Indonesian-led violence and ensuing denials.

Moving forward: resistance and self-formation

Like many other contributions to this book, this chapter has illustrated that state–corporate crimes and acts of resistance are intertwined. They evolve, and are undertaken, in relation to each other. Faced with ongoing terror, death and environmental destruction, Papuans have engaged in resistance strategies that are increasingly diverse, complex, 'loud' and global. Gone is the romanticized notion of 'rural guerrillas' fighting with bows and arrows; instead, Papuans creatively and assertively use public protest, international law and global information systems to advance their position. In doing so, they have had numerous 'successes': for instance, they have gained partial control over their land and resources; they have reasserted their cultural practices; their experiences of violation and calls for self-determination have gained an international audience; pressure has been placed on Indonesia to restrain its military actions and propel justice interventions; some corporations, observing the resistance to Freeport, have taken a more participatory attitude towards local engagement; and locals have consolidated a deep consciousness of, and active engagement in, West Papuan power and politics (including the development of a new generation of networked activists) (Braithwaite *et al.* 2010; MacLeod 2009).

Yet these acts of resistance also face significant restraints and unmet expectations. Papuans and their supporters have faced entrenched counter-resistance by violators, through which repression and restrictions are ratcheted up. Increased militarization, travel restrictions, torture and killings, diplomatic constraints, legal impunity, and so on, are endured by many people, at home and abroad. In the contestation of power, Indonesia has sustained a violent response that is shored up through law and media management.

At the same time, the future of West Papua rests upon cooperation with Indonesia. This is a key paradox of state crime – that the state commits or leads crime, but is also a central entity in propelling change. For West Papuan demands to be met, there would have to be a benign shift within the Indonesian leadership. Such an outcome is possible; states are not homogenous and there can be progressive periods of a state's existence. For instance, the so-called Papuan Spring – in which the Morning Star flag was accepted and some Papuan political structures were established – occurred during the 1999–2001 Presidency of the late Abdurrhaman Wahid (Hedman 2007). However, these moments are rare and one might surmise that a dramatic surge in pressure, from international and domestic quarters, would need to be sustained before Indonesia could be brought to the negotiating table (Braithwaite *et al.* 2010). Given the realpolitik of strategic, economic and political global relations, a strong international engagement with West Papua remains to be seen. While many international actors have begun to speak in support of human rights for Papuans, West Papua largely remains 'off the radar' in terms of influential political action to support resistance struggles (Kirksey 2011).

Moreover, any possibility of change raises the question of what current resistance strategies are directed towards. Many Papuans articulate the need for a referendum on independence, yet, within these claims, broader concerns around land, resources and human rights are evident. To put it simply, even if Indonesia were removed as the governing force in West Papua, Papuans would still endure 'crimes of globalization', 'eco-crimes' or 'corporate crimes', whereby multinational corporations and new migrants dominate their country's resources and opportunities. What might be regarded as a significant 'victory' against the crimes of the powerful might turn out to be pyrrhic, as violations may re-emerge in different forms (see Chapter 1, this volume, for a further discussion on this point). In relation to contemporary resistance, then, West Papuans need to progress beyond issues of strict governance to attend to the 'elephant in the room': the dominance of advanced global capitalism (Urquhart 2011).[13]

These are undoubtedly difficult endeavours, particularly in a local context where corruption and weak political and economic institutions dominate, and an international context in which international financial institutions reflect the interests of powerful global economic players. Yet this kind of self-formation, in which alternatives to prevailing structures of power and governance are pursued, is a critical form of resistance as it acknowledges that the challenge cannot be directed only at the use of force but also at the 'very system' itself (Thompson 2003: 118). In this respect, West Papuan campaigns on labour rights, women's rights, cultural rights, environmental justice and education, among other issues, reflect a broader commitment to respond to entrenched economic, social and cultural violations of human rights. Such actions, albeit in their infancy, demonstrate that resistance is not only an *acting against*, but is also about *becoming*. That is, without resistant acts that contest multiple forms of domination and simultaneously build and sustain a way of life, in which real capacity and resilience are developed within future community structures, any victories experienced by Papuans may be relatively short-lived.

Notes

1 I would like to thank Budi Hernawan, Maire Leadbeater and Jude McCulloch for ideas, information and encouragement.
2 The terms 'West Papua' and 'Papuans' in this chapter refer to the Indonesian administrative provinces of Papua and West Papua, and the Indigenous populations of these provinces, respectively.
3 The amount provided to local Amungme and Kamoro villagers is contested – from an initial US$250,000 with an extra US$100,000 on an annual basis (Perlez 2006) to an initial US$2.5 million with an extra US$1 million annually (FCX 2010).
4 Transfers from Jakarta to West Papua have increased since 2000 (Hernawan 2011). Between 2002 and 2006, an estimated US$240 million per annum was channelled to the region (Hernawan 2011).
5 The proposed Merauke Integrated Food and Energy Estate (MIFEE) is a case in point. With no local consultation, the Indonesian government has recently provided 36 companies with permits for more than two million hectares of land to be redesignated as commercial plantations (to include oil palm, maize and rice). Launched as a means to provide food security for Indonesia, the plan will displace Indigenous villagers, impact upon protected landscape areas and bring thousands of new migrant workers into the region. The UN Committee on the Elimination of Racial Discrimination has called for a suspension of MIFEE until the Indigenous people have given their free, informed consent for any land or resource development (Down to Earth 2011).
6 The Suharto government engaged a policy of transmigration from Indonesia – 'non-Papuans' represented 2.5 per cent of the population on West Papua in 1960, 4 per cent in 1971 and 51 per cent in 2010, and are forecast to form 71 per cent of the population by 2020 (Chauvel 2007; Elmslie 2010; Rees *et al.* 2008). This massive demographic change has increasingly marginalized Papuans as they struggle to compete for work with more skilled migrants.
7 During protests at the Freeport mines in October 2011, two strikers were shot dead by police (Asian Human Rights Commission 2011).
8 Resistance is quelled by the need for Papuans to support, or capitulate to, Indonesian structures and military practices (Braithwaite *et al.* 2010). Those who take an oppositional approach will not be elected to political office. In other circumstances, tribal leaders are 'bought' by the military through bribes, alcohol and sex workers (Braithwaite *et al.* 2010).
9 Including the Papua Peace Network, West Papua National Committee, National Coalition for Liberation and the Democratic Forum for Papuan People's Resistance.
10 This occurred in Timor-Leste. The 1991 global broadcasting of the 'Santa Cruz' massacre – in which approximately 270 people were killed by Indonesian soldiers in a Dili cemetery – deepened international resistance to Indonesian state violence.
11 English-language sites include 'West Papua Media', 'Tapol', 'Info Papua', 'Free West Papua', 'Pacific Scoop', 'Pacific Media Centre' and 'ETAN'.
12 Including Benny Wenda (a central figure in Britain) and Paula Makabory (who works across Australasia), among countless others.

13 Although not discussed here, gendered violence is another 'elephant' that needs to be dealt with. Jarangga and Wandita (2011) have highlighted the continuum of violence suffered by Papuan women, at the hands of military officials and family members, over the past 40 years.

References

Andriyanto, H. (2010) 'Papua Tribe Files $32b Lawsuit against Freeport', *The Jakarta Globe*, 8 March.

Asian Human Rights Commission (2010) *Files Show Kopassus Targets Papuan Churches*, available at www.pacific.scoop.co.nz, accessed 16 November 2010.

Asian Human Rights Commission (2011) *Indonesia: Another Protester Dies Amidst the Tense Situation at Freeport*, 15 December, AHRC-UAU-049–2011, Hong Kong: AHRC.

Ballard, C. (2002) 'The Signature of Terror: Violence, Memory, and Landscape at Freeport', in B. David and M. Wilson (eds), *Inscribed Landscapes: Marking and Making Place*, Honolulu: University of Hawai'i Press.

Banivanua-Mar, T. (2008) '"A Thousand Miles of Cannibal Lands": Imagining Away Genocide in the Re-colonization of West Papua', *Journal of Genocide Research*, 10(4), 583–602.

Bertrand, J. (2007) 'Papua and Indonesian Nationalisms: Can They Be Reconciled?' in E. Hedman (ed.), *Dynamics of Conflict and Displacement in Papua, Indonesia*, Refugee Studies Centre Working Paper No. 42, Oxford: Department of International Development.

Braithwaite, J., Braithwaite, V., Cookson, M. and Dunn, L. (2010) *Anomie and Violence: Non-Truth and Reconciliation in Indonesian Peacebuilding*, Canberra: ANU E-Press.

Chauvel, R. (2007) 'Refuge, Displacement and Dispossession', in E. Hedman (ed.), *Dynamics of Conflict and Displacement in Papua, Indonesia*, Refugee Studies Centre Working Paper No. 42, Oxford: Department of International Development.

Chesterfield, N. (2010) *West Papua: Ignored Struggle Set to Explode on Our Doorstep*, available at www.pacific.scoop.co.nz, accessed 22 December 2010.

Chesterfield, N. (2011a) *PNG Troops Burn Down Border West Papua Refugee Camps as Refugees Flee to the Jungle*, West Papua Media, 28 January.

Chesterfield, N. (2011b) *Free the People? Free the Media!*, Paper presented at the University of Sydney Centre for Peace and Conflict Studies 'Comprehending Papua Conference', 22–23 February 2011.

Chesterfield, N. and Kareni, R. (2011) *Large Rally against Torture Held Serui*, West Papua Media Alerts, 23 June.

Down to Earth (2011) *The Land of Papua: A Continuing Struggle for Land and Livelihoods*, Newsletter 89–90, November, Hallbankgate: DTE.

Drooglever, P. (2011) 'The Pro- and Anti-Plebiscite Campaigns in West Papua: Before and After 1969', in P. King, J. Elmslie and C. Webb-Gannon (eds), *Comprehending West Papua*, Sydney: Centre for Peace and Conflict Studies.

Elmslie, J. (2010) *West Papuan Demographic Transition and the 2010 Indonesian Census: 'Slow Motion Genocide' or Not?*, CPACS Working Paper No. 11/1, Sydney: University of Sydney.

Elmslie, J. and Gannon, C. with King, P. (2010) *Get Up, Stand Up: West Papua Stands up for Its Rights*, Sydney: Centre for Peace and Conflict Studies.

FCX, Freeport McMoRan Copper and Gold (2010) *History*, available at www.fcx.com/company/history.htm, accessed 28 September 2010.

Foucault, M. (1981) *History of Sexuality, Vol. 1: An Introduction*, (trans. R. Hurley), London: Penguin.

Hedman, E. (2007) 'Papua: The Last Frontier for Democratization, Demilitarization and Decentralization in Indonesia', in E. Hedman (ed.), *Dynamics of Conflict and Displacement in Papua, Indonesia*, Refugee Studies Centre Working Paper No. 42, Oxford: Department of International Development.

Hernawan, B. (2009) *Terror, Resistance and Trauma in Papua (Indonesia)*, Issues Paper 14, Centre for International Governance and Justice, Canberra: Australian National University.

Hernawan, B. (2011) *Managing Papuan Expectations after Handing Back Special Autonomy*, Paper No. 16, Centre for International Governance and Justice Issues, Canberra: Australian National University.

Horatio Alger (2011) *James R. Moffett*, available at www.horatioalger.org/member_info.cfm?memberid=mof90, accessed 13 January 2012.

Human Rights Watch (2009) *'What Did I Do Wrong?' Papuans in Merauke Face Abuses by Indonesian Special Forces*, New York: Human Rights Watch.

Jarangga, F. and Wandita, G. (2011) *West Papua: Violence against Indigenous Women*, AHRC-FAT-021–2011, Jakarta: Asian Human Rights Commission.

King, P. (2010) *West Papua and Indonesia in the 21st Century: Resilient Minnow? Implacable Minotaur?*, Papua Paper No. 1, Sydney: University of Sydney.

Kirksey, S. E. (2011) 'Reclaiming the Messianic Promise', in P. King, J. Elmslie and C. Webb-Gannon (eds), *Comprehending West Papua*, Sydney: Centre for Peace and Conflict Studies.

Leaver, R. (2010) *West Papua: Journalists Become Targets for Playing with Fire*, available at www.pacific.scoop.co.nz, accessed 11 November 2010.

Leith, D. (2002) 'Freeport and the Suharto Regime, 1965–1998', *The Contemporary Pacific*, 14(1), 69–100.

MacLeod, J. (2009) 'The Role of Strategy in Advancing Nonviolent Resistance in West Papua', in L. Reychler, J. Deckard and K. Villanueva (eds), *Building Sustainable Futures*, Bilbao: University of Duesto.

Makur, M. (2010) *Papuans Rally to Gain International Support for UN Political Review*, available at www.pacific.scoop.co.nz, accessed 29 January 2010.

Margold, J. A. (1999) 'From "Cultures of Fear and Terror" to the Normalization of Violence', *Critique of Anthropology*, 19(1), 63–88.

Perlez, J. (2006) 'The Papuans Say, This Land and its Ores are Ours', *New York Times*, 5 April, available at www.nytimes.com/2006/04/05/world/asia/05letter.html?_r=1&pagewanted=all, accessed 3 December 2009.

Pilger, J. (2009) 'Let the Bird of Paradise Go Free', *New Statesman*, 12 November.

PMC News Desk (2011) *Indonesian Soldier Shot Dead Amid more West Papuan Unrest*, available at www.pacific.scoop.co.nz, accessed 4 August 2011.

Rees, S. J., Van de Pas, R., Silove, D. and Kareth, M. (2008) 'Health and Human Security in West Papua', *Medical Journal of Australia*, 189(11/12), 641–3.

Roberts, A. (2009) 'Introduction', in A. Roberts and T. Ash (eds), *Civil Resistance and Power Politics*, Oxford: Oxford University Press.

Saltford, J. (2006) *The United Nations and the Indonesian Takeover of West Papua, 1962–1969: The Anatomy of Betrayal*, London: Routledge.

Saltford, J. (2011) *Presentation at the 'West Papua: The Road to Freedom Conference'*, Oxford, available at http://soundcloud.com/free-west-papua/west-papua-road-to-freedom, accessed 2 August 2011.

Stanley, E. (2012) 'Indonesian State Terror in Timor-Leste and West Papua', in S. Poynting and D. Whyte (eds), *Counter-Terrorism and State Political Violence*, London: Routledge.

Stephan, M. and Chenoweth, E. (2008) 'Why Civil Resistance Works: The Strategic Logic of Nonviolent Conflict', *International Security*, 33(1), 7–44.

Tapol (2009) *Tapol Supports Amungme People's Lawsuit against Freeport*, available at www.tapol.gn.apc.org, accessed 20 July 2009.

Tebay, N. (2005) *West Papua: The Struggle for Peace with Justice*, London: Catholic Institute for International Relations.

Tebay, N. (2010) *Indonesia/West Papua: Papuans Want a Negotiated Solution*, available at www.pacific.scoop.co.nz, accessed 5 July 2010.

Thompson, E. (1975) *Whigs and Hunters: The Origin of the Black Act*, New York: Pantheon Books.

Thompson, K. (2003) 'Forms of Resistance: Foucault on Tactical Reversal and Self-Formation', *Continental Philosophy Review*, 36, 113–38.

UNDP (2005) *Broadening Opportunities: Assessing the Needs of Papua*, available at http://undp.or.id/factsheets/fs_ciu_papua.pdf, accessed 30 September 2010.

Urquhart, B. (2011) 'Revolution without Violence?' *New York Review of Books*, LVIII, 37–40.

US Congressmen Faleomavaega and Payne (2010) 'West Papua: 50 Congressmen Urge Obama to Make West Papua a Priority Concern', Media Release, available at www.pacific.scoop.co.nz, accessed 4 August 2010.

Wainggai, H. (2011) 'The Resistance Struggle of the West Papuan People Organisationally Requires Trias Politica', in P. King, J. Elmslie and C. Webb-Gannon (eds), *Comprehending West Papua*, Sydney: Centre for Peace and Conflict Studies.

Webb-Gannon, C. (2011) 'Culture as Strategy: Being West Papuan "the Melanesian Way"', in P. King, J. Elmslie and C. Webb-Gannon (eds), *Comprehending West Papua*, Sydney: Centre for Peace and Conflict Studies.

West Papua Advocacy Team [WPAT] (2009) 'Papuans Proceed with Lawsuits vs Freeport-McMoRan', available at www.pacific.scoop.co.nz, accessed 3 November 2009.

WPAT (2012) *West Papua Report*, February, available at www.etan.org/issues/wpapua/2012/1202wpap.htm, accessed 6 February 2012.

West Papua Media (2010a) 'Video Released of Torture Killings by Indonesia Forces', available at www.pacific.scoop.co.nz, accessed 18 October 2010.

West Papua Media (2010b) 'British Deputy Prime Minister raised "Grave Concerns" over Human Rights and Restricted Press Access to West Papua during Meeting with Indonesian Government officials', available at http://westpapuamedia.info/, accessed 22 December 2010.

West Papua Media (2011a) 'Papua: A Paradise for Corrupt Officials', available at www.pacific.scoop.co.nz, accessed 30 June 2011.

West Papua Media (2011b) 'Open Letter: Free Youth Activists and Respect Human Rights of the People of West Papua', available at http://westpapuamedia.info/, accessed 16 June 2011.

8   The race to defraud

State crime and the immiseration of Indigenous people

Chris Cunneen

Introduction

Most analysis of state crime focuses on state violence – ranging from torture and terror through to genocide. This chapter is an exploration of state crime in the form of systematic state-sponsored fraud and related breaches of human rights. It derives from a more general project on the relationship between colonization in settler societies and state crime (Cunneen 2008). Analysis of the ongoing effects of colonization on Indigenous populations reveals that one of the major factors in bringing about their contemporary immiseration has been the long-term and systematic exploitation of Indigenous labour. I am not thinking here of exploitation of labour in the strictly Marxist sense of the expropriation of surplus value (which applied to all workers), but rather exploitation through the organized system of a racialized, state-controlled labour market which includes specific fraudulent misappropriation of money (including wages, trust funds and other payments). The specific example drawn upon in this chapter is the exploitation of Indigenous people in Australia. However, the defrauding and gross mismanagement of trust funds established by the state for the benefit of Indigenous peoples has been evident in other settler states, such as the United States (US), where in 2009 there was a $3.4 billion settlement to a class action relating to the mismanagement of hundreds of thousands of American Indian trust accounts (Riccardi 2009; see also Kidd 2006: 28–35).

The exploitation of Indigenous workers and their families includes:

- the setting, control and enforcement of wage levels on the basis of race
- the systematic underpayment or non-payment of Indigenous workers
- the defrauding of compulsory trust funds and savings accounts established and controlled by the state for the benefit of Indigenous peoples
- the systematic underpayment or non-payment of state social security benefits on the basis of race.

There are two aspects to the argument for including the exploitation of Indigenous labour and misappropriation of Indigenous people's moneys within an understanding of state crime. These relate first to the criminal offence of fraud, and second to the contextualization of the offence of fraud within a legislative framework that supports pervasive racial discrimination. There is no doubt that fraud is a crime. The offence of fraud is broadly understood as obtaining property by deception. However, it is not limited to property and can include dishonestly obtaining benefit or dishonestly causing detriment by deception. Dishonesty offences can include obtaining benefit through exploiting positions of advantage. While a considerable focus of the regulation of modern fraud offences is to control frauds aimed at government and public officials (Bronitt and McSherry 2005: 699), the focus of this chapter is fraud conducted *by public officials*. It is argued that the systematic nature of fraud conducted by state officials transforms the 'individual' crimes into an example of organized state criminal activity – and a state crime that has had long-term intergenerational effects.

The state's involvement in fraud also raises questions about resistance. As shown below, in our Australian case study there was knowledge that fraudulent activity was taking place, both among Indigenous people who failed to receive their due entitlements and among government officials and parliaments through various inquiries and reports. However, the relative powerlessness of Indigenous peoples and government complacency largely prevented effective action – denial of citizenship rights meant that legal redress was difficult, and direct action was dealt with through punitive, colonial systems of criminal justice and administrative control. Indigenous resistance in more recent times has involved seeking redress through both individual litigation and collective reparations – yet both actions have achieved limited success and have caused ongoing political protests. Thus, clearly there have been different forms of resistance to such fraud in the Australian context.

In Australia, there were individual acts of resistance to the control of wages and entitlements (although these by their nature are less well documented) and organized challenges by Indigenous political groups (sometimes assisted by non-Indigenous supporters, including labour unions) throughout much of the twentieth century. Resistance against the exploitative practices outlined in this chapter also occurred both contemporaneously (that is, throughout the period under review) and retrospectively. By 'retrospective' resistance, I am referring to the more recent and current demands to redress past wrongs, largely sought through political and legal means.

Colonialism and state crime

Acknowledgement of the broader context of colonialism is necessary in understanding state fraud against Indigenous people. Elsewhere I have argued that our knowledge of state crime needs to be mediated through an appreciation of colonial processes (Cunneen 2007, 2008). The historical relationship between Indigenous people and the development of modern nation-states raises the problem of the extent to which contemporary liberal democracies like Australia, New Zealand (NZ), Canada or the US were founded on processes we might now regard as state crime. However, this is not simply a matter of judging the past by the standards of the present, or of retrospectively applying contemporary human rights standards to past actions. As will be demonstrated in this chapter, state agents were clearly engaged in activities that were defined *at the time* as unlawful (such as breaches of fiduciary or guardianship duties) and in many cases were clearly criminal (acts of fraud).

It is widely acknowledged that the modern political state has been integral to the commission of genocide and other state crimes (Bauman 1989). The colonial context adds a further dimension to how we understand the connection between the development of the modern political state and the globalized nature of gross violations of human rights and state crime. Indeed, the 'modernity' of genocide might also be located in the formations of colonial states across various continents and nations through the eighteenth and nineteenth centuries.[1] Many contemporary states are built on crimes committed against colonized and formerly enslaved peoples. Indigenous people have been victims of profound historical injustices and human rights abuses which can be understood in the context of state crimes committed in the pursuit of colonial domination. The claims concerning historical injustices and human rights abuses against Indigenous peoples are multilayered. At the highest level is the claim that particular colonial practices against Indigenous peoples constituted genocide in specific contexts. Alongside this claim are others of mass murder, racism, ethnocide (or cultural genocide), slavery, forced labour, forced removals and relocations, the denial of property rights, systematic fraud and the denial of civil and political rights.

To the extent that there has been analysis of state crime in relation to colonized and enslaved peoples, it has tended to focus on questions of genocide and mass murder – the most egregious of state crimes. Overwhelmingly, discussions on state crime concentrate on the use of force – and there is clearly a good reason for this given the role of the modern state in the murder of vast numbers of people (Green and Ward 2004: 1). However, it is the purpose of this chapter to open up a way of seeing state crimes against Indigenous peoples through an understanding of the systematic defrauding of Indigenous moneys and the non-payment or comparative underpayment of Indigenous labour, which itself has had a profound effect on entrenching a deep contemporary disadvantage across all social and economic measures.

The civilizing mission

A key component of the colonial process, and one that was to provide a legitimating and motivating discourse, was the 'civilizing mission' to transform native 'savages' into civilized Christians. It was a brutal task that occupied European empires over several centuries and caused horrific death tolls and dislocation: from deaths through disease, starvation and mistreatment (Stannard 1993: 138) to the forced removal of Indigenous children from their communities and families (NISATSIC 1997; Milloy 1999). The civilizing mission incorporated foundational beliefs of racial superiority and inferiority. Racism was a precondition for the colonial genocides and the systematic abuse of human rights of

Indigenous peoples in Australasia and the Americas, and provided an overarching basis for governmental law and policy towards Indigenous people throughout much of the eighteenth, nineteenth and twentieth centuries. The suspension of the rule of law and the use of terror and violence by colonial authorities was contextualized and legitimated within racialized constructions of Indigenous people as inferior, lesser human beings. Although ideas around race changed during the eighteenth, nineteenth and twentieth centuries and competing views about race were often prevalent at the same time (McGregor 1997), racism inevitably facilitated institutionalized and legalized discrimination and intervention, whether designed to eradicate, protect or assimilate the 'native'. Furthermore, legal protections could be suspended and otherwise unlawful behaviour could be ignored in the higher interest of the betterment, protection or control of Indigenous peoples. The suspension of the rule of law essentially placed Indigenous people outside 'legitimate' systems of legal redress, making resistance more difficult but certainly not impossible.

It was typically the case that settler colonial states put in place restrictions on the civil and political rights exercised by Indigenous peoples (Chesterman and Galligan 1997). Thus, the foundations of liberal democracies were built on various exclusionary measures aimed at the original owners and occupiers of the land. The discriminatory restrictions were justified on the basis of race, although often said to be motivated by the aim to protect the best interests of Indigenous people, as defined by the state (NISATSIC 1997). In Australia, the denial of civil and political rights included numerous legislative controls and restrictions on movement, residence, education, healthcare, employment, voting, workers compensation and welfare/social security entitlements. Many of these restrictions continued into the second half of the twentieth century (Chesterman and Galligan 1997). Indigenous people who struggled against these controls could be arbitrarily 'relocated' or detained. Places like Palm Island in Queensland (QLD) became notorious 'reserves' for troublesome Indigenous people and were also the sites of further resistance, such as the 1957 Palm Island strike over forced labour on the building of a new jail (Rosser 1978; Watson 1995).

The developments that we associate with the rise of modern social welfare-oriented liberal democracies during the course of the twentieth century need to be reconsidered against the backdrop of a range of exclusionary practices which were essentially derived from the colonial experience. For example, Aboriginal people in Australia were largely excluded from the right to social security: a number of federal statutes explicitly disqualified Aboriginal people from receiving government entitlements claimable by non-Indigenous Australians. These included:

- the *Invalid and Old-Age Pensions Act 1908*, which barred 'aboriginal natives' of Australia and the Pacific from receiving an old-age and/or invalid pension
- the *Maternity Allowance Act 1912*, which disqualified 'women who are aboriginal natives of Australia' from receiving the maternity allowance

- the *Child Endowment Act 1941*, which prohibited the payment of the benefit to an 'aboriginal native of Australia' who was nomadic or dependent on Commonwealth or state support
- the *Widows' Pensions Act 1942*, which denied the pension to any 'aboriginal native of Australia'.

Aboriginal people were generally prohibited from receiving social security allowances when they were first introduced. However, there developed a mosaic of legislation and regulations which entitled some Aboriginal people and not others to social security payments. For example, 'nomadic' Aboriginal people were not entitled to child endowment (introduced in 1941) until the restrictions were removed in 1966. Maternity allowances (introduced in 1912) originally excluded women who were 'Asiatics, Aboriginal natives of Australia, Papua or the Islands of the Pacific'. The maternity allowance legislation continued to exclude 'nomadic' or 'primitive' mothers until the provisions were repealed in 1966 (Senate Standing Committee on Legal and Constitutional Affairs [hereafter, Standing Committee] 2006: 35). Thus, discriminatory restrictions on eligibility for social security benefits were not completely lifted until 1966 – the same year the United Nations (UN) adopted the *Convention on the Elimination of all Forms of Racial Discrimination* (Chesterman and Galligan 1997). These changes also reflected the successful campaign work of organizations like the Federal Council for the Advancement of Aborigines and Torres Strait Islanders (FCAATSI) in its struggle for equality during the 1950s and 1960s, and direct political action, such as the Freedom Rides of 1965 and 1966 led by Aboriginal activist Charles Perkins (Behrendt *et al.* 2009: 260; Curthoys 2002).

For those Aboriginal people who were entitled to child endowment or maternity allowances prior to 1966 (that is, those who were not defined as nomadic or primitive), state governments diverted the federal entitlements away from individual Aboriginal recipients (Chesterman and Galligan 1997: 165). There were provisions for allowances to be paid 'indirectly' to a third party. For example, QLD had its missions and settlements defined as 'institutions' so that bulk quarterly federal endowment payments were received on behalf of settlement mothers. State government grants to the missions and settlements were reduced by the amount of the incoming federal revenue. Similar diversion of entitlements occurred with maternity allowances, invalid, old age and widows' pensions. In South Australia, federal social security entitlements to Aboriginal people were used to pay rent back to the state government authority, and for medical expenses, clothes and other items (Standing Committee 2006: 31, 51). On the large pastoral stations in Western Australia and the Northern Territory, the station itself received Aboriginal child endowment, old age and other pensions 'on behalf' of Aboriginal employees and their families. These were regarded as a form of station subsidy (Standing Committee 2006: 32, 36).

As noted above, some of the restrictions on Indigenous people's entitlement to social security remained in place for nearly 20 years after the UN's *Universal Declaration of Human Rights* in 1948 affirmed equality before the law and racial equality as fundamental human rights. The broad legislative controls which restricted or denied citizenship entitlements might be viewed as state crimes in themselves, particularly after the adoption of the Universal Declaration by the UN General Assembly. However, for the purposes of this chapter, I aim to develop a more focused argument specifically on state fraud. The denial of civil and political rights, and the consequent denial of eligibility to social security, was the broader framework within which state fraud could take place in a relatively open manner and without legal consequence.

Forced labour and government fraud

The denial of civil and political rights outlined above forms the context in which the state was involved in vast fraudulent schemes against Indigenous people who were under its care and protection. These schemes involved such matters as stolen wages, missing trust monies and underpayment. Part of the precondition for this fraudulent activity was state control over Indigenous labour, which had been exercised through a range of 'protection' laws enacted in the late nineteenth and early twentieth centuries (Rowley 1972; Haebich 2000). Various Australian governments put in place legislative and administrative controls over the employment, working conditions and wages of Indigenous workers. These controls allowed for the non-payment of wages to some Aboriginal workers, the underpayment of wages to others and the diversion of wages into trust and savings accounts (Standing Committee 2006: 3). There were negligent and, at times, corrupt and dishonest practices which led to the withholding of moneys from Aboriginal wages that had been paid into savings accounts and trust funds.

With the perpetuation of the view that Indigenous people were 'doomed' to extinction, various legislation enacted extensive control in the name of protection. However, the regulation of the Indigenous labour market was more in the interests of capital than it was in the interests of protecting Indigenous people. For example, Aboriginal workers could be jailed for up to five years for breach of employment contracts compared to a maximum of three months for non-Indigenous workers. Aboriginal men and boys could be whipped as punishment, although the practice had been abolished for non-Indigenous offenders many decades previously (Haebich 2000: 210). The 'regulation' of Aboriginal labour amounted to forced labour and bordered on a type of slavery in some cases. Many Aboriginal workers in Western Australia (WA) were not paid wages and were primarily remunerated through rations such as flour, tea, tobacco and clothing. As late as the early 1960s, Aboriginal workers employed as stockmen were given 'perhaps two shirts and two pairs of trousers a year, working boots, hat, canvas swag, and a couple of blankets … no money' (Toussaint 1995: 259). The exploitation of Aboriginal workers in the pastoral industry was often considered to be 'unpaid slavery' at the time (Haebich 1992: 150). Australia was clearly in contravention of International Labour Organization conventions. In 1932, Australia ratified the Forced Labour Convention, which generally prohibited forced labour and working only for rations, although the practice of Indigenous people working for rations in Australia was to last in some areas until the 1960s (Toussaint 1995: 259; Standing Committee 2006: 60–1).

The defrauding of trust funds and savings accounts appears to have been widespread. Kidd (1997, 2000) conducted extensive research in QLD on the way corruption and financial abuse by police 'protectors' and other state officials led to the diversion of Aboriginal money from trust funds into the pockets of the protectors.[2] In December 2006, the Australian Senate Standing Committee on Legal and Constitutional Affairs (hereafter, the Standing Committee) released the report of its inquiry into what had become known as Indigenous 'stolen wages'. The inquiry itself was the outcome of many years of Indigenous political agitation around the issue (see Kidd 2006). The inquiry took a broad view of 'wages' to include wages, savings, entitlements and other monies due to Indigenous people. The Standing Committee (2006: 4) vindicated Indigenous concerns and found that there is:

> compelling evidence that governments systematically withheld and mismanaged Indigenous wages and entitlements over decades. In addition, there is evidence of Indigenous people being underpaid or not paid at all for their work. These practices were implemented from the late 19th century onwards and, in some cases, were still in place in the 1980s.

Typically, state protection legislation set out controls on Indigenous workers whereby they could only be employed under a permit granted by a local protector. Minimum wages were set for Indigenous workers who held a permit. For example, in QLD the wage was set at less than one-eighth of the 'white wage' and protectors could instruct the employer to pay the wages of the Indigenous worker directly to the protector. Monies held by the protector were to be deposited in the worker's name into a government bank account where accounts of expenditure were to be kept. Some small percentage of the worker's wage could be given to the worker as pocket money, by either the employer or the protector.

In QLD, further deductions could be taken from the wages of Indigenous workers to be placed in an Aboriginal Provident Fund (later the Aboriginal Welfare Fund), which was established for the 'relief of natives'. In the Northern Territory, protectors could direct an employer to pay a portion of an Aboriginal worker's wages to the protector to be subsequently held in a trust account. However, it was also the case that, after 1933, employers of Aboriginal workers could be exempted from paying *any* wages if the protector was satisfied that the employer was supporting the relatives and dependants of the Aboriginal employee.

In New South Wales (NSW), the focus of control of the Aborigines Protection Board was the apprenticeship (or indenture) of Aboriginal children. The power of the Board to apprentice Aboriginal children 'on such terms and conditions as it may think under the circumstances of the case are desirable' continued until 1969 (Standing Committee 2006: 15). The protection legislation set the wages for Aboriginal apprentices and directed that a small percentage be given as pocket money to the apprentice and that the remainder go into a trust account to be paid out to the apprentice at the end of their apprenticeship, usually at the age of 21. Many Aboriginal people failed to receive either their pocket money or their wages (Standing Committee 2006: 41–56; Kidd 2006: 71–103). Aboriginal people were not notified of their entitlements and were expected to actively seek any entitlement from the Aboriginal Welfare Board. In some cases, employers had failed to pay the required wages into trust accounts, so there was no money available upon the worker's completion of their apprenticeship (Standing Committee 2006: 56).

Indigenous organizations from the early part of the twentieth century were engaged in mobilizing resistance to the exploitative systems of government control. In NSW in the 1920s, the Australian Aboriginal Progressive Association (later named the Aboriginal Progressive Association, or APA) fought against the removal of children and the apprenticing system, and called for 'emancipation' and the extension of full citizenship rights (Goodall 1996: 149–66). In WA, the Natives' Union made similar demands for equality rights (Attwood and Markus 1999: 91). Formed in Victoria, the Aboriginal Advancement League (AAL) continued this struggle for full citizenship rights during the 1930s. Two organizations (the APA and AAL) held the National Day of Mourning and Protest in Sydney on 26 January 1938, demanding, inter alia, to receive 'the benefits of labour legislation', 'the full benefits of workers compensation and insurance', 'wages in cash ... and not by rations or apprenticeship systems', 'to own land and property and to be allowed to save money in personal banking accounts' and 'to receive the benefits of old-age and invalid pension' (Attwood and Markus 1999: 91). There is a direct line of continuous political agitation by Indigenous organizations from the period of the 1920s through to contemporary demands for redress discussed below. Full citizenship rights and compensation for losses arising from the denial of those rights has been a core part of Indigenous resistance for nearly a century.

Individuals also undertook their own acts of resistance to the oppressive regime of control, and the daily humiliation and degradation of, for example, requesting pocket money from a protector or employer and being refused, or asked why the money was required and being allowed only a certain amount at the discretion of the protector or employer. Some individuals were able to successfully leave their communities, although this inevitably involved loss of family and kin. Others undertook local action, such as strikes, or made demands for control over their payments and accounts. Some individuals were able to lobby local politicians and undertake successful court action to access their money (Kidd 2006: 84). There were also isolated cases where employers of Aboriginal labour subverted the systems of control and paid wages directly to Aboriginal employees (see generally, Standing Committee 2006: 66–7).

The transformation of individual corrupt behaviour into systemic fraud

Governments had put in place compulsory regimes for the regulation of Indigenous money, including compulsory contributions to savings and trust fund accounts. However, the state failed to ensure that Indigenous people received the money they were entitled to and failed to ensure that the savings and trust fund accounts were properly protected from misappropriation and fraud. There were particular obligations on the state given that it had constructed a legal relationship of 'protection' for many Aboriginal people: under the various protection laws, Aboriginal people were legally placed in a position of enforced dependency on the state. The Standing Committee found that:

> Misuse of money included misappropriation by governments, fraud by protectors and employers, and non-payment or underpayment of wages by employers. Although the protection boards, protectors and governments were under obligations to keep proper records and account for all Indigenous monies, these obligations were often not complied with.
>
> (2006: 49)

Examples of the misappropriation of Indigenous money included the use, in QLD, of Indigenous savings accounts and trust funds to pay for expenses related to the administration and maintenance of reserves, such as infrastructure costs; and during the Great Depression, Aboriginal monies were used to cover consolidated revenue shortfalls.

The Senate inquiry received many allegations of fraud and noted the difficulty of proving these allegations. However, the inquiry also noted the widespread and long-running nature of the complaints concerning fraud and the poor administration of the finances of Indigenous people under various Protections Acts (Standing Committee 2006: 4). In QLD, the government commissioned an independent report on the stolen wages issue in 1991 (Consultancy Bureau 1991). The report noted that until 1965 control mechanisms in the Savings Bank were ineffective in guarding against errors, fraud and misappropriation:

> Large frauds on the Savings Bank were detected from time to time, and the Department admitted that, even in these cases, the extent of the fraud could only be reliably determined by the admissions of the persons involved in the frauds. It is realistic to assume that detected frauds comprised only those which were large enough to draw attention to the perpetrators.
>
> (Consultancy Bureau 1991: 8)

In the early part of the twentieth century, the extent of police fraud in relation to the accounts was debated in the QLD state parliament and a thumb-printing and witnessing procedure was introduced in 1921 in an attempt to safeguard against future fraudulent practices by police (Standing Committee 2006: 52). However, two years later, a public service investigation revealed that half of all records on deductions by protectors were inaccurate (Standing Committee 2006: 52). Another investigation in 1941 revealed that incompetence was endemic in the system (Kidd 2006: 84). In the Northern Territory, a 1919 Royal Commission into the administration of the territory showed the ease with which Aboriginal trust funds could be defrauded (Standing Committee 2006: 76). In NSW, there were two investigations in the late 1930s which considered the (mis)management of Indigenous monies (Standing Committee 2006: 74).

In addition to the misappropriation of Indigenous money and the commission of fraud by state officials, there was also widespread non-payment and underpayment of wages to Indigenous workers by employers. In QLD, the government was well aware, at least from the 1930s to the 1960s, that Indigenous workers were not receiving their 'pocket money' from employers. Indeed, the government rejected the auditor's recommendations to tighten the system. Decade after decade, the government was notified by auditors and others that the system of pocket money was a 'farce', was 'useless', that Aboriginal workers were being 'cheated' and that they were 'entirely at the mercy' of employers (Standing Committee 2006: 55; Kidd 2006: 81). As noted previously, in NSW Aboriginal apprentices often were not paid their savings when they reached the age of 21. There were a few parliamentarians and senior bureaucrats who, from the 1930s, described the condition of Aboriginal workers as a form of slavery. Kidd estimated that in QLD perhaps half of all of the wages of the regulated Aboriginal workforce were lost over a 60-year period 'through entrenched official negligence' (cited in Standing Committee 2006: 55).

All of the evidence strongly suggests that the defrauding of Aboriginal people was widespread and that it was ignored by various governments, despite attention being drawn regularly to the ongoing problems over a long period of time by Indigenous organizations, government auditors, members of parliament and other Indigenous and non-Indigenous individuals (see generally, Standing Committee 2006; Kidd 2006).

Resistance and redress

The resistance by Indigenous people to government control, the loss of their land and the exploitation of their labour has a long history. During the twentieth century, there were numerous attempts through strike action to achieve equal wages and conditions, such as the 1946 strike in the Pilbara region by Aboriginal pastoral workers (Toussaint 1995: 259). However, it was not until the direct action in the Gurindji strike for equal wages at Wave Hill in the 1960s, and the subsequent Northern Territory Cattle Industry Case (1966), that wage equality and award conditions were finally extended to Aboriginal men working in the cattle industry. The case was brought by the Northern Australian Workers Union. Resistance has involved direct action, such as strikes, and political action for equality and redress, historically by Indigenous organizations like the APA, the AAL and FCAATSI, and more recently by statutory bodies like the Aboriginal and Torres Strait Islander Commission and community-based bodies like the Foundation for Aboriginal and Islander Research Action (FAIRA). The struggle for legal redress for past wrongs has occurred both individually through the courts and collectively through demands for reparations. Indigenous organizations have played a continuing role from the early part of the twentieth century through to the present in these various forms of political, industrial and legal struggles.

There are many barriers to Indigenous people receiving individual compensation through the legal system for the losses incurred through negligent, corrupt and criminal activity (see Cunneen and Grix 2004). These legal barriers include statutory limitation periods, establishing specific liability, and the financial cost of litigation. However, one of the key issues has been the problem of records. In relation to stolen wages and missing trust funds, the Standing Committee (2006) identified two difficulties: first, records and files that have been lost or are missing; and second, the complexity and number of records involved in trying to piece together information on any one individual. In WA, QLD and NSW, many records are either missing or inconsistent or were never created (Standing Committee 2006: 79–89). In WA, the Aboriginal Legal Service estimated that, as a result of archival destruction, some 21 per cent of the 15,400 personal dossier files created between 1926 and 1959 has been deliberately destroyed (Standing Committee 2006: 84). There are likely to be similar problems in other Australian jurisdictions related to the destruction of individual records.

Some litigation has led to moderately successful outcomes for Indigenous people and their organizations. Palm Island Indigenous people, provided with legal assistance by FAIRA, claimed before the Australian Human Rights Commission that they had been racially discriminated against because they were paid at a lower rate than they would have been if they were not Indigenous (Kidd 2006: 2). Litigation of this type has only related to racial discrimination occurring *after* the introduction of the federal *Racial Discrimination Act 1975*. The Commission found in the applicants' favour and awarded them $7000 each. In presenting his reasons for the decision, Commissioner Carter found that the QLD government had 'intentionally, deliberately and knowingly discriminated' against the Indigenous complainants.

It was clear that the low wages paid to Palm Island Indigenous people brought about great hardship:

> Figures on the department files show that in 1969 when the dole was $23.25, an [Indigenous] sawmiller with nine children was paid only $16, a truck driver with eight children got $18.50. By 1972 the average wage on Palm Island had increased to $23.80 but the basic wage had risen to $43.65.
>
> (Kidd 1997: 83)

As a result of the successful litigation, and the lodging of more than 350 additional claims by FAIRA, in 1999 the QLD government introduced a broader scheme to provide a payment of $7000 to Indigenous workers who had been employed on Indigenous reserves after 1975 and paid at lower rates than non-Indigenous workers. This scheme did nothing for Indigenous people who had their income controlled prior to the introduction of the Racial Discrimination Act in 1975. As a result of Indigenous agitation and further litigation, in 2002, the QLD government made an offer of a one-off payment through the QLD

Indigenous Wages and Savings Reparations Scheme for Indigenous workers who could demonstrate that their wages and savings had been controlled under QLD's Protection Acts (Behrendt *et al.* 2009: 63). The offer included payments to individuals, a written apology from the government and a statement in parliament that publicly recognized past injustices on the basis of race. However, the payment was insultingly low: ranging from $2000 to $4000 for decades of financial losses. Indigenous organizations publicly denounced the offer,[3] and the Australian Human Rights Commission criticized the reparations as being based on balancing the state's budget rather than any principled application of criteria for entitlement or assessment of losses (Jonas 2002). NSW also introduced a repayment scheme which, while slightly more generous than that of the QLD government, failed to recognize the enormity of loss when assessing the financial payment. Neither the federal government nor other Australian state governments have made any effort to offer reparation or compensation for losses.

Many Indigenous people were forced to accept the 'repayments' on offer because of their current age, poverty and often ill-health. Some examples of Indigenous people in QLD who accepted the money included Fred Edwards, who had worked for 50 years on cattle stations where he was not paid his wages; Mabel Williams, who was sent out to work in domestic service at the age of 11 and never received payment; and Percy Bedourie, who worked on properties for more than ten years from the age of 12 for which she only received rations. In each of these, and many other, cases (Kidd 2006: 84–5), individuals begrudgingly and resentfully accepted the $4000. As Vera Hill, who had worked as a domestic servant from the age of 15 for pocket money and rations, stated, 'I really didn't want to take the $4000 but I thought if I didn't take it I'd get nothing' (cited in Kidd 2006: 85). Indigenous activism forced a state response, but that response has been far from satisfactory.

Conclusion

The Senate Standing Committee inquiry into stolen wages found that Indigenous people had been 'seriously disadvantaged by these practices across generations' (Standing Committee 2006: 4) and that a cycle of poverty was created through the denial of wages. Given what we know of the depth of contemporary Indigenous detriment across all social, educational, health and economic indicators (Steering Committee for the Review of Government Service Provision 2009), and the active role played by the state in controlling Aboriginal access to wages, I prefer to describe the outcome as a process of *immiseration*. Historian Anna Haebich begins to capture some of the long-term impacts in the following:

> Aboriginal people played a major role in building the [WA] state economy. ... It was the state government's discriminatory employment system that prevented Aboriginal workers from benefiting from the Australian labour system.... Aboriginal people were subject to a disabling system which denied them proper wages, protection from exploitation and abuse, proper

living conditions, and adequate education and training. So while other Australians were able to build financial security and an economic future for their families, Aboriginal workers were hindered by these controls. Aboriginal poverty in Western Australia today is a direct consequence of this discriminatory treatment.

(Cited in Standing Committee 2006: 68)

The effect of the wages of Indigenous people having been stolen, and of the subsequent immiseration arising from this exploitation, is fundamental to understanding the contemporary situation of Indigenous people in Australia. Housing overcrowding, low incomes, chronic health issues, lower life expectancies, poor educational outcomes, higher incidences of child protection matters and domestic violence can all be related to some extent to the historical process of immiseration. Thus, the long-term impact of government policy in the realm of financial controls over Indigenous people has been devastating.

There are compelling arguments for considering systematic government fraud as a state crime. As indicated in this chapter there are at least three factors that transform the individual criminal behaviour of officials into state crime. First, there was public knowledge of this systematic and widespread abuse. Second, governments failed to ensure proper record-keeping and accounting mechanisms for moneys they were holding in trust for the beneficiaries. And, third, basic principles of equality before the law were suspended. While the liberal democratic principles of inclusionary citizenship were seen as applicable to most Australians, those principles were suspended for Indigenous peoples. Indigenous people were presumed not to be able to participate equally in the social benefits of a welfare state, or to be capable of managing their own affairs or protecting their own interests.

Finally, the struggle by Indigenous peoples to receive compensation and reparation for these historical wrongs raises important questions for how we define and mobilize for adequate remedies to state crime. While there has been much written on truth commissions, restorative justice and reparations, most of this work has not dealt with how historical wrongs should be dealt with within liberal democracies like Australia, NZ, Canada or the US. Certainly, the Australian example reveals a tardiness to confront historical wrongs within the heartland of the nation and a mean-spirited response on the part of the state when forced to consider compensation or reparation. And it has only been the political, social and legal strategies of Indigenous people and their organizations and supporters that have forced governments to respond at all to these wrongs. It is clear that Indigenous resistance has continued for decades. The resistance took various forms, both at an individual, localized level and through Indigenous organizations. Resistance has involved political agitation to change discriminatory laws, policies and practices, as well as seeking compensation and redress for past wrongs. Resistance through collective direct action, such as strikes, has also been a fundamental component in forcing change, and raising public awareness of the issues. However, it is clear that the state has absorbed these challenges and responded in ways that have tended to offer at best partial victories. Resistance, like colonization, is a continuing process and events like the 2007 Northern Territory Emergency Response[4] demonstrate, for example, that even fundamental rights such as non-discrimination on the basis of race can be easily 'suspended' when it suits government interests.

Notes

1 I am not suggesting that the whole colonial project was genocidal, but rather that colonialism brought about specific genocides at particular times and places (see Moses 2000; Barkan 2003).
2 Under 'protection' legislation, local protectors were appointed to enforce the legislation. These were typically police or specially appointed public officials.
3 See, for example, the Stolen Wages Working Group, which was partly funded through Australians for Native Title and Reconciliation and trade unions.
4 The NT Emergency Response was instigated by the federal government in the Northern Territory of Australia. Ostensibly a response to child abuse allegations within Aboriginal communities, it involved far-reaching changes, including forced takeover of Indigenous land, control of welfare payments and the suspension of human rights.

References

Attwood, B. and Markus, A. (1999) *The Struggle for Aboriginal Rights*, St Leonards: Allen and Unwin.

Barkan, E. (2003) 'Genocides of Indigenous Peoples: Rhetoric of Human Rights', in R. Gellately and B. Kiernan (eds), *The Spectre of Genocide: Mass Murder in Historical Perspective*, Cambridge: Cambridge University Press.

Bauman, Z. (1989) *Modernity and the Holocaust*, Cambridge: Polity Press.

Behrendt, B., Cunneen, C. and Libesman, T. (2009) *Indigenous Legal Relations in Australia*, Melbourne: Oxford University Press.

Bronitt, S. and McSherry, B. (2005) *Principles of Criminal Law*, Thomson Law Book.

Chesterman, J. and Galligan, B. (1997) *Citizens Without Rights*, Melbourne: Cambridge University Press.

Consultancy Bureau (Firm) (1991) *Final Report: Investigation of the Aborigines Welfare Fund and the Aboriginal Accounts*, Brisbane: Consultancy Bureau.

Cunneen, C. (2007) 'Criminology, Human Rights and Indigenous Peoples', in S. Parmentier and E. G. M. Weitekamp (eds), *Crime and Human Rights* (pp. 239–63), Oxford: Elsevier.

Cunneen, C. (2008) 'State Crime, the Colonial Question and Indigenous Peoples', in A. Smuelers and R. Haveman (eds), *Supranational Criminology: Towards a Criminology of International Crimes* (pp. 159–80), Antwerp: Intersentia Press.

Cunneen, C. and Grix, J. (2004) *The Limitations of Litigation in Stolen Generations Cases*, Research Discussion Paper 15, Canberra: Australia Institute of Aboriginal and Torres Strait Island Studies.

Curthoys, A. (2002) *Freedom Ride: A Freedom Rider Remembers*, St Leonards: Allen and Unwin.

Goodall, H. (1996) *Invasion to Embassy*, St Leonards: Allen and Unwin.

Green, P. and Ward, T. (2004) *State Crime: Governments, Violence and Corruption*, London: Pluto Press.

Haebich, A. (1992) *For Their Own Good: Aborigines and Government in the South West of Western Australia 1900–1940*, Perth: University of Western Australia Press.

Haebich, A. (2000) *Broken Circles*, Freemantle: Freemantle Arts Centre Press.

Jonas, W. (2002) 'First the Wages Were Stolen, Now Justice Has Been Lost', *National Indigenous Times*, 2 December, available at http://eniar.org/news/stolenwages4.html, accessed 1 November 2011.

Kidd, R. (1997) 'Profiting from Poverty: State Policies and Aboriginal Deprivation', *Queensland Review*, 4(1), 81–6.

Kidd, R. (2000) *Black Lives, Government Lies*, Sydney: University of New South Wales Press.

Kidd, R. (2006) *Trustees on Trial: Recovering the Stolen Wages*, Canberra: Aboriginal Studies Press.

McGregor, R. (1997) *Imagined Destinies: Aboriginal Australians and the Doomed Race Theory, 1880–1939*, Carlton South: Melbourne University Press.

Milloy, J. (1999) *A National Crime: The Canadian Government and the Residential School System 1879 to 1986*, Winnipeg: The University of Manitoba Press.

Moses, D. (2000) 'An Antipodean Genocide? The Origins of the Genocidal Moment in the Colonisation of Australia', *Journal of Genocide Research*, 2(1), 89–106.

National Inquiry into the Separation of Aboriginal and Torres Strait Islander Children from Their Families (NISATSIC) (1997) *Bringing Them Home*, Report of the National Inquiry into the Separation of Aboriginal and Torres Strait Islander Children from Their Families, Sydney: Human Rights and Equal Opportunity Commission.

Riccardi, L. (2009) 'U.S. Settles Indian Trust Account Lawsuit', *Los Angeles Times*, 9 December, available at http://articles.latimes.com/2009/dec/09/nation/la-na-indian-settlement9-2009dec09, accessed 1 November 2011.

Rosser, B. (1978) *This is Palm Island*, Canberra: Australian Institute of Aboriginal Studies.

Rowley, C. (1972) *The Destruction of Aboriginal Society*, Ringwood: Penguin.

Senate Standing Committee on Legal and Constitutional Affairs (2006) *Unfinished Business: Indigenous Stolen Wages*, Canberra: Commonwealth of Australia.

Stannard, D. (1993) *American Holocaust*, New York: Oxford University Press.

Steering Committee for the Review of Government Service Provision (2009) *Overcoming Indigenous Disadvantage: Key Indicators 2009*, Productivity Commission.

Toussaint, S. (1995) 'Western Australia', in A. McGrath (ed.), *Contested Ground*, St Leonards: Allen and Unwin.

Watson, J. (1995) '"We Couldn't Tolerate Any More": The Palm Island Strike of 1957', *Labour History: A Journal of Labour and Social History*, 69 (November), 149–70.

9 'Frameworks of resistance'

Challenging the UK's securitization agenda

Christina Pantazis and Simon Pemberton

The period following the events of September 2001 marked a major watershed in the relationship between the British state and individuals living within its borders. In what can be described as a 'frenzied' approach to law-making, the last United Kingdom (UK) government, led by the Labour Party, enacted five major pieces of counter-terrorism legislation between 2000 and 2008. In the context of the heightened security environment, the legislation sought to enhance the collective security of the nation by promoting the freedoms of the so-called law-abiding majority at the expense of the civil liberties of the 'suspect' minority (Pantazis and Pemberton 2011a).

Driving the processes of securitization has been a centre-right political consensus, an alliance between the 'Blairites' within the Labour Party and the 'Tory hawks' within the Conservative Party (Lambert 2011). A remarkably resilient 'security hegemony', resting on the powerful 'new terrorism' discourse, formed to augment populist opinion behind these reforms (Pantazis and Pemberton 2011a). This discourse purports that the new threat is both qualitatively and quantitatively different from past types of terror and is motivated by an extremist religious ideology, which shows no bounds in terms of the damage it is capable of inflicting (HM Government 2010, 2011). The 'new terrorism' discourse offers a platform from which other discourses may be built, insofar as the current threat requires a rebalancing of security and civil liberties – with the former serving to endanger the latter through its rationale of modernizing the criminal justice system by expanding counter-terrorism powers and encouraging a shift towards 'pre-emption' within the criminal justice system (McCulloch and Pickering 2009).

Without doubt, the 'new terrorism' discourse served to legitimate the British state's undermining of the most fundamental individual liberties, including the right to a fair trial, freedom from torture, freedom from discrimination and the right to liberty. However, it would be misleading to suggest that these encroachments have been untrammelled. Indeed, the Labour government was embarrassingly forced to retreat in a number of crucial areas of its counter-terrorism policy, for example, over its use of indefinite detention of terrorist suspects – a situation likened to the US's Guantanamo Bay (Liberty 2003), while the policy of indiscriminate police stop-and-search tactics has since undergone significant revision. We contend that the worst excesses of the securitization agenda, which unfolded over the past decade, have been slowly dismantled. Explanation for this lies in the frameworks of resistance that have emerged during this period to challenge the prevailing security hegemony.

In this chapter, we identity three dominant frameworks of resistance, constituted by material practices and social action, as well as a series of discourses that have sought to contest these legislative developments. First, the 'human rights framework' has directly challenged the encroachment of individual liberty by the state by invoking human rights norms and instruments. These have been mobilized and have formed critical sites of resistance for a diverse range of actors, including politicians, judges and non-government organizations (NGOs). A second dominant framework revolves around the promotion of 'freedom'. This framework defends a negative notion of freedom (Berlin 1958), seeking the removal of constraints on the ability of individuals to act and promoting the idea of being free from the 'big state'. The Muslim community, in all its diverse forms, through representative bodies, as well as others, including policymakers, NGOs and academics (Hickman *et al.* 2010; Kundnani 2009; Pantazis and Pemberton 2009a; Choudhury and Fenwick 2011), has been instrumental in promoting the third major resistance framework, which focuses on the 'criminalization of communities'. Here, the attention is on the corrosive impacts of expanded counter-terrorism powers on the religious and ethnic groups disproportionately affected, highlighting how 'suspicion' has come to define the experiences of ordinary law-abiding Muslims and other minority groups.

The chapter seeks to evaluate the ways in which the security agenda outlined so far has been contested by these resistance frameworks. In doing so, three principal themes run throughout our analysis and form the basis of our conclusion. First, through an analysis of the strategies that are embedded within these frameworks, we can better understand their transformative capacity. Drawing on Michalowski's metaphor of the 'master's tools' (Chapter 16, this volume), a key concern we address is the extent to which these strategies become subsumed within the existing security agenda, therefore serving to legitimate the status quo. If, as Foucault (1981) suggests, resistance strategies should be considered as embedded within existing fields of power, the nature of power necessitates that we seek to identify which strategies are best placed to minimize the pervasive impacts of the security agenda. Second, the extent to which these frameworks represent a coalition of interests is explored. While the frameworks represent a broad resistance strategy, they are constituted by a wide range of 'social audiences' (Green and Ward 2000) with an array of interests and goals that at times conflict and potentially contradict one another. Third, drawing on Stanley and McCulloch (Chapter 1, this volume), we can assess the success of resistance frameworks in a variety of ways. Within this context, success can most obviously be defined in terms of the resulting reforms in counter-terrorism powers. Key indicators of success would include the removal of counter-terrorism powers, the reduction in the level of discretion on which powers are based, and the reversal of the shift towards pre-emption. However, in many respects, these would represent limited incursions into the security agenda. We contend that a more significant and sustained transformative project would also serve to undermine the security hegemony which has augmented populist support behind these counter-terrorism powers.

Frameworks of resistance (1): human rights

The deployment of a human rights framework to reign in the excesses of the UK's counter-terrorism agenda can be observed at a number of different policy levels, including at the highest level of global policymaking, where a number of actors and bodies, including human rights experts, chairs of human rights treaty bodies and the United Nations (UN) Commission on Human Rights, have raised concerns about the lack of a human rights perspective in the counter-terrorism stance taken by the United Nations Security Council (UNSC) since 2001 (Pantazis and Pemberton 2009b).

A more significant role, however, has been the influence of European human rights on the development of the UK's counter-terrorism legislation. Britain's protracted engagement with counter-terrorism in Northern Ireland brought the state into regular conflict with European law and, more specifically, the European Court of Human Rights (ECHR) in Strasbourg (Gearty 2005). By incorporating the European Convention of Human Rights into British law with the introduction of the *Human Rights Act 1998*, the influence of European law developed in fresh and dramatic ways when the newly elected Labour government promised the British public 'access to the rights which should be theirs in the first place' (Straw 1997).

The Human Rights Act – a ' "higher law", to which all other laws and policies must conform where "possible" ' (Klug and Wildbore 2007: 231) – allows courts to adjudicate and declare legislation incompatible with human rights norms. Crucially, the Human Rights Act requires ministers to produce a compatibility statement when proposing new legislation (s 19) and courts to interpret the legislation's compatibility with the human rights legislation where possible (s 3), while provisions in Schedule 2 allow for a 'remedial order' to be introduced by government to address any incompatibility issues. Even before the Human Rights Act was fully enforced, Gearty (2005) notes, it served an early role in constraining the scope of the Terrorism Bill, which preceded the *Terrorism Act 2000*.

The Human Rights Act has been referred to as a 'dialogue model' that engages the courts, government and parliament in human rights protection (Klug and Wildbore 2007). Hiebert (2006) describes it as a 'parliamentary rights model' – an innovative approach to the protection of rights. Central to these models has been the role of the Joint Committee on Human Rights (JCHR), a non-departmental select committee established in the wake of the enactment of the Human Rights Act in 1998, and inaugurated in 2001, with the aim of strengthening parliamentary scrutiny of human rights. It became a thorn in the side of the Labour government (*Guardian* 2010a) as it prioritized the scrutiny of all bills (including counter-terrorism bills) and made inquiries into thematic concerns, including counter-terrorism.

The JCHR had a significant impact on the Anti-Terrorism, Crime and Security Bill, introduced in November 2001 in the wake of the US attacks (Hiebert 2006). The JCHR voiced its concerns over a number of potential compatibility issues in relation to the Bill, reserving its fiercest critique for the controversial proposal to indefinitely detain foreign nationals suspected of terrorist involvement (JCHR 2002: para 21). These were individuals who could not be deported safely back to their country of origin (art 3), but for whom the criminal evidence against them would not hold up in a criminal court if they were brought to trial. This proposal had led the government to derogate from the ECHR (art 5), which was only possible by declaring that the UK faced a public emergency that threatened the life of the nation, following the attacks against the US. The JCHR queried why the government felt that this was necessary when no other state member of the Council of Europe had done so (para 30). It raised concerns about the broad definition of 'terrorist', the lack of a requirement of reasonableness in determining terrorist suspects, and the potential risk of discriminatory practices against foreign nationals, particularly in the context of the nature of the deprivation being proposed (para 34). The British government did not acquiesce to the JCHR's concerns about derogation but it did amend the Bill to introduce 'reasonable grounds' of suspicion of involvement with 'international terrorism' as a requirement for an individual to be detained, tighten up the definition of a terrorist suspect and introduce a sunset clause for the detention measures, meaning that they would be subject to parliamentary renewal (Hiebert 2006).

If the JCHR provides one important element of the 'dialogue model', which the Human Rights Act supposedly promotes, then British courts provide another. Section 4 of the Human Rights Act allows the courts to make a declaration of incompatibility. Perhaps in anticipation of the concerns raised by the JCHR, the clearest example of this was the December 2004 House of Lords' declaration (in a vote of eight to one) that section 23 of the *Anti-Terrorism, Crime and Security Act 2001*, which allows for non-UK citizens suspected of terrorism to be placed under indefinite detention without trial, was incompatible with articles 5 and 14 of the Human Rights Act. To quote Lord Bingham, who led the declaration, incompatibility was announced 'insofar as [the measure] is disproportionate and permits detention of suspected international terrorists in a way that discriminates on the ground of nationality or immigration status' (UK House of Lords 2004: para 73). While it would be misleading to portray the Law Lords as actively resisting these shifts towards authoritarianism, they nevertheless performed a highly important role in challenging counter-terrorism through their interpretation of human rights instruments. As Lord Bingham's declaration made clear: 'the function of independent judges charged to interpret and apply the law is universally recognised as a cardinal feature of the modern democratic state, a cornerstone of the rule of law itself" (UK House of Lords 2004: para 42). It is for this reason that Bingham was described as 'the radical who [led] a new English revolution' (*Guardian* 2004).

The reaction against the Law Lords' verdict by the government and the Conservative Opposition Party was instructive. Michael Howard, the then Conservative Shadow Home Secretary, warned in an article in the *Daily Telegraph* against the new tide of 'judicial activism', putting the blame squarely on the Human Rights Act:

> Given that judicial activism seems to have reached unprecedented levels in thwarting the wishes of Parliament, it is time, I believe, to go back to first principles ... the Human Rights Act has drawn British judges into areas of political controversy through no fault of their own. It is vital ... that the judiciary exercises these powers with self-restraint...
>
> Parliament must be supreme. Aggressive judicial activism will not only undermine the public's confidence in the impartiality of our judiciary, but it could also put *our security at risk* – and with it the freedoms the judges seek to defend. That would be a price we cannot be expected to pay.
>
> (Howard 2005, italics added)

Not only is Howard here critical of the role bestowed upon judges by the Human Rights Act, he is also alluding to the heightened risks of terrorism that might follow from this exercise of judicial flexing. However, despite the resulting furore about parliamentary sovereignty being undermined, and the then Home Secretary, Charles Clarke, stating that he had no intention of repealing section 23 (cited in Hansard 2004), the government did not renew the controversial measure and the nine remaining prisoners were eventually released from detention and placed under the Control Order regime following the introduction of the *Prevention of Terrorism Act 2005*.

The 'human rights framework' draws upon a range of 'social audiences' beyond parliament and the courts, and a loose network of human rights bodies (such as Liberty, Statewatch, Amnesty International and the Islamic Human Rights Commission) have played a central role in promoting human rights and defending civil liberties in relation to the government's counter-terrorism agenda through their campaigning, lobbying and policy work. At the helm of this human rights network has been Liberty. Under Sharmi Chakrabarti's directorship, Liberty became almost a household name during the height of the controversy over particular measures, such as the indefinite detention and pre-charge detention of terror suspects: 'Chakrabarti found herself becoming the most prominent mouthpiece for a disparate network of politicians from both the right and the left, human-rights groups and millions of concerned citizens who felt voiceless' (*Guardian* 2008).

One of the most successful actions taken by Liberty was providing legal representation to a journalist and a peace protester. The legal action (*Gillan and Quinton* v. *UK*) resulted in the January 2010 ECHR unanimous ruling that section 44 of the Terrorism Act breached respect for private and family life (art 8), thereby overturning an earlier domestic court decision. Kevin Gillan and Pennie Quinton had been stopped and searched by the police without the requirement of reasonable suspicion while on their way to a demonstration outside the annual arms fair at the ExCeL centre, in London's Docklands in September 2003. The Court raised a number of concerns regarding the use of these powers and the lack of sufficient safeguards in place to prevent the abuse of civil liberties, declaring that 'there is a clear risk of arbitrariness in the grant of such a broad discretion to the police officer' (*Gillan and Quinton* v. *UK*: para 85). The impact of Liberty's legal action, as well as the ruling itself, has been immense. Even before the decision, the Metropolitan Police Force, which out of the 43 police forces in England and Wales was the most prolific user of section 44 powers, reduced its use of section 44 searches in 2009 as a 'calculated attempt to avoid this outcome at the European Court' (*Guardian* 2010b). However, the most dramatic fall occurred after July 2010 when the new Conservative Home Secretary, Theresa May, introduced interim measures bringing section 44 powers into line with the European Court ruling (May 2010). Thus, between July and September 2010, there was a 98 per cent reduction in the use of stop-and-search powers compared to the same period one year earlier (a staggering fall from 30,070 to 666) (*Guardian* 2011).

Frameworks of resistance (2): 'freedom' from the big state

The second framework revolves around the notion of 'freedom'. This framework promotes a negative notion of liberty and seeks to stifle state interference in both private and public forms of life. It underpinned several of the Law Lords' statements in the 2004 judgement against indefinite detention without trial:

> The real threat to the life of the nation, in the sense of a people living in accordance with its traditional laws and political values, comes not from terrorism but from laws such as these.
>
> (UK House of Lords 2004: Lord Hoffman, para 97)

Chief advocates of the freedom framework include members of the Conservative Party, particularly those who favour a disposition towards libertarianism. While in opposition, for example, the Conservatives decided to side with the Liberal Democrats in the parliamentary vote on the 2008 Counter-Terrorism Bill, to challenge Labour's key provisions to extend detention without charge from 28 to 42 days. Significant too was the then Shadow Home Secretary David Davis's decision to resign in protest at Labour's proposals, thereby effectively forcing a by-election on the issue of civil liberties. Interestingly, the leader of the Conservative Party, David Cameron, failed to come out in support of Davis's decision, thus exposing Cameron's populist agenda and the limits of how far he would promote his defence of freedom in the context of a populist-driven counter-terrorism discourse (Pantazis and Pemberton 2011a).

The freedom framework became more ascendant in the immediate aftermath of the May 2010 election, with the establishment of the coalition government led by the Conservative Party and supported by the Liberal Democrats, who have contemporaneously aligned themselves to a civil liberties agenda. The coalition sought to respond to the 'respectable fears' of the 'law-abiding majority' relating to the perceived 'normalization' of counter-terrorism powers. Specific concerns arose from the 'audience from below' about the 'net-widening' impact on different groups (such as professional photographers experiencing stop-and-search powers). Thus, the Coalition's Programme for Government, the document setting out the coalition's vision, promised to 'be strong in defence of freedom', advocating the scrapping of the identity card scheme and offering 'safeguards against the misuse of anti-terrorism legislation' (HM Government 2010: 11). The new government instigated a review of counter-terrorism powers (HM Government 2011), which preceded the 2011 Protection of Freedoms Bill, aimed at reforming the most controversial of the powers introduced by the Labour government. These included amending the widely abused police powers to stop and search individuals without the requirement of reasonable suspicion and reducing the pre-detention of terrorist suspects to a maximum of 14 days. The coalition government also introduced legislation in 2011 which abolished the use of control orders against terrorist suspects and replaced them with a new regime known as TPIM (Terrorism Prevention and Investigation Measures). The government has claimed that this minimizes the limits to freedom but maintains and extends the system of surveillance. However, the new regime continues to maintain the worst elements of the previous measures – for example, by continuing to deny terrorist suspects the right to a fair trial.

The freedom framework may appear to resonate with the human rights framework, but historical lineage differentiates the two approaches in significant ways. While the latter has its origins in European and American visions of a new world order developed in the post-World War II period, which rejected the horrors of the war and the events leading up to it, the freedom framework is firmly rooted in Britain's bygone era of the Magna Carta. In a clear encapsulation of the freedom framework, David Cameron, as Opposition leader, acknowledged its historical trajectory:

> David Davis and I are fiercely determined to protect Britain's security with tough and intelligent action to fight crime and to fight terrorism. But in doing so, we will never be casual about our freedoms. We understand that freedom is central to the *British way of life*. It is a vital part of our history and our heritage. We feel it in our bones.
>
> (Cameron 2006, italics added)

Moreover, some advocates of the freedom framework have gone to some lengths to distinguish between contemporary human rights, as embodied within the Human Rights Act, and the freedoms supposedly ingrained within the British legal tradition. As David Cameron further noted:

> The Human Rights Act has made it harder to protect our security. And it's done little to protect some of our liberties ... Tony Blair recognises this. It is

why he keeps talking about reviewing the Human Rights Act and rebalancing the criminal justice system.

(Cameron 2006)

This issue is a source of major tension among the current coalition partners; while the Conservative Party remains unequivocal in its opposition to the Human Rights Act and wishes to replace it with a British Bill of Rights, the Liberal Democrats appear committed to maintaining the Act. Dissonance with the Human Rights Act among Conservative Party members is based on the ideological construction of the Act as a European import that undermines British parliamentary sovereignty and British values, as well the security of the nation. However, it seems somewhat ironic that advocates of the freedom framework actively favour the rejection of contemporary human rights norms as currently embedded. This is particularly so as the Human Rights Act makes readily available the machinery necessary for legal challenges to the operation of counter-terrorism powers. Ultimately, the appeal to Britain's unique civil liberties tradition seeks to discursively square the circle imposed by the securitization agenda – that rights should exist but should not fetter the operation of counter-terrorism powers. However, it goes without saying that rights that are incapable of curtailing state power are essentially impotent – an inescapable contradiction which lies at the heart of the attempt to rebalance civil liberties and security (Pantazis and Pemberton 2011a).

Frameworks of resistance (3): the criminalization of (Muslim) communities

The third framework we identify revolves around the corrosive impacts of counter-terrorism legislation on the communities most affected. It is a resistance framework rooted in perspectives 'from below' and involves both individuals and civil society organizations (such as the Muslim Council of Britain, the Islamic Human Rights Commission, the Campaign Against the Criminalisation of Communities and the Institute of Race Relations). This resistance framework consists of a 'weaker' and a 'stronger' version. The former stresses the deleterious impact of the legislation and powers in terms of community relations and community cohesion, where the concern is on the potentially adverse consequences for how different ethnic and religious communities relate to, and treat, each other. Concern is also expressed about the decline in trust between the criminalized communities and public authorities. This is especially the case in relation to the police, whose tactics have often been identified as counterproductive, particularly where intelligence gathering is made more difficult as a result. Thus, in the aftermath of September 2001 and the British state's response to the threat of violence, concerns were raised by the House of Commons Home Affairs Committee (2005), which had sought the views of community organizations about the impact of counter-terrorism powers on community relations. Parallels were drawn between the experiences of the Irish community and those of the Muslim population in the UK, although the Committee stopped short of describing the experiences of the Muslim population as being perceived as the new 'enemy within'.

The 'stronger' version focuses much more explicitly on the experiences and grievances of the Muslim population as a 'suspect community'. Researching the Irish community's experience of UK anti-terrorism powers during the 1970s, Hillyard (1993) claimed that counter-terrorism legislation had created a 'suspect community'. In 2009, we argued that the identification of Islamic fanaticism as the main threat facing Western democracies had resulted in the Muslim community replacing the Irish as the principal suspect community for the British state (Pantazis and Pemberton 2009a). Just as was the case for the Irish population, religious identity and other related signifiers (such as ethnicity and dress) rather than evidence of criminal wrongdoing became the main factors determining whether an individual is to be 'singled out for state attention as being "problematic"' (Pantazis and Pemberton 2009a: 649).

We argued that suspicion should be understood as a diffuse social phenomenon incorporating a range of social practices, interactions and discourses that operate both within and outside the law and legal processes (Pantazis and Pemberton 2009a, 2011b). We stated that, supported by a highly charged political and media discourse, the new array of legal powers – particularly those contained in the Terrorism Act relating to the open-ended nature of the definition of terrorism (ss 1 and 2), the proscription of 'terrorist' groups (s 3) and the unfettered discretion of police officers to stop and search anyone or any vehicle in connection with terrorism (ss 44 [1] and [2]) – were instrumental in creating the legislative conditions in which Muslims became identified as a suspect community (Pantazis and Pemberton 2009a).

Choudhury and Fenwick's (2011: v) empirical study for the Equality and Human Rights Commission provided further evidence of how the Muslim community itself began to experience its treatment by the state and its agents as suspicious:

> Muslims and non-Muslims from the same local areas who participated in this research appear to live 'parallel lives'.... Many participants, while not referring to specific laws or policies, felt that counter-terrorism law and policy generally was contributing towards hostility to Muslims by treating Muslims as a 'suspect group', and creating a climate of fear and suspicion towards them.

With the implementation of the legislation, it is hardly surprising that Muslims came to feel that they were treated differently from others, thus becoming part of a suspect community. This was most readily observed in the police treatment of Muslims in their rapid and escalating use of stop-and-search powers. We revealed, for example, how Asian and black people were three times more likely to be stopped and searched than white people under section 44 powers (Pantazis and Pemberton 2009a). Although the data did not allow us to draw any firm conclusions about the religious identity of those stopped, other sources of evidence present at the time suggested that Muslims felt they were being stopped disproportionately (Pantazis and Pemberton 2009a). The fact that these stops and searches resulted in less than 1 per cent of arrests, and even fewer charges, let alone any successful convictions, provided further evidence that these powers were being used randomly and without adequate justification against minority groups (Pantazis and Pemberton 2009a). Moreover, statements from government ministers that Muslims would bear the brunt of counter-terrorism powers because it reflected the 'reality of the situation' (Blears cited by House of Commons Home Affairs Committee 2005: 46) certainly did little to reassure the Muslim community that it was not being racially and religiously profiled by the police.

The furore surrounding Muslims' experiences of policing climaxed with the publication of the Metropolitan Police Authority's inquiry *Counter-Terrorism: the London Debate* in 2007 (MPA 2007). The inquiry claimed that 'anti-terrorism stop and search is doing untold damage to certain communities' confidence in the police, and its effectiveness in countering terrorism is in serious doubt' (MPA 2007: 4). Among its 73 recommendations, the inquiry urged the Metropolitan Police Service (MPS) to undertake an urgent review of section 44 powers. The MPS's *Tactical Use* Review (MPS 2009) recommended a three-layered approach to the use of stop-and-search powers, which effectively ended the blanket use of this power (para 14). Its consultation confirmed 'suggestions that the power is seen as controversial and has the potential to have a negative impact, particularly on minority communities' (para 13). The inquiry further reported that it would undertake race and equality impact reviews to monitor and evaluate the use of the powers on communities (section D). In an interview with Human Right Watch, the Detective Chief Superintendent leading the MPS review emphasized the need to ensure that the powers were not seen as disproportionately affecting some groups (Human Rights Watch 2010). In the light of these tensions, as well as legal pressure (highlighted above), section 44 stop-and-search powers have been subject to rapid national reform.

Following the government's *Review of Counter-Terrorism and Security Powers* (HM Government 2011), Home Secretary Theresa May made a statement to parliament in which she declared that 'too much of [counter-terrorism legislation] was excessive and unnecessary. At times it gave the impression of criminalising entire communities' (May 2011). She promised to repeal section 44 and to replace it with a more limited power in the Protection of Freedoms Bill, but in response to the Review's recommendation to ensure that new powers would be available more quickly, the Home Secretary has in the meantime introduced the *Terrorism Act 2000 (Remedial) Order 2011* and a new section 47A Schedule 6B of the Terrorism Act. The Order replaces existing powers with a more targeted and proportionate power that allows authorizations for stops and searches without reasonable suspicion to occur where their authorizer considers that a terrorist act will take place and views these powers as necessary to prevent terrorism from taking place (Home Office 2011). Despite the tighter provisions contained in the Order, the JCHR (2011) nevertheless expressed concerns about the lack of detailed evidence on the circumstances that would demonstrate the need for the use of stop-and-search powers without the requirement of reasonable suspicion. It also raised the spectre of further compatibility issues, urging that the authorizer should have 'reasonable basis' for their belief concerning the necessity for an authorization and recommended strengthening the Code of Practice in order to address concerns about racial discrimination.

Conclusion

The three frameworks of resistance outlined above have all coalesced to instigate the reform of counter-terrorism powers in the UK. It is important to note that these frameworks may not have enjoyed the same measures of success had the UK experienced further violence since 2005. Without a climate of fear, sustained by such incidents, spaces for resistance have developed in which a perpetual state of emergency has begun to unravel (*Guardian* 2009). With this in mind, we must be realistic about the future transformative potential of these frameworks. Nevertheless, these frameworks appear to offer contrasting 'degrees of resistance' which relate to their varied abilities to minimize the insidious influence of the securitization agenda.

The freedom framework, constituted largely by the Conservative Party and 'establishment' interests, is focused on removing the 'excesses' of state interference in order to return to what is considered to be the traditional cornerstones of the British legal system. Excessive powers are seen to be impacting on the freedoms of the 'law-abiding majority' as state interference incrementally creeps into their lives (as demonstrated by the increasing use of counter-terrorism powers by local authorities in a number of different spheres of life). By removing seemingly 'unnecessary' powers, the framework in fact serves to consolidate the security paradigm.

The security paradigm, because of the UK's commitment to the ECHR, has been required to confront the demands of the human rights framework. However, human rights are far from embedded within the security apparatus, as the intractable debate on how to reconcile security and civil liberties has demonstrated (Pantazis and Pemberton 2011a). Of course, if human rights norms were to be fully embedded within counter-terrorism policing, then we might expect to see a very different set of outcomes. Nevertheless, as a strategy, it is restricted by the tools it commands. It can lead to perverse outcomes, as was demonstrated in the 2004 Law Lords judgement, which found indefinite detention to be unlawful because it only applied to foreign nationals. The resulting outcome was the inclusion of UK citizens in the new Control Orders which were introduced. The sites of resistance offered by this framework remain firmly grounded in the material practices and discourses of the law and have proved incapable of effectively challenging the broader hegemonic processes that have sustained the securitization agenda.

We contend that the 'criminalizing communities' framework, informed largely by the audience from below (Green and Ward 2000), has the greatest transformative potential. In both its weaker and stronger versions, the framework allows a shift in focus from the fettered forms of individual liberty to attention to the corrosive impact on entire communities. While the transformative possibilities offered by the weaker version may be restricted to improved police–community relations, the stronger version focused on the experiences of the community as suspect opens up a wider range of possibilities in seeking to exploit spaces of resistance beyond legal spheres. These provide a means to challenge the discursive components of the security hegemony and to offer alternative truths about the nature of the violence. Significantly, a different set of policy solutions have emerged which draw from the experiences of political violence in Northern Ireland. Crucially, this could involve a shift away from the securitization agenda towards a greater emphasis on political dialogue and negotiated settlement to address grievances and processes of radicalization that ultimately serve to undermine our security.

References

Berlin, I. (1958) *Two Concepts of Liberty*, Oxford: Clarendon Press.

Cameron, D. (2006) *Balancing Freedom and Security – A Modern British Bill of Rights*, 26 June, available at www.conservatives.com/News/Speeches/2006/06/Cameron_Balancing_freedom_and_security__A_modern_British_Bill_of_Rights.aspx.

Choudhury, T. and Fenwick, H. (2011) *The Impact of Counter-Terrorism Measures on Muslim Communities*, Research Report No. 72, London: Equality and Human Rights Commission.

Foucault, M. (1981) *The History of Sexuality: Vol. 1*, London: Penguin.

Gearty, C. (2005) '11 September 2001, Counter-terrorism, and the Human Rights Act', *Journal of Law and Society*, 32(1), 18–33.

Gillan and Quinton v. *United Kingdom* [2009] ECHR 28 (12 January 2010).

Green, P. and Ward, T. (2000) 'State Crime, Human Rights and the Limits of Criminology', *Social Justice*, 27(1), 101–15.

Guardian (2004) 'The Radical Who Is Leading a New English Revolution', *Guardian*, 21 December, available at www.guardian.co.uk/politics/2004/dec/21/humanrights.britainand911?INTCMP=ILCNETTXT3487.

Guardian (2008) 'Profile: Shami Chakrabarti: The Undaunted Freedom Fight', *Guardian*, 22 June, available at www.guardian.co.uk/world/2008/jun/22/humanrights.civilliberties.

Guardian (2009) 'Terror Laws Built Up after 9/11 and 7/7 May Be Scaled Back, Says Jack Straw', *Guardian*, 13 May, available at www.guardian.co.uk/politics/2009/may/13/terrorism-legislation-jack-straw.

Guardian (2010a) 'What Next for the UK Parliament Joint Committee on Human Rights?', *Guardian*, 5 July, available at www.guardian.co.uk/law/2010/jul/05/human-rights-human-rights-act.

Guardian (2010b) 'European Court Condemns Police Misuse of Stop and Search', *Guardian*, 12 January, available at www.guardian.co.uk/uk/2010/jan/12/euorpean-court-police-misuse-stop-search?INTCMP=SRCH.

Guardian (2011) 'Stop and Search Numbers Fall after Change to Counterterrorism Powers', *Guardian*, 24 February, available at www.guardian.co.uk/law/2011/feb/24/stop-and-search-fall-counterterrorism-powers?INTCMP=SRCH.

Hansard (2004) *House of Lords Judgment on A & Others and The Secretary of State for the Home Department*, 16 December, Column 151WS, available at www.publications.parliament.uk/pa/cm200405/cmhansrd/vo041216/wmstext/41216m03.htm.

Hickman, M., Silvestri, S. and Thomas, L. (2010) *A Comparative Study of the Representations of 'Suspect' Communities in Multi-ethnic Britain and of Their Impact on Muslim and Irish Communities*, ESRC End of Award Report, RES-062–23–1066, Swindon: ESRC.

Hiebert, J. L. (2006) 'Parliament and the Human Rights Act: Can the JCHR Help Facilitate a Culture of Rights?', *International Journal of Constitutional Law*, 4, 1–38.

Hillyard, P. (1993) *Suspect Community: People's Experiences of the Prevention of Terrorism Acts in Britain*, London: Pluto Press.

HM Government (2010) *The Coalition: Our Programme for Government*, London: Cabinet Office.

HM Government (2011) *Review of Counter-Terrorism and Security Powers: Review Findings and Recommendations*, Cm 8004, London: The Stationery Office.

Home Office (2011) *Operation of Police Powers under the Terrorism Act 2000 and Subsequent Legislation: Arrests, Outcomes and Stops and Searches*, Home Office Statistical Bulletin, 2010–11, HOSB 15/11, London: Home Office.

House of Commons Home Affairs Committee (2005) *Terrorism and Community Relations*, Sixth Report of Session 2004–05 Volume I Report, together with formal minutes and Appendix, London: Stationery Office.

Howard, M. (2005) 'Judges Must Bow to the Will of Parliament', *Daily Telegraph*, 10 August, available at www.telegraph.co.uk/comment/personal-view/3618954/Judges-must-bow-to-the-will-of-Parliament.html.

Human Rights Watch (2010) *Without Suspicion: Stop and Search under the Terrorism Act*, London: Human Rights Watch.

Joint Committee on Human Rights (2002) *Second Report, Anti-terrorism, Crime and Security Bill*, 2001–02, available at www.publications.parliament.uk/pa/jt200102/jtselect/jtrights/037/3703.htm#a1.

Joint Committee on Human Rights (2011) *Terrorism Act 2000 (Remedial) Order 2011: Stop and Search without Reasonable Suspicion*, Fourteenth Report of Session 2010–12, HL Paper 155, HC 1141, London: The Stationery Office.

Klug, F. and Wildbore, H. (2007) 'Breaking New Ground: The Joint Committee on Human Rights and the Role of Parliament in Human Rights Compliance', *European Human Rights Law*, 3, 231–50.

Kundnani, A. (2009) *Spooked: How Not to Prevent Violent Extremism*, London: Institute of Race Relations.

Lambert, R. (2011) 'Cameron and Blair: the Real Counter-Terrorism Coalition', *New Statesman*, 6 June, available at www.newstatesman.com/blogs/the-staggers/2011/06/cameron-clegg-muslim-blair.

Liberty (2003) 'It's Time to Release or Charge without Delay', Media Release, 18 December, available at www.liberty-human-rights.org.uk/media/press/2003/its-time-to-release-or-charge-without-delay.php.

McCulloch, J. and Pickering, S. (2009) 'Pre-Crime and Counter-Terrorism: Imagining Future Crime in the "War on Terror"', *British Journal of Criminology*, 49(5), 628–45.

May, T. (2010) *Statement by the Home Secretary on Stop and Search Powers under the*

Terrorism Act 2000 (section 44), 8 July, available at www.homeoffice.gov.uk/publications/about-us/parliamentary-business/oral-statements/stop-and-search-statement/?view=Standard&pubID=821759.

May, T. (2011) *Oral Statement of Theresa May: Review of Counter Terrorism and Security Powers*, 26 January, available at www.homeoffice.gov.uk/publications/about-us/parliamentary-business/oral-statements/.

Metropolitan Police Authority (2007) *Counter-Terrorism: The London Debate*, MPA: London.

Metropolitan Police Service (2009) *Section 44 Terrorism Act 2000: Tactical Use Review*, Report 10, 7 May, available at www.mpa.gov.uk/committees/sop/2009/090507/10/.

Pantazis, C. and Pemberton, S. (2009a) 'From the "Old" to the "New" Suspect Communities: Examining the Impact of Recent UK Counter-terrorist Legislation', *British Journal of Criminology*, 49, 646–66.

Pantazis, C. and Pemberton, S. (2009b) 'Policy Transfer and the UK's "War on Terror": A Political Economy Approach', *Policy & Politics*, 37(3), 363–87.

Pantazis, C. and Pemberton, S. (2011a) 'Reconfiguring Security and Liberty: Political Discourses and Public Opinion in the New Century', *British Journal of Criminology*, 52(3), 651–67.

Pantazis, C. and Pemberton, S. (2011b) 'Re-stating the Case for the Suspect Community: A Reply to Greer', *British Journal of Criminology*, 51(6), 1054–62.

Straw, J. (1997) *Speech at the 1997 Labour Party Conference*, available at www.prnewswire.co.uk/cgi/news/release?id=33162.

United Kingdom House of Lords (2004) *Judgments: A (FC) and others (FC) (Appellants) v. Secretary of State for the Home Department (Respondent)*, SESSION 2004–05, UKHL 56.

10 Environmental activism and resistance to state–corporate crime

Rob White

Introduction

This chapter explores the tactics and strategies employed by environmental activists to resist and respond to instances of state–corporate activity associated with environmental harm. There is frequently a close nexus between the state and corporations when it comes to environmentally harmful practices, and elements of denial and facilitation on the part of the state are vital to the pursuance of such activities. Resistance to such harms takes a number of forms, ranging from civil disobedience to appeals for international support and condemnation via the media. Conversely, state responses to environmental activism may include litigation, criminalization, control over information and the use of counter-terrorism powers.

The chapter considers the tactical and strategic dance between activists and dominant social interests, the ways in which environmental activists attempt to subvert formal state power and official representations of legitimacy and legality, and the bounce-back from this on the part of the powerful. From cooperation and compromise to confrontation and conflict, there are many avenues for activist intervention and varying responses on the part of powerful economic and political bodies to environmental activist agendas.

The intellectual and practical context for this chapter is the dearth of adequate controls and regulatory actions within official criminal justice and state offices on matters pertaining to environmental harm. To put it simply, not enough is being done to prevent, prosecute and respond to environmental crime (see White 2010, 2011a). Accordingly, it is very often transnational environmental activists who have stepped into the breach, exposing instances of ecological and species harm, providing details of poor regulation and enforcement practices, and contributing both formally and informally to crime reduction and prosecution processes. As increasingly important players in the world of environmental protection, conservation and management, environmental activists frequently have to both confront powerful social, economic and political interests, and work with and alongside powerful groups, organizations and state apparatus. This chapter describes some aspects of this complicated but essential work.

The tactics of social change

Environmental activism involves many different individuals, groups and organizations, with diverse aims and missions, employing a wide variety of tactics and strategies. Key international non-government organizations (NGOs) include:

- Friends of the Earth
- Greenpeace
- World Wide Fund for Nature
- Sea Shepherd
- Bird Life International
- Climate Action Network
- Biodiversity Action Network
- Humane Society International
- Sierra Club
- Environmental Investigations Agency
- Basel Action Network
- Environmental Justice Foundation.

This list of named organizations extends into the hundreds (indeed, the thousands) and includes local neighbourhood action groups through to transnational or global NGOs.

The focus of activists varies greatly (White 2008). 'Brown' issues tend to be defined in terms of urban life and pollution (such as air quality), 'green' issues mainly relate to wilderness areas and conservation matters (like logging practices), and 'white' issues refer to science laboratories and the impact of new technologies (such as genetically modified organisms). There is generally a link between environmental action (usually involving distinct types of community and environmental groups) and particular sites (such as urban centres, wilderness areas or seacoast regions). Groups are also demarcated by the particular notions of justice they hold, including notions relating to environmental justice (for example, specific human communities), to ecological justice (such as the protection and conservation of particular ecosystems) and to species justice (like animal rights and welfare).

There are major tensions within environmental social movements, and among them (White 2008; Pezzullo and Sandler 2007). These are due to differences in ideology, as well as contrasting views on the tactics and strategies seen as most suitable or effective in any given circumstance. Nonetheless, when it comes to significant environmental reform, it is environmental activism, rather than, say, state environmental regulation, that is the most fundamental pillar of substantive change (Buttel 2003).

Environmental activism seeks to address acts and omissions that are already criminalized and prohibited, such as illegal fishing or the illegal dumping of toxic waste. It also comes to grips with events that have yet to be designated officially as 'harmful', but that show evidence of exhibiting potentially negative consequences. It thus deals with different kinds of harms and risks, as these affect humans, local and global environments, and nonhuman animals. The politics of ecological sustainability will inevitably collide with the interests of economic growth, since greater adherence to environmental, ecological and species justice, and to the precautionary principle, will almost always lead to the curtailment of existing profit-making enterprises (White 2011a).

Not surprisingly, very often the target for action, and the object of change, is the state. In part this is because much environmental destruction globally is supported by particular nation-states in collusion with powerful corporations. This harm can take the form of acts of commission or acts of omission (see Kauzlarich *et al.* 2003). For example, some acts of harm are perfectly allowable and receive the approval of state authorities (such as clear-fell logging). Other acts are formally illegal but, without adequate state resources directed at enforcement, are allowed to occur as a matter of course (like the disposal of hazardous waste). Specific types of transnational environmental crime are basically linked in some way to the nature and extent of state intervention (or non-intervention), which in turn depends on the geographic location and political-economic importance of the specific activities in question.

Activism usually occurs within a moral climate in which certain justifications are made in support of particular actions. This opens the door to some interesting observations and debates over how the moral high ground is constructed, by whom and with what consequences. Williams (1996: 36), for instance, has noted that:

> If, between states and between state and citizen, the need to ensure human security 'must prevail' over justice norms as reflected in international or domestic law, and we accept the inference that military force may then legitimately be used against the entity posing the threat to human security, do we then accept that the principle extends to violence by community activists against the threat posed by the lead smelter down the road?

The degree to which the aims justify certain means, and the precise relationship between means and ends, is subject to intense scrutiny and debate within environmental social movements. Different groups will construe their activities as 'righteous' and 'appropriate under the circumstances' according to their particular philosophical criteria and ideological leanings.

What also influences action taken on the ground are factors such as how particular nation-states act, react or do not act in relation to environmental issues. This, too, helps to shape local, regional and transnational activist campaigns. For instance, different jurisdictions view and respond to acts of environmental 'resistance' in different ways. In the United States, the recent tendency has been to brand damage-causing acts of protest as forms of eco-sabotage (or 'ecotage') or environmental terrorism, and to prosecute and sanction offenders heavily (Rovics 2007; Brisman 2008). By contrast, a court case in England that involved six Greenpeace activists charged with criminal damage after being involved in scaling and defacing a chimney at a coal-fired plant at Kingsnorth saw the jury deciding that the activists were justified in causing damage to the power station due to the larger threat posed by global warming (McCarthy 2008). How nation-states respond to activism provides impetus for the adoption of different kinds of activist tactics and strategies. Depending upon the issue, and the activist, the interplay between state and society sometimes leads to extremism and the conscious stretching of the boundaries of existing law. Thus, a wide variety of activist approaches are apparent.

The social construction of environmental activism is a collective process involving many different players and interests. The justification for both legal and illegal actions around environmental and animal issues relates to perceptions that many presently legal activities in fact constitute crimes against nature, whether this is logging a forest or 'harvesting' certain animals (see, for example, Green *et al.* 2007). Conversely, some of the types of actions undertaken in protest against these alleged crimes are themselves subject to considerable criticism on the basis of their present illegality and, indeed, the harm they pose to others.

Come what may, most environmental activism includes a combination of tactics and strategies that involve confrontational as well as more conciliatory or conventional activities. The former include mass mobilizations and protest actions, sit-ins and blocking of roads. The latter include petitions, leafleting of suburbs and shopping centres, websites and information stalls. What works best depends upon the context, although specific organizations may disagree on overall strategic directions.

There is a particular dialectic of subversion and engagement between activists and the state and corporations. Interventions can involve the symbolic (in the form of media stunts and clever use of propaganda), the technological (in the form of the Internet and the active use of social media) or the applied (in the form of collaboration with certain state agencies or the use of satellite images to expose wrongdoing). Activists use a wide variety of measures in pursuing their goals. But so, too, do states and corporations.

Indeed, the use of both confrontational and conciliatory tactics is apparent when considering the actions of activists, states and corporations (see Figure 10.1). When it comes to confrontation, activists engage in measures such as mass mobilizations, protest demonstrations, trespass, breaking and entering, and even eco-sabotage. For their part, states (at varying levels, up to the national) may utilize tactics such as abrogation of regulation (deregulation), not entering into any discussions with those who dissent, cracking down on activists and relying upon arrest and imprisonment to quell resistance. Corporations engage in reluctant rule compliance, job blackmail (for example, establishing an opposition between jobs and the environment), citing the threat of capital flight and suing protesters. Confrontation is not the preserve of any one party.

Nor is conciliation limited to selected participants. Activists are known to engage in closed-door negotiations, to undertake their own investigations into the illegal wildlife trade and to lobby politicians and corporate bosses. The state

Confrontational

activists	*state*	*corporate*
mass mobilization	deregulation	reluctant rule compliance
protest actions	no discussions	job blackmail
trespass and breaking in	crackdown on dissent	threat of capital flight
eco-sabotage	arrest, imprisonment	law suits

Conciliatory

activists	*state*	*corporate*
closed-door cooperation	negotiation	negotiation
petitions	environmental regulation	green public relations
information website	green campaigns	green industries
lobbying of politicians	lobbying NGOs	alliances with NGOs

Figure 10.1 Types of engagement.

may be open to negotiation with diverse parties, including NGOs and community groups, to enact particular forms of environmental regulation, to promote 'green' campaigns (such as those around recycling) and to, in effect, lobby and rely upon NGOs. Likewise, corporations can be drawn into community negotiations, engage in 'green' public relations, form alliances with certain NGOs and seek business opportunities in developing 'green' industries.

Thus, there are complex relations between activists, states and corporations, relations that shift and change as individuals, groups and agendas are transformed over time. Tactical flexibility is therefore critical to maintaining sectoral interests, and navigating specific issues demands a well-honed consciousness of what works under which circumstances, and why.

What works

From an activist point of view, in order to gauge which actions will work, it is useful to consider what specific companies or states view as especially threatening, damaging or confounding (see White 2011b). Generally speaking, the struggle between opposing parties occurs on two different levels. First of all, it is the *actions* of the environmental activists and organizations that pose the problem, and such activities include varying forms of civil disobedience that may involve breaches of civil and criminal law.

Second, the *ideas* of activists and their organizations are seen as problematic. Here, what is at stake are the notions of 'interests' (as measured by different moral and economic criteria) and 'reputation' (as manifest in concerns with the messages being conveyed about the operations and ethics of a company). In essence, this is about the ideology and politics of environmental debate and the terms under which the debate is carried out.

Activists

Four main areas of campaign activity have been identified as illustrative of 'what works' from an activist perspective (White 2011b). These include:

- campaigns and actions that directly disrupt company operations (such as logging and the transportation of wood products)
- corporate vilification campaigns that undermine their 'clean', 'green' image (for example, publicly challenging a company's 'green' credentials)
- campaigns against overseas customers of corporate products (especially business customers, such as purchasers of woodchip products, who depend upon a degree of positive community sentiment to ensure the success of their sales strategies)
- corporate campaigns targeting shareholders, investors and banks (such as those groups and organizations that hold strategic decision-making vis-à-vis financial planning and expenditure).

A multifaceted, long-term and energetic campaign can have major negative repercussions for targeted businesses.

Ideological interventions can include portraying activism as an important form of global citizenship. For example, ecological notions of rights and justice see humans as but one component of complex ecosystems that should be preserved for their own sake and are supported by the concept of the rights of the environment (Smith 1998). Ecological justice demands that human interaction with the environment be evaluated in relation to potential harms and risks to specific creatures and specific locales, as well as to the biosphere generally.

There is a strong link between the ideas of ecological justice and ecological citizenship. The notion of 'universal human interests' is useful here in contradistinction to sectoral human interests ('business interests') and narrowly defined notions of the 'national interest'. In the course of ostensibly protecting or promoting the 'national interest', for instance, the state frequently engages in conduct that violates human rights and degrades and destroys environments and species. These environmental harms are justified by the state on the basis that the net result will be for the benefit of the majority, even though the main beneficiaries tend to be transnational corporations and local business firms. The result is the systemic and intensive violation of human rights and the undermining of overall environmental wellbeing (Boekhout van Solinge 2010; Clark 2009; Robin 2010). While everybody on the planet has a common interest in the survival of the human race, the specific commercial interests of companies and transnational corporations mean that they are reluctant to implement or enact strategies and policies that further common human interests. The state continues to play a prominent role in protecting the interests of the elite and ruling classes, both at a domestic country level and through transnational consortiums and international agreements governing commercial activities.

From an activist perspective, global ecological citizenship provides a general philosophical viewpoint from which to assess the performance of a state in relation to environmental matters. Processual accounts can be useful in evaluating the overall human and ecological rights performance of a state over time. For instance, Ward and Green (2000) describe a process whereby states may be involved in either a 'virtuous' spiral or a 'vicious' spiral in relation to gross violations of human rights. Each spiral reflects the dynamic ways in which norms about the institutionalization of human rights are either reinforced or abandoned, depending upon the political context. A similar processual analysis can be made in regards to state crimes relating to the environment. Towards this end, a framework of ecological citizenship provides an ideological and symbolic platform from which to challenge narrowly defined 'national interests' and specific state interventions that degrade and destroy environments.

Ecological citizenship positions the actor as an international citizen, a status that allows them to transcend narrow state interests (as defined by local elites), yet to still make claims on the state according to notions of universal human interests (as reflected in the Universal Declaration of Human Rights, for example). From the perspective of ecological citizenship, state laws and actions (and omissions) should be tempered by the imperative that human interests are intimately bound up with the wellbeing of the planet as a whole. Human intervention, of any kind, needs to be considered in this light.

At the level of practical interventions, activists engage in varying types of successful tactics. Some organizations engage in militant and spectacular actions, such as the Greenpeace and Sea Shepherd anti-whaling campaigns. Others focus on specific issues and work closely with governments and international regulatory bodies to enact change. For example, the Antarctic and South Ocean Coalition is an NGO established in 1976 to coordinate the activities of over 250 conservation groups on matters such as Patagonian toothfish management. In so doing, it works closely with governments in confronting issues associated with illegal, unreported and unregulated fishing. So, too, do groups such as the Environmental Investigations Agency and the Freeland Foundation for Human Rights and Wildlife, which engage in independent investigations of illegal environmental activities, gathering evidence that is eventually handed over to local police authorities and which is suitable for prosecutions in relevant jurisdictions and courts.

Other groups, such as the Animal Liberation Front, use a variety of tactics that raise awareness about systematic animal cruelty. Breaking the law (such as illegal entry into animal laboratories or battery hen farms) is considered legitimate if it means that public consciousness is heightened and immediate harms to animals are diminished through such actions. Some groups resort to tactics that have been described as eco-terrorism. Earth First!, for instance, has advocated a form of 'strategic ecotage' – that is, environmentally related sabotage – that has involved sabotaging the machines that destroy forests (such as monkey-wrenching). Direct action by environmental activist groups has included blockades of logging roads, tree sit-ins, demonstrations, protests and the destruction of machinery, including through tree spiking (putting iron or steel spikes through trees so that cutting machinery breaks upon contact).

Corporations/states

For their part, corporations and states likewise utilize a range of tactics in pursuing their sectional interests. Five particular tactics have been identified in this regard, as summarized below (Bruno *et al.* 1999):

- Deny (for example, the Global Climate Coalition formed to spread the notion that global warming is a dangerous myth)
- Delay (for example, we do not know enough about climate change, so for the sake of immediate financial prosperity, environmental decisions that threaten existing industries, such as coal-fired power stations, will be delayed)
- Divide (for example, jobs versus the environment)
- Dump (for example, exporting a product, such as pesticide, to developing countries even after its use has been banned in the US or Australia)
- Dupe (for example, posing as a friend of the environment, or greenwashing).

Ideological interventions tend to involve various kinds of 'spin', public relations exercises that reflect specific sectoral interests and which vary depending upon the state–community nexus. For example, in the area of environmental regulation, there is business support for the idea that persuasion, not coercion, is or ought to be the key regulatory mechanism. This is usually associated with the ideology of 'self-regulation' (see, for example, Grabosky 1995). Here, it is argued that corporate regulation should be informed by the idea of enlisting 'private interests' in regulatory activity via 'inducements', such as adopting waste minimization programmes that translate into more efficient production, or earning a good reputation among consumers for environmental responsibility. Such proposals and strategies basically fail to acknowledge the structural imperatives of consumer capitalism, both in its general tendencies (that is, to expand) and in the daily operations of specific capitals (to compete effectively in producing commodities and realizing surplus value). At the centre of changes to environmental regulation has been the movement towards 'corporate ownership' of the definitions, and responses to, environmental problems.

The ways in which corporations communicate about environmental issues and concerns play a big part in what is conveyed to the general public and in building popular support for particular industries and company practices. The study of corporate reporting and communication strategies points to great variability in how individual firms report – what they report, how they report it and to whom they report (Topalov 1999; Hughes 2004). It would appear that this variability in communication and corporate reporting stems in part from the fact that there may be no uniform rules governing the public disclosure of environmental impacts of corporate activity and no legal requirement or process for the independent verification of the information reported (Hughes 2004). A further issue is that, even when the reporting is well structured and presented, this does not mean that the company in question necessarily translates environmental considerations into actual operating strategies.

The issue of corporate communication also demands recognition of how firms engage in systematic propaganda campaigns. Inadequate corporate reporting mechanisms may be reinforced by concerted attempts to greenwash issues (this pulp mill will be the most environmentally friendly ever built, claimed a prominent Tasmania-based company, which then proceeded to whittle away each safeguard that was central to the initial claim) and companies simply asserting their virtues (we do everything in a sustainable and environmentally friendly way, says the same company). Greenwashing is basically about public relations and is today a significant part of any corporate image-making (see Athanasiou 1996; Beder 1998). Assessing environmental harm is difficult if the issues are clouded and obscured from the beginning.

The corporate and state sectors also engage in many different practical interventions designed to stifle dissent and convey positive messages about what are essentially environmentally destructive activities. These include legal manoeuvres, such as the use of freedom-of-information legislation to drag up personal information about activists that can be used to discredit them, and strategic lawsuits against public participation that have the consequence of soaking up activist time, energy and money in fruitless endeavour (Ogle 2005). Explicit propaganda campaigns are conducted by states and their corporate partners in support of projects and to thwart environmental controls and accountability. States are also implicated in coercive policing of protesters and activists, as well as denying them access to publicly provided free legal services (Baker 2011; Kuehn 2000).

Losing and finding our way

Negotiating the tactical and strategic minefields of activist politics requires appreciation of the constantly shifting ground. This demands a modicum of tactical and strategic nous, and an ability to compromise and choose the right thing to do at the right moment. Importantly, there is a certain dialectic to social change (and maintenance of the status quo) marked by a constant shift in the tactics and strategies adopted by key protagonists, the use of a wide range of measures across the relevant domains and persistent ideological struggles over core values and diverse interests. This is represented in Figure 10.2.

Public spaces are battlegrounds for public opinion, and the tactical use of 'space' is reflected in attempts to open it up for democratic purposes (for example, social networking or mass demonstrations), to restrict it according to the security dictates of public order policing (such as penning techniques) and to close it off completely under the rubric of private property (like corporate buildings and grounds) (Baker 2011). Measures of activism and counter-activism range from the mild to the extreme: from the delivery of pamphlets through to ecotage on the part of activists; from arrest to the use of counter-terrorism powers and torture on the part of some states; and greenwashing through to the violation of human rights (including extra-judicial killings and the rape of local villagers) on the part of corporations (Boekhout van Solinge 2010; Clark 2009; Robin 2010).

The ideological struggle has many different components. It can include differing emphasis on ecological citizenship (from popular concerns to appeals to planetary benefits), the national interest (for example, the narrow chauvinist concerns of the state elite) and economic interest (for example, which benefits profit-oriented enterprises). The public interest may be set against public order concerns, which in turn may be linked to neoliberal exaltations to support specifically bourgeois notions of private property (that separate private rights from questions of the public good). For activists, the counter-revolution may take the form of state emphasis on 'eco-terrorism' and the destructive things done by eco-activists in support of their goals. Meanwhile, as corporate bodies continually trot out the 'threat to jobs' refrain to rebut environmental activist concerns, activists in some places now speak about the 'green scare' – the contemporary equivalent of the 'red scare' of 1950s America (Rovics 2007). According to this script, it is now the greenies who represent the forces of darkness, as they strive to remould modern post-industrial societies in their own image according to an insidious agenda of new political correctness and group conformity.

In the midst of this toing and froing of activist politics and intervention, it is essential to hold on to several key guiding principles and concepts. In this regard, it is useful to distinguish between 'progressive' work and 'transformative' interventions. The first serves to ameliorate the worst, most regressive aspects of contemporary practices, such as blatant examples of animal cruelty or

Changes in tactics and strategies over time

activists	state	corporate
mass demonstrations in public spaces	policing practices that narrow spaces	private ownership of spaces

Range of measures

activist	state	corporate
pamphlets	arrest	greenwashing
direct action	counter-terrorism	litigation
ecotage	torture	violation of human rights

Ideological struggles

activist	state	corporate
ecological citizenship	national interest	economic interest
public interest	public order	private property
green scare	eco-terrorism	threat to jobs

Figure 10.2 Environmental activism and resistance: the dialectic of social change.

the destruction of forests. The second attempts to push the boundaries of the current system, and to change the system as a whole in substantial ways – for example, through enhancing public accountability and building effective social movements. The challenge is to develop 'transitional' political paths that will bridge the gap between holding the line and building a new, alternative future. Testing the waters of intervention, and using whatever resources we can access, is one way in which a critical praxis can be achieved.

It is also important to acknowledge the paradoxes and challenges of confrontation and conciliation. Three issues illustrate these. First of all, the state is not a monolith. That is, while much activism is directed at the state, not all actions by the state are 'bad', nor are all sections of a state implicated in environmentally destructive acts or omissions. For the activist, the tactical issue is to figure out when, where and why to work in, with and against the state. This is not pre-given, but determined by context and circumstance.

Second, and related to the first point, specific issues give rise to different social and political dynamics. Illegal trade in wildlife, for instance, is officially recognized in various international conventions and is actively pursued as an issue of concern by different 'official' bodies, such as Interpol. There are many ways in which transnational environmental activist groups can work with official agencies and personnel to achieve similar goals, including the sharing of intelligence and joint efforts to gather evidence against wrongdoers. On the other hand, in countries and regions where legal and illegal logging is built into the fabric of state–corporate collusion, it may well be the policing of anti-logging activists that predominates. There is a specificity to intervention and activism here that demands careful attention. This is an especially important consideration given that, particularly in some contexts, activists can find themselves subject to serious repression, including death.

Third, one should not assume a binary moral calculus that stipulates that all things that the state and corporations do are 'bad' and all things that activists do are 'good'. After all, the road to hell is paved with good intentions as well as bad. This is demonstrated in the actions of well-meaning Western NGOs that are attempting to preserve and conserve forests in places such as Africa and Latin America. In some instances, they are doing so without any interaction with or sensitivity towards local traditional users of the forests. One consequence of their actions, coordinated and managed from afar, is to exclude these users from utilizing what for many generations has been their birthright; another is to criminalize those who in fact are the victims of both environmental destruction and state coercion (Duffy 2010).

Conclusion

The tactics and strategies employed by states and corporations to stifle dissent and limit popular resistance to actions and events that threaten and destroy social and ecological wellbeing change over time. Just as activist engagement becomes more sophisticated and varied, so too does the push-back from the top.

Fundamentally, there is a need to expand democratic space in order to change society – as evidenced by the role of the social media in the Arab Spring – often against those who wish to restrict discursive space. How to do so and what to actually do in this space is of perennial concern to activists and powerful interests alike.

Social revolution is a complex process, with ebbs and flows, and uncertain outcomes. The challenge is to navigate the twists and turns of the tactical flows in ways that will make a difference. As this chapter has demonstrated, this demands a sophisticated understanding of 'what works' for activists, as well as what works against activists. After all, it takes two to tango – and one cannot always be sure whether the dance is a struggle or an embrace.

References

Athanasiou, T. (1996) *Divided Planet: The Ecology of Rich and Poor*, Boston: Little, Brown and Company.

Baker, D. (2011) 'A Case Study of Policing Responses to Camps for Climate Action: Variations, Perplexities, and Challenges for Policing', *International Journal of Comparative and Applied Criminal Justice*, 35(2), 141–65.

Beder, S. (1998) *Global Spin: The Corporate Assault on Environmentalism*, Melbourne: Scribe Publications.

Boekhout van Solinge, T. (2010) 'Equatorial Deforestation as a Harmful Practice and a Criminological Issue', in R. White (ed.), *Global Environmental Harm: Criminological Perspectives*, Devon: Willan Publishing.

Brisman, A. (2008) 'Crime–Environment Relationships and Environmental Justice', *Seattle Journal for Social Justice*, 6(2), 727–817.

Bruno, K, Karliner, J. and Brotsky, C. (1999) *Greenhouse Gangsters vs. Climate Justice*, San Francisco: Transnational Resource & Action Centre.

Buttel, F. (2003) 'Environmental Sociology and the Explanation of Environmental Reform', *Organization and Environment*, 16(3), 306–44.

Clark, R. (2009) 'Environmental Disputes and Human Rights Violations: A Role for Criminologists', *Contemporary Justice Review*, 12(2), 129–46.

Duffy, R. (2010) *Nature Crime: How We're Getting Conservation Wrong*, New Haven: Yale University Press.

Grabosky, P. (1995) 'Regulation by Reward: On the Use of Incentives as Regulatory Instruments', *Law & Policy*, 17(3), 256–79.

Green, P., Ward, T. and McConnachie, K. (2007) 'Logging and Legality: Environmental Crime, Civil Society, and the State', *Social Justice*, 34(2), 94–110.

Hughes, S. D. (2004) 'The Current Status of Environmental Performance Reporting', *National Environmental Law Review*, 4, 41–58.

Kauzlarich, D., Mullins, C. and Matthews, R. (2003) 'A Complicity Continuum of State Crime', *Contemporary Justice Review*, 6(3), 241–54.

Kuehn, R. (2000) 'Denying Access to Legal Representation: The Attack on the Tulane Environmental Law Clinic', *Journal of Law and Policy*, 4(1), 33–147.

McCarthy, M. (2008) 'Cleared: Jury Decides that Threat of Global Warming Justifies Breaking the Law', *Independent*, 11 September, available at www.commondreams.org/headline/2008/09/11-6, accessed 10 October 2008.

Ogle, G. (2005) *Gunning for Change: The Need for Public Participation Law Reform*, Hobart: Wilderness Society.

Pezzullo, P. and Sandler, R. (2007) 'Introduction: Revisiting the Environmental Justice Challenge to Environmentalism', in R. Sandler and P. Pezzullo (eds), *Environmental Justice and Environmentalism: The Social Justice Challenge to the Environmental Movement*, Cambridge, Massachusetts: The MIT Press.

Robin, M.-M. (2010) *The World According to Monsanto: Pollution, Corruption and the Control of Our Food Supply*, New York: The New Press.

Rovics, D. (2007) 'Pivotal Moment in the Green Scare', *Capitalism Nature Socialism*, 18(3), 8–16.

Smith, M. (1998) *Ecologism: Towards Ecological Citizenship*, Minneapolis: University of Minnesota Press.

Topalov, A. (1999) 'Environmental Reporting by Australian Corporations', *Griffith Law Review*, 8(2), 411–38.

Ward, T. and Green, P. (2000) 'Legitimacy, Civil Society, and State Crime', *Social Justice*, 27(4), 76–93.

White, R. (2008) *Crimes Against Nature: Environmental Criminology and Ecological Justice*, Devon: Willan.

White, R. (2010) 'Prosecution and Sentencing in Relation to Environmental Crime: Recent Socio-Legal Developments', *Crime, Law and Social Change*, 53(4), 365–81.

White, R. (2011a) *Transnational Environmental Crime: Towards an Eco-Global Criminology*, London: Routledge.

White, R. (2011b) 'The Right to Dissent: The Gunns 20 Legal Case', in F. Gale (ed.), *Pulp Friction*, Launceston: Pencil Pine Press.

Williams, C. (1996) 'An Environmental Victimology', *Social Justice*, 23(4), 16–40.

11 Witnessing the gorgon

Remarks on normative visuality in confronting state crime

Wayne Morrison

> We who survived the Camps are not true witnesses. We are those who, through prevarication, skill or luck, never touched bottom. Those who have, and who have seen the face of the Gorgon, did not return, or returned wordless.
>
> (Levi 1988: 83–4)

> Urgent. Send two metal rolls of film for 6x9 as fast as possible. Have possibility of taking photos. Sending you [4] photos of Birkenau showing prisoners sent to gas chambers. One photo shows one of the stakes at which bodies were burned when the crematorium could not manage to burn all the bodies. The bodies in the foreground are waiting to be thrown into the fire. Another picture shows one of the places in the forest where people undress before 'showering' – as they were told – and then go to the gas chambers. Send film roll as fast as you can. Send the enclosed photos to Tell – we think enlargement of the photos can be sent further.
>
> (Text accompanying four photographs taken by members of the Jewish Sonderkommando ['special labour detail'] with small camera and film smuggled into Auschwitz-Birkenau by Polish Resistance, cited in Didi-Huberman 2008: 16–17)

Witnessing Auschwitz: resisting state control of vision

The perfect crime is one where there is no trace, no presence, no record and no archive: absent the (documentary or human) witness, no trial and no verdict; hence no existence. So the continuing controversies over the fate of the Armenians at the end of the Ottoman Empire (in 1915) and the debates over how many died and who knew the human consequences of Mao's 'Great Leap Forward'. Even with the most extreme case of state crime – the Holocaust – where a range of trials could take place and considerable evidence put into a public record since for a time Germany was occupied by victorious forces, there are those who invoke the absence of the full witness. Thus have the revisionists emerged – such as Faurission, who contends that he has 'tried in vain to find a single former deportee capable of proving to me that he really has seen, with his own eyes, a gas chamber' (cited in Lyotard 1988: 3). Lyotard's answer to this was to explain the underlying distorted logic:

in order for a place to be identified as a gas chamber, the only eyewitness I will accept would be a victim of this gas chamber; now, according to my opponent, there is no victim that is not dead; otherwise, this gas chamber would not be what he or she claims it to be. There is, therefore, no gas chamber.

(Lyotard 1988: 3–4)

The logic may be distorted but the charge partly underlies the writings of Primo Levi, that articulate and anguished Jewish survivor. He feels the import of the words of an SS guard: 'even if some proof should remain or some of you survive, people will say that the events you describe are too monstrous to be believed' (said to Simon Wiesenthal, quoted in Levi 1988: 11–12). Levi declares that he cannot be a true witness, for he did not plumb the depths; those who did were indeed consumed, or returned wordless, unable to articulate.

Communication and recording are in themselves acts of resistance; hence, the importance of producing and saving images – images to which we can claim some reality. They are open to interpretation, yes, but not able to be extinguished from the archive. While today we may inhabit a global order mediated by mass communication and awash with images (which itself offers opportunities for stimulating and continuing resistance – see Friedrichs, Chapter 2 this volume), it is important to understand the legacy of the struggle to gain images and the basis for the ethical or normative visuality that such images may offer (or may distort).

We have a considerable range of photographs that the Germans took of the Ghettos, the mobile killing squads and Reserve Police Battalions at work, and of the personnel of the concentration (labour and death) camps, which are frightening in their normalcy (see, for example, Morrison 2006; Struk 2003; Zelizer 1998). Yet, there are four photographs, badly composed, somewhat blurred, taken by victims. One shows inmates undressing ready for the gas chambers, one the burning of corpses; they are the sole and priceless evidence of a witnessing of the death process. They represent an act of resistance by that most compromised group – the Jewish Sonderkommando of Auschwitz (the Sonderkommando were the 'special labour detail' – Jewish inmates who, in order to survive for a while, worked for the Nazis, led the unsuspecting victims to the gas chambers, cleared out the bodies, took out the teeth from the gassed, cut off the hair, burnt the corpses and so on). These photos were accompanied by a brief message: 'Send ... to Tell', the code name for Teresa Lasocka-Estreicher, a Krakow-based member of a secret committee of aid working for those in concentration camps. There is no record of any other photograph being produced, only four photos taken by the dead – four images that were not meant to be. 'We think enlargement of the photos can be sent further': a plea to reach a Western world that either ignored or disbelieved the accounts of the industrial killings within the concentration camps.[1]

The name 'Auschwitz' denotes a place, the death camp part of the Auschwitz-Birkenau 'industrial' complex – a complex of slave labour, of the industrial manufacture of products, of death, of corpses and the *Muselmann* (or 'Muslim', which in the coarse language of the camps described the exhausted inmate who had lost the will to live, who would have had little in-depth knowledge of Islamic practices, but whose stooped and folded posture was seen to resemble a Muslim at prayer, as the Arabic word 'Muslim' was understood to mean one who submits unconditionally to the will of God [Agamben 2002]). Auschwitz is now a museum, a site of representation, a place of homage. It is also a cipher for our realization of the power of the organized modern state to kill, to utilize thousands upon thousands of people in a process of identification, confiscation, concentration and annihilation. What marks the Holocaust off from other crimes conducted in the name of, or the shadow of, the state was the intention to annihilate; rational and utilitarian arguments for the usefulness of Jewish labour or how the annihilation process took scarce resources away from the war effort provided only temporary reprieves. There was no talk of 're-education'; instead, the labels were of 'vermin' and 'lice' that were to be destroyed, 'cargo' to be processed. To annihilate millions in a modern, industrial manner requires order and efficiency: cooperation must be maximized, resistance minimized. The process used ideological and visual techniques of identification of the Jews as *Untermenschen* (literally under-man, sub-human), as agents responsible for attacks on culture, progress and German strength, along with numbing strategies to encourage and legitimate action against them and lower the psychological barrier to participating.

For Levi, perhaps the Nazis' greatest crime was to construct a system wherein the victims, and for his and our purposes, the Jews, participated in their own destruction. This participation spanned a continuum from: (i) not understanding the stakes when laws were passed that stripped Jews of citizenship and defined being Jewish as a matter of race, rather than religious affiliation – laws that depended for their operation on an acceptance of their validity; to (ii) Jewish Councils and Jewish policemen who obeyed the orders of the Reich and ran the Ghettos in occupied Europe; and to (iii) the *Karpos* (prisoner guards, usually ex-convicts or political prisoners, whose brutality often outdid that of the SS) and the Jewish *Sonderkommando* – 'miserable manual labourers of the slaughter ... who from one shift to another preferred a few more weeks of life (what a life) to immediate death, but in no instance induced themselves, or were induced to kill with their own hands' (Levi 1988: 59).

Friedrichs (2009) has pointed out that an exception to the relative gap in scholarship on resistance to state crime is the literature on resistance and the Holocaust. However, the findings in this field are on the whole deeply disturbing; while there are good case studies, the literature is weakly theorized and understandably desperate to provide evidence of resistance, yet it underplays the degree to which the operational power of the Nazis rested on acceptance by others of their power and authority. One argument was that the Jews became complicit in their own destruction at the hands of the Nazis by reverting to traditional strategies of accommodation with their persecutors, who had always been far more powerful. Contradictions abound: the Jewish writers Raul Hilberg and

Hannah Arendt, for example, were attacked as 'self-loathing Jews' for empha-sizing Jewish complicity, while at the same time 'Zionist rhetoric itself main-tained that, with a few heroic exceptions ... the Jews went like sheep to the slaughter precisely because of the very Diaspora mentality that Zionism was striving mightily to transform' (Bartov 2000: 178).

It was fashionable for a time to describe the Nazi state in terms of a gang of criminals, who through trickery and street violence took over the governmental system of a civilized society, destroyed the rule of law and ruled through terror. Although some still refuse to face up to the lessons of the Holocaust by repeating this 'myth', we now see the Nazi project of rebuilding Germany and strengthening the *Volk* (and their positive and negative eugenics) as enjoying wide support and drawing upon racial and biological conceptions that are recognizable and shared in many societies other than that of Germany. The Nazi state not only ordered and decreed processes and events, many of which, such as the sterilization laws of 1933, were seen as progressive elsewhere, it also created spaces wherein thousands of individuals, such as the doctors who performed medical experiments in the camps, could pursue projects that others could only secretly dream of. Seduction and terror were siblings. And if hell on earth was ultimately created, it was full of law and scientific discourse, aspects of which were thoroughly modern: 'the holo-caust was an accomplishment in every respect superior, if measured by the stand-ard that this society has preached and institutionalised' (Bauman 1989: 89). Yet the Nazi order was also reactionary, an act of resistance against perceived cultural, moral and physical degeneration and the modernist cultural movement; this com-plexity must be acknowledged if we are to understand the spirals of coordination and obedience that occurred, as well as the obvious resistance. Kaplan's statement that the Jews 'expected the worst; they did not expect the unthinkable' (1998: 236) reflects the fact that throughout history Jews had been targets of Western religious and existential fears and prejudices, expulsion, massacre and discrimination. Only in hindsight can we see the difference: the twentieth century was a period during which the reality of what it was possible for men to do to fellow men (and women) outstripped the imagination. Thus the cry of the Jewish Pioneer Youth Group in the Vilna Ghetto in 1942 – 'Let us not go as sheep to the slaughter' – was only pos-sible when that group admitted that the Jews were already doomed and that the tactic of accommodation, and thereby trying to save one's close family or at least a minority of the group, had failed (Bartov 2000: 176). If one could not conceive that annihilation was the goal (as some, including historians, still cannot conceive), then tactics of accommodation – and of passive, symbolic or personal resistance – made sense.

> If gentile [armed] resistance was motivated by the prospect of liberation and national resurrection, Jewish [armed] resistance was an expression of despair, a final gesture by a slaughtered people. Especially in those parts of eastern Europe and western Russia where the vast majority of Jews lived, fighting meant choosing how to die, not how to live.
>
> (Bartov 2000: 177)

To hope to survive meant not to fight and not to commit suicide. Thus, the extreme position of the *Sonderkommando* (the forced labour groups), who comprised 12 groups in total, up to several hundred individuals, who were themselves killed after six months; around 40 individuals survived, being the last group and still operating at the time the Russian advance finally caused the SS Guards to flee. Levi hints that the 'souls' of this elite afflicted group had died: yet we now know from the collected writing of the scattered remains – sections of diaries and fragments of writing that members buried in the grounds – that these were men with souls, and many were sensitive and deeply distraught. One task was to make sure that the arriving Jews would undress as quickly as possible, and then to lead them into the gassing chamber. Suspicious and nervous individuals had to be isolated in case they upset the others and made the process unpredictable. We learn of one who finds his mother in a new group arriving at the camp and, to reassure her, tells her that it is indeed a shower facility she is going to and takes some soap with him as he accompanies her, to be gassed together (see Greif 2005). For Sofsky (1997: 1157), this was a place without moral choices: 'any moral deed is impossible where absolute evil has become an institution'. Is it therefore impossible to judge the morality of behaviour inside the camp? Levi gives us an image of the 'grey zone' in which the inmates move yet cling to the absolute necessity of asserting the moral consequences of every tiny act and he is confident, moreover, that evil existed in the game of football that took place between members of the SS and the *Sonderkommando* (Levi 1988: 55). To insert normalcy into this place – to have these two groups 'play' – was itself barbaric.

Morality is present in the act of smuggling in a camera and a member of the *Sonderkommando* taking four photographs (for which he had actually to stand in a gas chamber) that were then smuggled out of Auschwitz. Resistance is present in the attempts of the *Sonderkommando* to communicate (leaving, for example, written accounts on whatever scraps of paper they could obtain and burying them in shoes dug into the ground): these prisoners were kept in isolation, such that contact with other prisoners was rare (they mainly stayed in barracks with guards at the gates, the latrines and bathing facilities were for their use only and everything was organized to minimize their contact with other prisoners). If they operated often as robots, numbed, they were also capable of articulating love and horror in such a deeply compromised state: only the act of pouring Zyklon B into the gas chamber was performed solely by German *Sanitäter* (medical orderlies); all the other processing of the Jewish bodies was their realm of horror (see the accounts in Greif 2005 for descriptions of their humanity).

Resisting Auschwitz: the ambivalence of visuality

In addition Hauptsturmfuhrer Lange said to us that the orders to exterminate the Jews had been issued by Hitler and Himmler. We had been drilled in such a way that we viewed all orders issued by the head of state as lawful and correct. We police went by the phrase, 'Whatever serves the state is right; whatever harms the state is wrong'. I would also like to say that it never even entered my head that these orders could be wrong. Although I am aware that it is the duty of the police to protect the innocent I was however at that time convinced that the Jewish people were not innocent but guilty. I believed all the propaganda that Jews were criminals and subhuman [*Untermenschen*] and that they were the cause of Germany's decline after the First World War. The thought that one should oppose or evade the order to take part in the extermination of the Jews never entered my head either. I followed these orders because they came from the highest leaders of the state and not because I was in any way afraid.

(Kurt Mobius, Schutzpolizist, Police Battalion, cited in Klee *et al.*,
1991: 220–1)

It serves us well to take these words seriously: this policeman says he killed defenceless Jews because he accepted the orders of the head of state as lawful and *correct*. He believed that all Jews were guilty of harming the state, that they were *criminals* and *sub-human*, and that they were the cause of Germany's decline after World War I. So, when this man lined up Jewish men, women and children to shoot, he did not see fellow humans, and nor did he experience what Levinas defines as the ethical appeal of the 'face' of the other, with its injunction 'do not kill me!'

While visuality is an empirical feature of homo sapiens as a species, state crime is a modern trope, the very definition of which is contestable in scope and meaning. Such contestability is inevitable, reflecting the concept of state crime's aspirational nature. Authors, such as Green and Ward (2004), look to broader, global norms to counter state power and to make claims of crime and deviance for state and state-sponsored actions and omissions; for Green and Ward (2004), state crime is state organizational deviance involving the violation of human rights. Thus, the trope 'state crime' invokes a new universal – human rights – by reference to which the correctness of state or state-sponsored actions of omissions can be gauged. This is a contested foundation: for while it is true that the discourse of human rights has now approached the status of a new *lingua franca*, it remains difficult to see the *grounds* on which this language exists. International conventions, for example, claim that the foundation of human rights is the inherent dignity of 'man', but for philosophers such as Michael Perry the premise that every human possesses innate dignity, which is somehow sacred or inviolable, is inescapably religious. Thus, according to Perry, there is ontological fragility to the idea of human rights and the question he continually poses is: in a culture in which it is widely believed that there is no God or metaphysical order of any kind, what can provide a valid foundation so that the idea of human rights can survive (Perry 1998, 2007)?

For Perry, ultimately 'we affirm the morality of human rights *because* we affirm it' (2007: 34), and we know the terrible reality of human existence without these criteria, this moral reading of humanity. Therefore, attempts at resisting state crime by invoking the dignity of the human are not simply pragmatic ploys, emotive in nature and lacking overall coherence; they are based in our knowledge of history, of what we have seen humans doing to other humans. To what extent is dignity visual? Traditionally, the response was that humans possessed dignity because God had created man 'in his own image'; when we looked at man, we saw God's creation and order. Hitler's aesthetic response to this was that we should look to the image of man as the strong and beautiful, with Greek sculpture as our ideal, not the suffering image of Christ crucified, which was termed a Jewish-inspired image; thus, beauty and strength, not ugliness and suffering, denoted man's heroic dignity (see generally Spotts 2009).

In *Survival in Auschwitz* (1993: 105–6), Levi describes how he was turned into an image held at arm's reach, subjected to a gaze of expertise, that distinguished those who could be used for Kommando 98 (the chemistry work unit) from those who would be gassed. Levi, a chemist, was examined by Doktor Engineer Pannwitz:

> the look he gave me was not the way one man looks at another. If I could fully explain the nature of that look – it was as if through the glass of an aquarium directed at some creature belonging to a different world – I would be able to explain the great madness of the Third Reich, down to its very core...
>
> The brain commanding those blue eyes and manicured hands clearly said: 'This thing standing before me obviously belongs to a species that must be eliminated. But with this particular example, it is worth making sure that he has nothing we can use before we get rid of him.'

The phenomenology of the Nazi doctor's gaze has been analysed by Lifton (1986) in terms of the doubling and division of the self – and thus it was that the Auschwitz self looked at Levi. However, for those insights, there is more at stake. In propaganda leaflets distributed among the German troops on the eastern front, acts of seeing were tutored and responses conditioned:

> Anyone who has ever looked at the face of a red Commissar knows what the Bolsheviks are like. Here there is no need for theoretical expressions. We would insult the animals if we described these mostly Jewish men as beasts. They are the embodiment of the Satanic and insane hatred against the whole of noble humanity. The shape of these Commissars reveals to us the rebellion of the Untermenschen [under-man] against noble blood.
>
> (From Mitteilungen fur die Truppe, quoted in Bartov 1996: 83)

In these examples, the image is controlled. When Nazis looked at Jewish faces, they were reminded not to allow their subjectivity to constitute the others as humans making an ethical appeal to be treated as humans. The most infamous of the SS booklets is *Der Untermensch*, Berlin SS 1942, a fully illustrated small book with many images and guidance on how to spot the 'hidden Jew' who may look civilized. It is a guide to recognizable features of the civilized and of the sub-human: the visual tactics are similar to aspects of Lombroso's criminology (see Morrison 2006).

In its historical specificity, to see or to recognize, to avoid the recognition of the other as the similar, is a constituted activity. The Nazi gaze was essentially 'modern'. It involved separations of the self and actions: professional and bourgeois, detached choices, thoughtless thoughtfulness. Here, power has learnt to master the image, to impose a modernist interpretation. The result was that Jewish people found little protection.

The dualities of the state: the disenchanted liberal state or the romantic/organic state

> for in arousing passion from opinion ... not the truth, but the image, maketh passion: and a tragedy, well acted, affective no less than a murder.
>
> (Hobbes 1840, Vol. 4: 76)

It is a neglected feature of the Holocaust that the Nazi state came into existence largely through acts of resistance and protest against the terms and the social and economic consequences of the Treaty of Versailles (which imposed a notion of state criminality on the defeated German state), and more generally the jurisprudence and political ideals of the liberal–constitutional state that was set up with the Weimar Constitution. The Weimar Constitution gave individuals – all individuals – equal rights; the Nazi appeal was to an 'equality of kind' and the ties of 'German Blood and German Honour'. At the core of the Nazi vision are two contrasting ideas of the state and of the relationship of people to each other. The first is that of Hobbesian liberal modernity, in which the state (an artificial creation) comes about contractually in a disenchanted world – that is, a world in which nature gives us no values other than 'mere equality' of individuals. The state is little more than a legal personality, given form through its representation of the individuals who are brought together in the sovereign territory. In the second, a 'romantic' image of community prevails, such that humans are linked together in ties of blood and of soil, and legality is a barrier to the organic truths of community identity. We tend to downplay this second conception but it was core to the image of the Nazi state, identity, leadership and the expulsion of 'otherness'.

It is comforting to emphasize the idea of the Nazi order as a state controlled by criminals, with government forcing people to cooperate through terror but, to explain the coordination of so many, seduction is a more disturbing but apt motif. Hitler's style of politics was new – he commenced his first campaign from within a plane (see the opening scenes of the film *Triumph of the Will*, in which Leni Riefenstahl portrays Hitler arriving at the 1934 Nuremberg Party Rally like a God descending from above), and his messages were mediated through symbols, myth, rites, spectacles and personal dramatics. If he 'took away democratic government, he gave Germans what they clearly found a more meaningful sense of political participation, transforming them from spectators into participants in national socialist theatre' (Spotts 2009: xii). As a Marxist historian later reflected:

We failed to see that the fascist aesthetic itself reflected the needs and hopes of contemporary society, that what we brushed aside as the so-called [ideological] superstructure was in reality the means through which most people grasped the fascist message, transforming politics into a civil religion.

(Mosse 1996: 246)

Modernity can be conceived as largely constituted in term of the Hobbesian–Westphalian nexus: (nation-)states and sovereignty. For Hobbes, we must constrain the power of the image and passion, and assert the realm of rational and scientific language. The passions are the enemy of cool rationality in which the political ought to be cast. Post Hobbes, the founding of the modern liberal state is prone to contradictory forces. On the one hand, the modern state embodies a series of positive goals; these are premised on the rejection of social hierarchies, a belief in the equality of all before the procedures of the law and the accession to a realm of subjective freedom (ethics, morality) founded on reason and private desire. Yet, on the other hand, the authoritarian structure of the state reflects the fact that its subjects are radically uncertain about the nature of virtue and values; as a result, the subjects are susceptible to manipulation and control. Hence, the power of the passionate rhetorician is entrenched; those in a position to be labelled as the enemy are always weak.

The liberal state is intended to be a rational order, yet we know the weakness in the simple Hobbesian statement: the sovereign must control the language and symbols though which power operates. Thus, language becomes a mask, and the human body – as the site of pain – disappears, as it did in the thousands of memos in which the victims of the Holocaust were but 'units' or cargo. Today, there is hope in the democratization of the image that new technology (such as mobile phone cameras) allows, for while the body disappears from language, it reappears, for example, in the images from Iraq. The stream of images of abuses of power in Iraq – in part an inevitable consequence of a highly technologically empowered military establishment fighting an insurgency of shadows, suicide bombs and ambiguity – seems to attest to a claim that at least the camera is moral or, put another way, that the camera does not care enough to hide the events. But is there an active audience moved to care? And state power still creates its own images, such as those of the transporting of the detainees from Afghanistan to Guantanamo Bay, revealing hooded men in orange jumpsuits (so no face is visible), shackled, sitting in a reclined position, chained to the floor of a transport plane with military guards and the American flag above, which were meant to reassure by demonstrating the power of the state to fight terror.

The gorgon

Circling the center, ten strong rings of bronze with twenty disks of glittering tin set in, at the heart a boss of bulging blue steel and there like a crown the Gorgon's grim mask – the burning eyes, the stark, transforming horror – and round her strode the shapes of Rout and fear. (Homer, Iliad, 11.35 Fagles trans.: 1990: 297, referring to an earthly presentation of the killed Gorgon's head as a device on the shield of Agamemnon.)

Why do [survivors] speak of such inexplicable horror? They speak because they know they are witnesses in a trial of planetary and epochal dimensions.

(Levi 1988: 149)

Levi places seeing the face of the gorgon as the ultimate act of witnessing the Holocaust; he did not know that Hitler had placed three panels on his writing desk to face the visitor in his 'office' in the rebuilt Chancellery. One represented the crown of the gorgon Medusa (the others showed Mars, God of War, and Minerva, Goddess of War). For Hitler, the message was clear: 'I will destroy you if I please' (Spotts 2009: 365).

The Ancient Greeks warned that no one could look directly upon the gorgon and survive, to look turned men into stone. In Greek myth, Medusa, the mortal one of the gorgon sisters, drew upon ancient powers that came from Hades before the defeat of the Titans and the ascent of the Olympian gods. She was full of sexual energy, fearsome, madness personified, and incoherently uttered what may be a war cry but also angst. Yet she was subversive, seductive and drew one closer to the bestial than the human. Athena, by contrast, the Goddess of Order and Justice, was all that Medusa was not – no mud or blood marred her countenance. She provided Perseus with a polished shield so that he could manoeuvre himself by Medusa's reflection and thus orientated was able to kill her. In homage, Perseus gave the gorgon's head to Athena, who placed it on her Aegis (a cloak or shield) where the gorgon's frontal representation was a fearsome sight (and Athena allowed Agamemnon, the leader of the Greek army in the siege of Troy, to put a gorgon symbol on his shield). Thus, the 'beingness' of horror was subdued, turned into a badge of authority and a symbol of higher, non-human power.

Hitler borrowed from the symbolism of the gift of Athena; Levi referred to the horror inherent in the original act of seeing Medusa, who had taken us too close to the chaotic forces of life and death, to the existential abyss wherein the meaning of being human was undeterminable. Athena had restored the order of (Olympian) gods and men, but men were left subjects of the gods' unpredictable whims. In turn, as a young failed artist and political agitator faced with a court trying him for treason after the failed Munich Beer Putsch, Hitler denied the legitimacy of the court he was before or any other human court and claimed that he would be responsible only to the court presided over by the goddess of history, Clio, who would be his eternal judge (Snyder 1966: 164–5).

The twentieth century has rightly been called the 'age of atrocity' (Langer 1978); what was the gorgon that Levi invoked? The gorgon was not death, was not barbaric treatment, nor individual acts of torture (no matter how much the tortured sufferer surrenders his humanity, blabs [un]truths that condemn his fellows). The gorgon was the limit, the limit paradox of witnessing that which cannot and could not be witnessed: the non-human powers of creation. Those who looked directly at Medusa were turned to stone; and those who found themselves in Auschwitz were manufactured into ash, corpses or the *Muselmann*. Engineering, bureaucracy and science distorted powers that were (once) meant to reside in the invisible Hades – beyond the grasp of man – but were now turned on the living: the camps were 'laboratories in training people to become bundles of reactions ... eliminating from the human psychology every trace of spontaneity' (Arendt 1994: 242).

From the testimony of survivors, we learn that this production, this logic, 'was designed to produce in the victim a "self-disgust" to the point of wanting death' (Fackenhein 1994: 208–9). Levi knew he had to resist, to keep his dignity, as above all he feared becoming a *Muselmann*. These inmates had given up; manufactured by the will of the Nazis, they became 'the living dead', certain candidates for the gas chambers, walking symbols of the fate of every inmate and therefore the pariah of the camps. Some were so close to death that they no longer responded to the hunger impulse, while others did not even respond to beatings by the guards. Other inmates avoided the *Muselmann* and held them in disdain as, by giving up, they 'had marked the moving threshold in which man passed into non-man' (Agamben 2002: 47). 'A staggering corpse, a bundle of physical functions in its last convulsions', Amery (1980: 9) preferred to 'exclude him from our consciousness', as if nothing ethical can be learnt. And yet the *Muselmann* is the site of creation, of the beginning, between the human and the inhuman. So the *Muselmann*, the most terrible of all sights, blankness, lack of depth, lack of reaction, awaiting neither death nor having life, but processed, produced. Man had produced not only death (as was always in the province of man), but a middle form of death/life, human/non-human, life not fit to be called human. No wonder even the contemporary theorist of resistance and the hope of the left, Zizek, was disorientated: for him, following Levinas, the ethical bond is grounded in the capacity of the human subject to say 'Here I am!' But Zizek (2005) argues that the *Muselmann* can no longer say 'Here I am!', as he is an inhuman 'other'. Recalling that Primo Levi repeatedly uses the predicate faceless, Zizek asserts that:

> this term should be given its full Levinasian weight. When confronted with a Muselmann, one cannot discern in his face the trace of the abyss of the Other in his/her vulnerability, addressing us with the infinite call of our responsibility. What one gets instead is a kind of blind wall, lack of depth.
>
> (2005: 160)

Has the gorgon turned Zizek's humanity to stone? Yet this is the ultimate lesson of the attempt to resist the Holocaust: we cannot turn from the *Muselmann*; rather, we must – absolutely must – see and feel a fellow human and empathize. The moment that one withdraws from that ethical imperative is the moment that one accepts and thus allows the genocidal laws. If human rights are the 'soul' of the metaphysics of constructing a new global order, with individual human beings being accountable for the acts of 'states' in denying the dignity of humans, then the primary act of visualization must hold to this normative principle. In support of this, there are no guarantees: for we who appreciate and live within the nature and forms of globalization understand that human rights are founded not on the idea that God has made 'man' in his image, nor in philosophical concepts of human agency or choice, but on our knowledge of what humanity has done to humanity. The gorgon reappeared in modernity: our shield is our understanding that there is ultimately no foundation to the human condition, no justice, other than the continual exposing of what we are capable of, our resistance, and our demand that we, and all others, are equally worthy of dignity.

Note

1 These four images can be accessed via the online gallery of the Auschwitz-Birkenau museum. See the 'Photo gallery' section of the museum online at http://en.auschwitz. org/, look under 'extermination' in the Historical pictures and documents section, and note in particular 'Burning of bodies'.

References

Agamben, G. (2002) *Remnants of Auschwitz: The Witness and the Archive* (trans. Daniel Heller-Roazen), New York: Zone Books.

Amery, J. (1980) *At the Mind's Limits: Contemplations by a Survivor of Auschwitz and Its Realities* (trans. Sidney and Stella P. Rosenfeld), Bloomington: Indiana University Press.

Arendt, H. (1994) *Essays in Understanding 1930–1954* (ed. Jerome Kohn), London: Harcourt Brace & Co.

Bartov, O. (1996) *Murder in Our Midst: The Holocaust, Industrial Killing and Representation*, New York: Oxford University Press.

Bartov, O. (2000) *Mirrors of Destruction: War, Genocide and Modern Identity*, Oxford: Oxford University Press.

Bauman, Z. (1989) *Modernity and the Holocaust*, Cambridge: Polity Press.

Didi-Huberman, G. (2008) *Images in Spite of All: Four Photographs from Auschwitz*, Chicago: University of Chicago Press.

Fackenhein, E. (1994) *The Mend the World: Foundations of Post-Holocaust Jewish Thought*, Bloomington: Indiana University Press.

Friedrichs, D. (2009) 'On Resisting State Crime: Conceptual and Contextual Issues', *Social Justice*, 36(3), 4–27.

Green, P. and Ward, T. (2004) *State Crime*, London: Pluto Press.

Greif, G. (2005) *We Wept Without Tears: Testimonies of the Jewish Sonderkommando from Auschwitz*, London: New Haven Press.

Hobbes, T. (1840) 'Elements of Law', in Sir William Molesworth (ed.), *The English Works of Thomas Hobbes Vol. 4*, London: John Bohn.

Homer (1990) *The Iliad* (trans. R. Fagles), London: Penguin Books.

Kaplan, M. (1998) *Between Dignity and Despair: Jewish Life in Nazi Germany*, New York: Oxford University Press.

Klee, E., Dressen, W. and Riess, V. (eds) (1991) *'The Good Old Days': The Holocaust as Seen by Its Perpetrators and Bystanders*, New York: The Free Press.

Langer. L. L. (1978) *The Age of Atrocity*, Boston: Beacon Press.

Levi, P. (1988) *The Drowned and the Saved* (trans. R. Rosenthal), Abacus: London.

Levi, P. (1993) *Survival in Auschwitz* (trans. Stuart Woolf), New York: Vollier.

Lifton, R. J. (1986) *The Nazi Doctors: Medical Killing and the Psychology of Genocide*, USA: Basic Books.

Lyotard, J.-F. (1988) *The Differend: Phrases in Dispute*, Minneapolis: University of Minnesota Press.

Morrison, W. (2006) *Criminology, Civilisation and the New World Order*, London: Routledge.

Mosse, G. (1996) 'Fascist Aesthetics and Society: Some Considerations', *Journal of Contemporary History*, 31, 245–52.

Perry, M. (1998) *The Idea of Human Rights: Four Inquiries*, New York: Oxford University Press.

Perry, M. (2007) *Toward a Theory of Human Rights: Religion, Law, Courts*, Cambridge: Cambridge University Press.

Snyder, L. (1966) *The Weimar Republic: A History of Germany from Ebert to Hitler*, Princeton, NJ: D. Van Nostrand Co.

Sofsky, W. (1997) *The Order of Terror: The Concentration Camp* (trans. William Templer), Princeton, NJ: Princeton University Press.

Spotts, F. (2009) *Hitler and the Power of Aesthetics*, New York: The Overlook Press.

Struk, J. (2003) *Photographing the Holocaust: Interpretations of the Evidence*, London: I. B. Tauris.

Zelizer, B. (1998) *Remembering to Forget: Holocaust Memory through the Camera's Eye*, Chicago: University of Chicago Press.

Zizek, S. (2005) *The Neighbor: Three Inquiries into Political Theology*, Cambridge, MA: University of Chicago Press.

12 Music as resistance to state crime and violence

David Kauzlarich

Like any form of communication, music reflects a range of political and social ideologies and commentaries. In this chapter, musical authorship, performance, consumption and interaction are seen as potentially powerful activities of resistance to harmful state and corporate activities. The analysis is based on an ongoing ethnographic, auto-ethnographic, participant observation and interview research project with politically radical punk rock musicians in the United States (US), Canada and the United Kingdom (UK). Specifically, I explore the extent to which music constructions provide windows for collective opposition and resistance to forms of state crime and violence, such as war, human rights abuses, oppression, state–corporate collusion and corruption. The analysis raises questions about the utility of music as a tool of resistance but also identifies several ways in which it can be effective in developing critical consciousness and social action. The chapter concludes by presenting five general premises on the relationship between music and resistance to state crime and violence.

Few expressly criminological studies have been conducted on the relationship between music, politics and deviance. One exception is Hamm's (1995) impressive work on how music helps neo-Nazi skinhead groups recruit and sustain membership. Another critical criminological example can be found in the work of Finley (2002), who has shown that the band Rage Against the Machine created songs that were critical of mainstream criminal justice policy and that their art might be productively used to illustrate the spirit of radical criminology to students. Further, Muzzatti (2004) has examined how the defiant and confrontational music of Marilyn Manson was identified by some audiences as a cause of youth violence, especially the 1999 Columbine school shootings. However, there appears to be no systematic criminological examination of how modern popular music specifically relates to resistance to *state crime*. While there are some edited volumes in criminology that include discussion of punk music in relation to crime (see, for example, Deflem 2010), and passing references to punk music in the work of other criminologists (Ferrell 2001), there have been no scholarly analyses of state crime and non-mainstream music.

Maffesoli's (1996) work redirects ethnomusicology through two main concepts: sociality and neotribes. To him, society is increasingly chaotic, dispersed, fragmented and unpredictable, and young people in particular are constantly bouncing among ephemeral groupings in the search to declare sovereignty over their own lives. They do this not by joining formal social action groups bounded by bureaucratic rules, roles, regulations and hierarchy, but rather through some-times serendipitous, everyday associations with others who are also seeking autonomy from the structures and agents (such as parents, teachers and bosses) that regulate them at all other times. To Maffesoli (1996), society is not dead, but rather social essence has changed so that hedonism, celebration, spontaneity, release, venting, escapism and emotional epiphanies become the glue that binds young people together outside their formal regulated and obligatory everyday realities. This is not to be confused with a pure subcultural approach, as the groupings discussed here are not as tight-knit and distinct as subcultural theorists suggest.[1] Rather, the fluidity of everyday experience, mediated by structural and institutional forces, produces momentary collectives more than stable, opposi-tional social networks. In other words, instead of paying their dues, attending meetings and occupying a distinct role in an organization, young people prefer to seek out less demanding, shorter term solutions in their search for identity. In terms of independent punk music, this means going to or playing shows, possi-bly getting drunk and high, 'moshing' in the pit, occasional vulgar displays of hypermasculinity and, especially for performers, enjoying any bit of attention they might get from those in the audience during or after a performance. This, in a nutshell, is ephemeral individual solidarity reinforced and to a greater or lesser extent shared with others in a situational context. Contrast this with an instru-mental manoeuvre, such as joining a university student group or community organization, and working on some issue of political injustice. When viewed through the lenses of cultural criminology and Maffesoli's perspective, this kind of traditional social activism is increasingly seen by young people as boring and too reminiscent of the regulatory and rule-based climate they seek to escape in their everyday lives at school, at home and in the workplace.[2]

In addition to Maffesoli (1996), I follow a cultural criminological approach that reflects the work of those at the Birmingham School of Cultural Studies who investigated how inequality and alienation work to produce counter-hegemonic and oppositional resistance to mainstream practices and structures. Music, espe-cially oppositional forms of punk rock, can thus be viewed as forms of cultural engagement, which may take on political or social organizational purposes. As Ferrell (2001, 2003, 2006) found in his ethnographic studies of urban graffiti artists, dumpster divers and others on the street, 'crimes of style' are partly developed out of the desire to share creativity with others and to enact individual artistic expression (which is often quashed in schools, jobs and home life). At the same time, this drive often produces various forms of resistance to agencies of social control, such as the police, schools and government. This dovetails nicely with Maffesoli's (1996) position that young people are constantly seeking out others to share exciting experiences and situations in order to declare their independence from adult regulation.

Traditional scholarly writing about the political possibilities of music often frames the process as rational, goal-laden and palpable, as demonstrated by studies into the effects of protest music, for example, on ideology and attitudes toward state policies (Peddie 2006). Most research finds that music can be an important component of social movements in a variety of contexts (Bennett and Peterson 2004; Eyerman and Jamison 1998; Roberts and Moore 2009). For example, there is ample evidence to show that the historic work of popular musicians such as Bob Dylan, Woody Guthrie, Pete Seeger and John Lennon made some impact on more people than those who were already sympathetic to anti-war messages during the Vietnam War era (Lee 2009). Further, labour organizations, civil rights groups and the like have been found to benefit from the galvanizing power of words put to music (Eyerman and Jamison 1998). As discussed below, however, the cultural landscape in late modern societies has changed to become one of greater fluidity, in terms not only of commodities but also of social relationships and indeed music (Kauzlarich and Awsumb 2012). This has major implications for understanding the connection between present-day music and contemporary opposition to various state policies.

From the minds and mouths of musicians

The present analysis is limited to Western liberal forms of political punk music. While the emergence of punk rock in the 1960s and 1970s in the UK and the US is often characterized as unsophisticated, self-indulgent and hedonistic, a number of subgenres have since emerged that reveal how much the style has changed. Certainly there are still many punk bands that do not speak to serious political or social concerns, but an increasing number of artists over the past 20 years have organized their music around critiques of war, inequality, homophobia, state abuses and corporate capitalism. The most notable bands within this category are Propogandhi, Anti-Flag and Leftover Crack, whom I have previously analysed as ideal types of major radical-left punk rock artists (Kauzlarich and Awsumb 2012). As with most forms of Western rock music, overtly political discourses are in the minority within punk, but given the genre's somewhat unique place in history as a voice for alienated youth, it is not surprising that out of all of the styles of rock music, punk has the potential to create alternative visions and critiques of structural inequality and oppression.

I am currently conducting a large research project involving interviews with active and formerly active punk and rock musicians in the US, Canada and the UK. All of these artists have written and performed original songs that are critical of various forms of state and corporate crime and malfeasance.[3] In addition to writing songs critical of capitalism, sexism, homophobia and racism, these artists have produced music with strong themes against war, human rights abuses, governmental corruption, state–corporate crime and a number of other state crimes. Eighteen interviews have been completed. Here I will share the preliminary results from the interviews as well as my own experiences as a politically radical punk rock musician.

The first theme that has emerged from the interviews is that artists have very mixed experiences in connection to using their music as a form of resistance to state and corporate crime. For instance, several musicians who write political songs with explicitly radical lyrics are somewhat disappointed that their calculated message seems to be consumed hedonistically, not intellectually or rationally by their audience. These interviewees report that audience members will often dance, mosh and recite the lyrics during performances but little beyond this ephemeral catharsis seems to be accomplished. Bemoaning this reaction, Josh noted in one of the last punk songs he wrote:

> Another curtain closes on another night
> And I wonder if a thing has changed...
> If you take one thing home with you tonight
> Let it be a mind for change
> And take it to your workplace
> And take it to your school
> And do something great.[4]

Among the most radical of the musicians and activists I have interviewed, Josh has produced dozens of expressly political punk rock songs with titles such as 'System Overhaul', 'Reaction Dies Tonight' and 'Collateral Damage', but he recently retired from political punk rock performance and composition partly because he believed that his efforts to change minds through music had limited results.[5] However, he shared several stories of young people who seemed to be affected by the music he performed in his small town in Illinois. Josh emphasized that it was not the music alone that changed the minds of these young people, but also the discussions he and his bandmates had with them before and after their shows. This reveals a central theme in my research at this point, which is that music can be a part of social change, but is probably not alone sufficient to reach people on a political–intellectual level. Josh now occasionally plays acoustic sets at anti-war, social justice or worker gatherings, and believes this is probably a better way to use music than to try to convince the general public of the importance of structural and economic change. Beyond the fact that acoustic music seems to be more listenable given the public's current cultural palate, it is simply much easier to grab an acoustic guitar and sing during a protest than to set up a stage with amplifiers, microphones, public address systems, mixers, monitors and drums.

Another interviewee, Andy, who wrote and performed rather blatant and sophisticated anarchistic punk songs, has also experienced the frustration of not getting through to his audience: 'I was noticing people who knew the songs at shows – then talking to people afterwards and they voted Bush – they were conservative, and I said fuck this.'[6] He too became semi-retired from punk rock performances and now occasionally plays acoustic sets at expressly political events.

Turning to my own experiences as an activist-musician, my various bands have written, performed and recorded many original songs about exploitation, racism, inequality and other forms of social injustice. Our shows, usually performed on a bill with two other independent bands, are short 45–60 minute sets with an audience ranging from 15 to 100 people, depending on the venue. I perform for both personal and political reasons, like all of the interviewees in this study. On a personal level, it is enjoyable to share my creations with others, drink beer, laugh with my friends and become absorbed in playing very loud, distorted and aggressive guitar riffs. On a political level, I hope that the songs do much more than entertain by educating and helping produce something in the way of a collective understanding of inequality, whether through the telling of stories of struggling workers, of the oppression of racial and ethnic minorities, or of the victims of war crimes.

One song we perform is titled 'Stolen' and is a condemnation of the theft of Native American land and culture. The lyrics read:

> You thought in me was you
> That thought has died
> That dream you told was true
> Became a lie
> Your time has clearly come
> To face my eyes
> Peltier lives in my heart
> Despite your cry
> You took me from my home
> To make me like a clone
> Now that the world has grown, you're left with you.[7]

We have played this song dozens of times live and it has also been freely downloaded or listened to thousands of times over the Internet, but audience reactions seem to range from apathetic to a moderate degree of excitement over the content. Usually the excitement over the song is strong when the storyline and topic is clearly introduced before the music is played. Disappointingly, however, we have rarely been engaged by an audience member about the song's lyrics or meaning except by those who are already politically energized and active in radical social movement activities, which is entirely expected given what scholars know about the difficulties in changing entrenched political ideology (Lakoff 2004). Another example of the challenge music faces in being able to directly speak to political issues in both a recorded and live context is seen in a song we perform titled 'I Won't Die For You' – an indictment of war and exploitative military recruitment. The lyrics read:

> I won't die for you
> Can't trick me with the red, white and blue, 'cause I know you
> And if I fight for you
> I'd be a part of your brutality, so I reject you
> Hunt the poor so they hunt for you
> Keep them high so there is no coup
> When they talk back to you

Lock 'em up in a little room
TV glam and deceptive spam
Make them look like rock stars
They come back poorer than before
Another pest for you to ignore
So sad to hear what you won't say
About economic motives and the underclass
Printing money on a copy machine
But I'm guessing that you know what you're doing
Have to think about years of commitment
While my friends slowly die from your neglect
Ask me now where my loyalties lie
And I'll tell you what the heck did you expect?[8]

The reaction to this song when played live is similar to that for 'Stolen', but because we recorded 'I Won't Die For You' in a slower acoustic format – that is more musically accessible – the song is one of our most popular. Ironically, people with conservative views will compliment my band on this song, which makes me wonder, like many of my interviewees, whether anyone is really listening to the lyrics.

Other musicians in the study, even some who are disappointed in their attempts to incite collective social justice action, have some optimism about their efforts to educate and rally audiences along political lines. Eleanor, a young woman fronting a hard rock band in Los Angeles known as Rooftop Revolutionaries, told me that her goal is to plant seeds of critical thought and that, while she is occasionally engaged by audience members after live shows, the absence of such conversation does not necessarily mean she has not succeeded. 'You never know what kind of an impact you have on people', she said[9]; and as I argue in the last section of this chapter, the lack of collective action does not mean that the music has failed. Indeed, individual forms of micro-resistance are necessary for larger networks of coalescence. A Canadian interviewee whose band has toured on two continents echoed this sentiment, adding that a live show 'is its own space' and that reaching people in that space requires the delivery of relevant and practical information.[10] Too many bands, he believes, focus on global issues that people, especially young people, feel ill equipped to act on. His approach, similar to that adopted by several other interviewees, is to say through the music 'here is what you can do today' to challenge inequality and oppression. His band regularly makes available reading materials, such as pamphlets, flyers and books, on various social justice issues alongside the merchandise table at venues.

This leads to another theme that emerged from this research: because music elicits multiple physical and emotional responses, lyrics, unlike words in a book, can be secondary to the rhythm, melody, instrumentation, speed and overall feel of a song. Add to this the very personal and unpredictable tastes in genres and musical instruments (especially guitar, drum and vocal tones) and it is clear that music provides a more complex discourse than most political speeches or written works. Further, and as pointed out earlier, punk music has typically appealed to the young as the speed, heaviness and sometimes unmelodic delivery tends to be too intense and loud for most older adults to enjoy. To reach people via music, then, raises unique challenges compared to other forms of communication. As Steve from the UK notes:

> I suspect, however, that 'messages' come across better when performed by the 'traditional' singer-songwriter accompanied by an acoustic guitar than they do when set to a more danceable, technological backing of the sort that I use. Then again, the people who listen to that sort of music are probably more disposed to looking out for a message, for meaning.... If a song has any subtlety, most people will tend to interpret it in the light of their existing views.[11]

This is an important point because the most popular leftist musicians in the US, the Caribbean and Europe have produced what is known as 'accessible' or 'listenable' music, which involves softer instrumentation, clearly articulated vocal parts, fairly predictable melodies, standard 4/4 tempos and relatively slow beats. The music of Bob Marley, Woody Guthrie and Billy Bragg fits all of these criteria, and genres such as folk and reggae have strong histories of progressive vocal storytelling that is relatively absent in most other genres. Punk music is typically much heavier, faster and harder, and the hardcore variety in particular often contains lyrics that are almost undecipherable unless accompanied by lyric sheets. There is also an interesting difference between listening to recorded music and music that is performed live. Many independent punk bands do not have the luxury of a 'sound person' dedicated to delivering to the audience, or even to the performers through monitors, a well-balanced mix that ensures the vocals are clearly discernible above the musical instruments. Problems with sound mixes are not an issue in the case of recorded music as affordable and easily accessible computer programmes can produce balanced output without much labour.

Another emerging theme from this research is the importance of situating radical punk music in the context of other social protest activities or organizations and community groups devoted to social change. As digital technology and Internet social networking advances, major music labels have diminished rapidly and thousands of independent labels have surfaced in the past decade to provide artists with music distribution, booking and other services. No longer does it require significant capital to own musical instruments, buy recording equipment and go to a professional studio to get a high-quality sound and mix. This has opened up the opportunity for political radicals, and of course thousands of others, interested in music to develop specialized label rosters, whether by genre or message. One example of this is the Canadian label Rebel Time Records, which only works with leftist political bands. Their catalogue includes bands with obvious political messages, such as The Class War Kids. Interviews with the co-founders and co-owners of the label reveal that, while there is some optimism in terms of whether people are understanding the intended political messages, there is also some doubt.[12] On the positive side, the label owners and their bands are very involved with non-musical social action causes and organizations, which provides them with connections across Canada so that scheduling shows at social justice benefits, meetings and other organizational events provides a sizeable opportunity for the music to be heard. Further, the label is well-connected to like-minded activists who provide them with technical, computer and artwork services at no charge. The label seeks to sign bands that produce listenable (that is, not hardcore or with 'brutal' style vocals) and melodic instrumental and vocal music because these are what most musical listeners seem to prefer. Again, this is a common point raised by many of the interviewees in this study. As Andy notes: 'We were trying to teach through lyrics and we would create slogans for choruses that would be catchy versus just talk. This allowed for callbacks.'[13]

Another example of the salience of political music linked to social change organizations and activities is found in the Occupy Wall Street movement against massive income inequality, corporate control of government, and war. At the time of writing, roughly 100 cities around the globe are now home to leftist activists occupying streets, parks and other gathering points to raise consciousness about a series of social justice concerns. Music has been a central part of these protests. Activists bring their guitars, drums and other instruments to perform impromptu sets, while some cities have seen both famous and local musicians perform in solidarity with the cause. Some of the more notable musicians who have performed or otherwise allied their music with the movement are Justin Sane from the punk band Anti-Flag, indie artist Moby, R'n'B artist Kanye West, Tom Morello from the band Rage Against the Machine, and many others. Saint Louis, Missouri's Occupy group has had dozens of local bands perform at their occupation, some of whom are expressly political artists. Interestingly, some organizers have said that, as long as the bands playing at these events are not anti-movement, they are welcome to play because the occupiers need some entertainment, and rest and relaxation, and music can fill that need. This does, however, reveal a fundamental problem: there are not enough expressly leftist musicians in most areas. By way of example, Saint Louis, Missouri, has a total metropolitan population of over 2.3 million, yet there are only a handful of expressly political artists regularly playing shows.

Interviewees expressed additional concerns about the impact of their music depending on the setting. Many know full well that unless they are playing a set at a political event such as Occupy Wall Street, a community peace organization meeting or among friends, it is challenging to get people tuned in to the lyrics and the overall message. I asked all interviewees whether they try to overcome this problem by delivering speeches or commentary between songs. Some have indicated that they do not, for fear of alienating audiences by 'hitting them over the head'. One American interviewee, Ian from the band Voice of Addiction, indicated that at public venues the last thing people want is someone 'preachy', and he prefers to let the music do the talking while 'trying to help people open their eyes to injustices around them'.[14] Another interviewee has come to the conclusion that both political movements and those who write leftist music should not 'do anything to scare the public' because the message will then be ignored.

This tactic is somewhat surprising, although I have previously found support for this reluctance to use overt political discourse in public settings. Indeed, in my study of peace activists in the context of the second US Gulf War, many respondents indicated that calling former President Bush a war criminal would be counterproductive because it would be automatically seen as hyperbole by the media and general public, even though the activists, and myself, see this as an indisputable fact (Kauzlarich 2007). In the current study, many of the interviewees, while politically active and outspoken on YouTube, on blogs, in interviews, in their lyrics and on their websites, fear that an equal measure of critique on stage could cost them credibility, perhaps result in the audience leaving the venue or completely tuning out, the band not being invited back to play in that space or fewer CD sales. Interestingly, this latter economic concern is also shared by corporate radio stations and the remaining major labels, who often choose to avoid music with obvious political messages (Artz and Kamalipour 2003).

The final theme to arise out of the interviews with artists is the problematic audience–performer dichotomy. Some of the more radical musician-activists interviewed in this study reject the binary between audience and performer, preferring to see live music shared and created by all in attendance. One interviewee, Stephen, indicated that this is why his band did not play in many standard clubs or venues – the stage literally separated the band from the people.[15] Instead, his band would play house shows or rent out a cheap space (such as a local community centre) and this would provide both physical and performative proximity and equality. In fact, at every show, his band tries to have many microphones available so that anyone can join in at any point. Further, one artist, Andy, indicated that he invited audience members to bang on his guitar, hit the drummer's cymbals and place themselves between band members at any time they desired. Other interviewees have indicated that they make a special effort to play at the ground level whenever possible to diminish their physical separation from others. As one very experienced musician told me, 'It is much better to look people in the eyes when singing than to look down at them from a stage.'[16]

From my own experience, I have played shows in a range of physical environments, from large stages well removed from the audience to ground-floor performances in garages, alternative venues and basements with little room to manoeuvre around non-band members. There is a clear and palpable difference in the experience from both a musical and a social standpoint, as performing at a distance feels like a reified one-way conversation, while physical closeness with others feels like one is a momentary leader in a larger social moment of solidarity. Prior to the sixteenth century, most cultures practised a form of music that involved little if any distinction between performer and audience (Turino 2008). This changed with modernity, when the commodification of entertainment became a wage-labour relationship under capitalism in which profit could be made through musical performances (Turino 2008). Most of the interviewees, and certainly I, see the cultural corollaries of the economic commodification of music, such as the hegemonic rock star image and the concept of 'fans', to be to a greater or lesser extent counterproductive to using music as a political instrument for social change and critique. In other words, the interviewees view the cult of personality as a distraction from the real message of their music because it places the focus on the messenger rather than the issue.

Music and resistance premises

Music, like the written word, film and other forms of art, has many functions and meanings, and to expect that rationality and instrumentalism will necessarily emerge from even the most well-intentioned performances and dissemination is highly optimistic. Although music is clearly a powerful force in many social and individual contexts, caution should be employed when conceptualizing a direct relationship between punk music and resistance to state crime and violence. As an autonomous act of rebellion and outrage by musical individuals or bands, music can certainly operate as a vent and a voice. As Eleanor put it: 'It can add emotional weight and power to political arguments and movements.'[17] Further, political punk music is obviously salient to already like-minded people engaging in other forms of social activism, although some interviewees who perform for social justice or anti-war events feel like they are invited to perform less for their skills and more to keep the crowds coming. In this context, however, music can offer emotional, psychological and communal solidarity, and allow actors to become closer and more united. The real question, however, is the extent to which music can change undecided or antithetical minds on issues related to resistance to state and governmental abuses. Although my study is incomplete and this question cannot be fully answered until far more research has been conducted, I have found that there is cause for both optimism and scepticism. To conclude, I identify five premises to consider in future scholarly work on the relation between music and resistance to state crime and violence.

First, music as a force in resisting state crime and violence is most powerful when situated within other nested contexts of protest. As a moment on the radio, a song in a live set, a preview on iTunes or a link on a Facebook or Twitter account, a song with 'pleasing' instrumentation and vocal tone is more likely to be appealing to people not already predisposed to radical thought. The lyrics, and thus the message, are then secondary to other concerns. This empirical observation is consistent with Maffesoli's (1996) argument that people 'hop around' in social groups and possess an overriding penchant for immediate gratification. While some music listeners may be able to consume, digest, analyse and process lyrics, most cannot. This is especially notable when political punk bands play local shows not expressly organized for political change. Some in the audience are drunk or high, but most are simply looking to shed their work, school and/or family identities and to reclaim sovereignty over their own lives through dancing, moshing, fist-shaking and screaming. While Maffesoli's 'sociality' is still possible under these conditions, contemporary Western life is just as likely to result in brief texts, Facebook updates or Twitter feeds the next day, which are then likely to become lost in a sea of data and keystrokes.

Second, music cannot genuinely be a force for social change, notwithstanding the above, unless the audience–performer dichotomy becomes blurred and perhaps is ultimately dismantled. An inherently unequal power situation is created when one becomes the performer and the other becomes the audience. The audience is passive, the performer active. The audience receives and the performer gives. The audience has no voice, the performer all of the voice. Such a sharp and defined separation, as one interviewee noted, plays right into the dynamics and structure of larger forms of oppression and inequality, and is very much a microcosm of national and increasingly global political, economic and philosophical estrangement between the masses and the corporate state. Until people other than musician-activists become invested in creation and critique, the message and action cannot be truly social.

Third, music should be understood as a special form of communication but one that is bound by the same rules governing other forms of communication. This means that presentation is just as important as substance, and that being young means being more open to alternative forms of discourse. This relates to Maffesoli's (1996) assertion that youth search for sovereignty, and that having different musical tastes can be a form of social capital, an opportunity to raise one's status, while those older and more beholden to the status quo are more resistant to difference and change (North and Hargreaves 2007). The Occupy movement, mostly composed of young people, is an excellent example of this because of the organic and wide net of progressives being extended hearty welcomes to join the movement.

Fourth, while music can certainly play an important corollary role in social change, there any many types of resistance to state oppression and violence that do not result in a groundswell of collective action. As pointed out by Stanley and McCulloch (see Introduction in this volume), resistance can be very personal and emotional, such as when a musician writes a line, while sitting on her or his couch, that is critical of human rights abuses, or when a fan or two in the audience yells with enthusiasm after an artist introduces an anti-war song. Even the terse and often superficial communicative formats of Facebook and Twitter offer people the opportunity to share their ideas and provide a space for others to consider the discourse. Indeed, there are countless acts of what I shall call micro-resistance occurring around the world every day which can fuel further individual and collective energies to accelerate, spread or deepen these individual acts of rebellion. As Riley *et al.* (2010: 358–9) note in their Maffesolian analysis of electronic dance music scenes:

> Everyday politics can be understood as a cluster of values that orient around the pleasure of being together (including notions of hedonism, belonging, solidarity, sociality), in temporary social groups that form through

proxemics at the local level.... The lenses of everyday politics allow for an understanding of practices that enable sovereignty over one's own existence and a celebration of counter-hegemonic values as political, without these practices needing to be permanent or associated with ideologies of social change.

At the very least, as pointed out earlier, micro-resistance can solidify and spark small networks of oppositional cultures and thereby ensure the survival of replacement discourse in an increasingly muddled and confusing world of claims, data and representations.

Finally, it is not completely unfortunate that hedonism and intellectualism happen to be in the same room when people listen to, write or create oppositional music. As the charismatic speaker, passionate writer, enthusiastic teacher and energetic performer all know, substance can be successfully connected to the lives of others when it is accompanied by a dash of fun, smiles and excitement, especially given that young people, *à la* Maffesoli, are tired of the cold and staid sobriety of school, work and family life. My observations at various Occupy events, interviews with musician-activists and experiences as an active agent in music and politics suggest that the synergy of art and politics, with its mix of seriousness and flippancy, may be the strongest way for social movements to spread wider and deeper layers of oppositional challenges to state oppression.

Notes

1 There are many studies and commentaries on youth culture and subcultures which reveal the modernist/postmodernist tensions between post-subcultural, neotribal and traditional subcultural approaches to studying crime, deviance, music and art (Bennett 1999, 2005; Chaney 2004). As Martin (2009) notes, Maffesolian-inspired post-subcultural scholarship has been criticized for ignoring structural disadvantage and glorifying consumerism. I cannot seriously grapple with this theoretical debate here. See Blackman (2005), Hayward (2004) and Martin (2002) for a thorough treatment of this matter.
2 Ferrell's (2004: 294) charge that 'criminologists must continue to investigate the circumstances of collective boredom, circumstances both historically structured and situationally negotiated' is just as salient to understanding the dynamics of political resistance as it is crime causation.
3 Interviewees thus far range in age from 22 to 44, and the political positions with which they self-identify range from Marxist, anarchist, feminist and green, to 'progressive' and 'independent'. Most interviewees are men who have college or university degrees and identify themselves as working class.
4 'Are We Listening', by Softer Than Yesterday, lyrics by Josh Lucker.
5 Interview, 10 November 2011, St Louis, Missouri.
6 Interview, 27 October 2011, St Louis, Missouri.
7 Resoldered (2010) *Everybody in Between*. Independent release.
8 Resoldered (2010) *Everybody in Between*. Independent release.
9 Telephone interview, 25 September 2011.
10 Telephone interview, 8 September 2011. Name withheld by interviewee request.
11 Email correspondence/interview, 24 August 2011.

166   *D. Kauzlarich*

12 Telephone interview, 8 September 2011. Name withheld by interviewee request.
13 Interview, 27 October 2011, St Louis, Missouri. 'Callbacks' occur when audiences vocalize lyrics or words from the encouragement of performers.
14 Telephone interview, 23 October 2011.
15 Interview, 3 November 2011, St Louis, Missouri.
16 Interview, 10 November 2011, St Louis, Missouri. Name withheld by interviewee request.
17 Telephone interview, 25 September 2011.

References

Artz, L. and Kamalipour, Y. R. (2003) *The Globalization of Corporate Media Hegemony*, Albany, NY: SUNY Press.
Bennett, A. (1999) 'Subcultures or Neo-tribes? Rethinking the Relationship between Youth, Style and Musical Taste', *Sociology*, 33(3), 599–617.
Bennett, A. (2005) 'In Defence of Neo-tribes: A Response to Blackman and Hesmondhalgh', *Journal of Youth Studies*, 8(2), 255–9.
Bennett, A. and Peterson, R. A. (2004) *Music Scenes: Local, Translocal and Virtual*, Nashville, TN: Vanderbilt University Press.
Blackman, S. (2005) 'Youth Subcultural Theory: A Critical Engagement with the Concept, Its Origins and Politics, from the Chicago School to Postmodernism', *Journal of Youth Studies*, 8(1), 1–20.
Chaney, D. (2004) 'Fragmented Cultures and Subcultures', in A. Bennett and K. Kahn-Harris (eds), *After Subculture: Critical Studies in Contemporary Youth Culture* (pp. 36–48), Houndmills: Palgrave Macmillan.
Deflem, M. (2010) *Popular Culture, Crime and Social Control*, Bingley, UK: Emerald Group Publishing.
Eyerman, R. and Jamison, A. (1998) *Music and Social Movements: Mobilizing Traditions in the Twentieth Century*, Cambridge: Cambridge University Press.
Ferrell, J. (2001) *Tearing Down the Streets: Adventures in Urban Anarchy*, New York: Palgrave.
Ferrell, J. (2003) *Crimes of Style: Urban Graffiti and the Politics of Criminality*, New York: Garland.
Ferrell, J. (2004) 'Boredom, Crime and Criminology', *Theoretical Criminology*, 8(3), 287–302.
Ferrell, J. (2006) *Empire of Scrounge: Inside the Urban Underground of Dumpster Diving, Trash Picking, and Street Scavenging*, New York: New York University Press.
Finley, L. (2002) 'The Lyrics of Rage Against the Machine: A Study in Radical Criminology', *Journal of Criminal Justice and Popular Culture*, 9(3), 150–66.
Hamm, M. S. (1995) 'Hammer of the Gods Revisited: Neo-Nazi Skinheads, Domestic Terrorism, and the Rise of the New Protest Music', in J. Ferrell and C. R. Sanders (eds), *Cultural Criminology* (pp. 190–212), Boston: Northeastern University Press.
Hayward, K. (2004) *City Limits: Crime, Consumer Culture and the Urban Experience*, London: Glasshouse Press.
Kauzlarich, D. (2007) 'Seeing War as Criminal: Peace Activist Views and Critical Criminology', *Contemporary Justice Review*, 18, 67–85.
Kauzlarich, D. and Awsumb, C. M. (2012) 'Resisting State Violence: The Role of Music', in W. S. DeKeseredy and M. Dragiewicz (eds), *The Handbook of Critical Criminology*, London and New York: Routledge.

Lakoff, G. (2004) *Don't Think of an Elephant*, White River Junction, VT: Chelsea Green.

Lee, R. A. (2009) 'Protest Music as Alternative Media during the Vietnam Era', in P. M. Haridakis, B. S. Hugenberg and S. T. Wearden (eds), *War and the Media: Essays on News Reporting, Propaganda and Popular Culture* (pp. 24–40), Jefferson, NC: McFarland.

Maffesoli, M. (1996) *The Time of the Tribes: The Decline of Individualism in Mass Society*, London: Sage.

Martin, G. (2002) 'Conceptualizing Cultural Politics in Subcultural and Social Movement Studies', *Social Movement Studies*, 1(1), 73–88.

Martin, G. (2009) 'Subculture, Style, Chavs and Consumer Capitalism: Towards a Critical Cultural Criminology of Youth', *Crime Media Culture*, 5, 123–45.

Muzzatti, S. L. (2004) 'Criminalising Marginality and Resistance: Marilyn Manson, Columbine, and Cultural Criminology', in J. Ferrell, K. Hayward., W. Morrison and M. Presdee (eds), *Cultural Criminology Unleashed* (pp. 143–154), London: GlassHouse Press.

North, A. and Hargreaves, D. (2007) 'Lifestyle Correlates of Musical Preference: 2. Media, Leisure Time and Music', *Psychology of Music*, 35(2), 179–200.

Peddie, I. (2006) *The Resisting Muse: Popular Music and Social Protest*, Aldershot, UK: Ashgate.

Riley, S., Griffin, C. and Morey, Y. (2010) 'The Case for "Everyday Politics": Evaluating Neo-tribal Theory as a Way to Understand Alternative Forms of Political Participation, Using Electronic Dance Music Culture as an Example', *Sociology*, 44(2), 345–63.

Roberts, M. and Moore, R. (2009) 'Peace Punks and Punks against Racism: Resource Mobilization and Frame Construction in the Punk Movement', *Music and Arts in Action*, 2, 21–36.

Turino, T. (2008) *Music as Social Life: The Politics of Participation*, Chicago: The University of Chicago Press.

13 Law for justice

The history of Community Legal Centres in Australia

Jude McCulloch and Megan Blair

Introduction

This chapter aims to deepen understanding of resistance to state crime in a democratic context by examining the history of Community Legal Centres (CLCs) in Australia. Drawing on over 50 interviews with CLC workers and volunteers, it explores how this vibrant community law sector has challenged state crimes in many guises over a continuing history spanning 40 years.

The chapter describes the factors that led to the emergence of CLCs in the early 1970s and explores how CLCs reflect what we know about state crime and resistance, specifically civil resistance – that is, 'political action that relies on non-violent methods' (Roberts 2009: 2). Through an examination of some of the ways CLCs have resisted state crime, the chapter argues that the early history of CLCs shares much in common with typical patterns of civil resistance. These include forging novel alliances; building on the legacy of previous resistance; drawing inspiration from international precedents; harnessing the energy of young people; creativity; and the development of an identity based in opposition as well as common purpose. In addition, and likewise in common with civil resistance more broadly, we suggest that CLCs' achievements over 40 years are hard to capture with any precision, yet valuable in ways that defy easy measure.

CLCs – what are they?

CLCs are independent organizations that provide a range of services aiming to make the law accessible to the marginalized and to advance legal, social and political equality. They arose in response to government and market failure to provide the benefits of the law to all but the wealthiest members of society. From modest beginnings in the early 1970s, there are now approximately 200 CLCs in Australia. While individual case work and free legal services constitute a large part of what CLCs do, from the outset they worked to demystify the law and empower people. CLCs focus particularly upon preventative community legal education programmes aimed at developing problem-solving skills among clients. CLCs undertake community development projects, often in coalition with other social justice organizations, and campaign to redress injustices using advocacy, radical action and large test cases. They have evolved to meet the needs of different communities: generalist centres serve particular geographic areas, metropolitan as well as regional, rural and remote; while specialist centres serve discrete demographics (for example, women, those with intellectual or physical disabilities and people with psychiatric illnesses). They have also become inextricably linked to mainstream legal education: law courses rely upon CLCs to give students practical experience. CLCs were originally unfunded, yet are now government-funded, but continue to rely heavily upon volunteer networks (for an overview of CLCs, see Noone and Tomsen 2006: Ch. 7).

In Australia, until the early 1970s, there was no concept of public interest or community lawyers and almost no legal aid (Noone and Tomsen 2006: 231). When lawyers worked for free, it was considered charity. For most people, seeing a lawyer was an extraordinary event; for lawyers, assisting the poor was rare (Sexton and Maher 1982). One anecdote from the early days of CLCs offered by Julian Gardner, the first paid lawyer at the Fitzroy Legal Service (FLS), underlines the assumed association that was prevalent at the time between social respectability and lawyers:

> [There was an] old codger in the pub in Fitzroy who we overheard one night saying to this bloke at the bar, 'My lawyer told me...'. And the other guy said, 'What do you mean, your lawyer? You haven't got a lawyer!' And he said, 'Yes, I have, my lawyer told me...'. That story to me epitomized ... here was this old guy who'd never had a quid to his name, who was able to say, 'I've got a lawyer!'[1]

To fully appreciate how radical CLCs were, and the challenge to state crime they represented, it is necessary to understand legal culture and practice in the early 1970s. The legal profession was composed largely of wealthy, private school–educated men from Anglo-Saxon backgrounds. It also included strong 'hereditary and tribal aspects' (Noone and Tomsen 2006: 34; Sexton and Maher 1982: 8–9). At the time, to adopt Kerry Greenwood's description, the profession 'operated like an Old Boys' Club where all the members had fond memories of grinding each other's faces on the football field' (1994: 3). With no national legal aid system, it acted as a gatekeeper for legal services to those who could not afford them.

There were state-based legal aid systems but they were not widely advertised, so people were unlikely to know about them and thus would not apply (Sackville 1975: 148–9). The services offered across states differed in detail but the basics were similar. In Victoria, to take a typical example, there was very limited aid for criminal matters heard in the Magistrates' Court (Sackville 1975: 99). Eligibility criteria were vague and aid was 'in the absolute discretion' of the Legal Aid Committee, consisting of a panel of barristers and solicitors (Sackville 1975: 50). The Committee could, 'without giving any reason, refuse or withdraw assistance' (Sackville 1975: 54). When aid was granted, a decision on the applicant's contribution to costs was also at the discretion of the Committee (Sackville 1975: 55). Those granted aid had to 'agree to accept the advice of the solicitor and counsel to whom they are assigned on all matters' – a reversal of the usual client–lawyer relationship where the latter is obliged to act on the instructions of the former (Sackville 1975: 55). The Public Solicitor, responsible for aid in criminal matters, frequently rejected applications because of prior convictions and said 'unsuccessful applicants could be roughly classified as "habituals"' (Sackville 1975: 101). Legal aid prior to the advent of CLCs was obscure, bureaucratic, narrow, arbitrary, paternalistic and often unaffordable.

The politics of law

The activities in which CLCs engaged need to be located in an appropriate historical context to be understood as resistance. Today, legal information and services are far more widely available and the provision of these is not likely to be considered resistance. Yet the actions of CLC pioneers were political. As Mary Anne Noone reflected, 'it's forgotten now, how confrontational community legal centres' approach and model of operation were. ... It was extraordinarily radical at the time.'[2]

CLCs have come into the legal mainstream over the years. As one CLC pioneer, Mick O'Brien, observes:

> A mate of mine ... he said to me, 'Mick, this legal service you've started,' he said, 'It started as a maverick, and it just is getting so established and such a good name, you'll soon be respectable.' And I guess in a sense that that's the way it turned out.[3]

Many of the strategies pioneered by CLCs are now taken for granted. In the 1970s, however, a service providing free legal advice to all comers was startling enough to make headlines (Chesterman 1996). Judith Peirce, a law student at the time and an early CLC volunteer, remembers thinking about the opening of the FLS: "'Why would they do this?... there must be lots of this sort of thing around." But of course, there wasn't at all.'[4] Ian Boag, a founder of the Frankston North Legal Service, recalls the time before that service began in 1977: 'Legal advice wasn't accessible, it was too expensive. It wasn't available [to locals]. It was something they didn't understand. It was an enemy rather than a friend' (Boag cited in Erlichster 2007: 8).

In hindsight, the provision of free legal services might be seen as a legal rather than political development, placing CLCs outside the frame of civil resistance. However, as Chesterman (1996: 38) points out in his history of the FLS, changing society and making legal advice accessible 'were inextricably linked' in the minds of many. Some CLC pioneers saw access to law and lawyers as a step towards radical social change, while others believed that making legal services accessible was itself a radical change. Pioneers understood CLCs to be legal *and* political organizations. They recognized and used the law as a tool for 'political action' through 'non-violent' means, engaging in a form of civil resistance in keeping with Roberts' definition (2009: 2).

Exclusive law and state crime

Access to the law through the provision of legal information, advice and, in serious cases, representation was not considered a right in the early 1970s. Denial of access to the law can only be understood as a state crime retrospectively, when access to knowledge about the law and access to legal assistance – particularly in serious matters such as criminal trials – is now seen as a fundamental human right (see, for example, *Dietrich* v. *the Queen 1992*).[5] The provision of legal services to those who previously could not access such services illuminated previously hidden harms perpetrated by the state and its agents, contributing to the development of a social milieu in which access to the law is seen as a right.

Prior to the advent of CLCs, there was little legal assistance available to low-income people or for the types of legal matters that they most frequently confronted. Unable to access legal information or afford legal advice and representation, many people found themselves effectively without rights (Sackville 1975). Although CLCs rarely referred to the 'state' and certainly did not speak of resisting state crime, it is clear that much of the early impetus and activities of CLCs fit this frame (see Brown 1984 on CLCs and the state). One example is CLCs' sustained challenge to systemic police violence, abuse of power and impunity – activities widely regarded as state crime (Green and Ward 2004).

For those unable to afford legal services, police were routinely the final word in what and who were considered crimes and criminal. Despite formal due process protections, groups low on the social hierarchy, particularly working-class youth and Indigenous people, were essentially 'police property' (Reiner 2009: 230–2). The impunity of police as the 'law on the streets' facilitated the criminalization of the poor generally and Indigenous people in particular. Peter Faris, an important figure in early CLCs, maintained in a 1973 interview 'that jails in Australia were largely comprised of working-class people' and that 'the whole use of lawyers to the ruling-class and the courts is to keep their clients under control so that the process of sending people to jail is orderly' (Chesterman 1996: 173).

The first Australian CLC, the Aboriginal Legal Service (ALS), opened in 1970 in Redfern, New South Wales, to protect Indigenous people from systematic oppression by police, including a police-imposed curfew. Justice Wootten observed:

> I found, as most people do, it [the curfew] a little hard to believe.... The simple position was that any Aboriginal who was on the streets of Redfern at a quarter past ten was simply put into the paddy wagon and taken to the station and charged with drunkenness, and that was something that was just literally applied to every Aboriginal walking along the street, irrespective of any sign of drunkenness in his [sic] behaviour.
>
> (cited in Cunneen 1990: 1)

In Melbourne, law student Mick O'Brien saw the connection between a lack of legal representation and the imprisonment of working-class men during his time working with a Catholic Youth Group. He used his connections to organize free legal representation for incarcerated youth:

> [O]ne year I organized legal assistance for 68 young offenders who had appeared unrepresented in the Magistrates' Court, and of those 68 all had received terms of imprisonment. I organized legal aid for appeals for them, and of the 68, 67 of them, on appeal, received non-custodial dispositions.... So from then on I established a rapport with a couple of firms of solicitors. When we went to prison on a Sunday morning, we would take applications for legal assistance, and we would send them off to this firm, and they would send them into the Legal Aid Committee. Then the Legal Aid Committee accused this firm of touting [advertising], and I thought that was ridiculous because we'd shopped around and this was the only firm we'd found that was prepared to accept these cases.[6]

Despite these successes the systemic issues remained. As he had discovered,[7] and as research in the early 1970s confirmed, there is a strong and demonstrable relationship between legal representation and a positive outcome for people charged with criminal offences (Armstrong 1975).

O'Brien, who went on to be a founder of the FLS, comments:

> Our motivation [in starting the FLS] was for the young people ... and of the kids who ended up in Pentridge in the young offenders group, a number of them were from Fitzroy. So it was directed to helping them.[8]

Once the first non-Aboriginal Legal Centre opened its doors in Melbourne in December 1972, the extent of unmet legal needs was exposed. John Finlayson, another FLS founder, talks of these early days:

> We didn't know that we were doing groundbreaking action until a lot later. We also didn't know how great the need for free legal service was across the community at large. We knew that it was bad – the lack of legal resources for the community at large. But the people were queuing underneath the Fitzroy Town Hall in the basement and up the steps to the footpath, along the footpath and right around the town hall and down Moore Street, that's how long the queues were. Some of them would be waiting and not get heard until 10 or 11 at night and they were there at 5.30. It was like going to a footy game in a way.[9]

CLCs quickly proliferated, particularly in Victoria, so that within a decade there were dozens operating across Australia (Neal 1984). Together they posed a powerful challenge to the previously accepted notion that the state had no obligation to extend the protection of the law to the poor and otherwise marginalized. In doing so, they exposed the injustices perpetrated by the state.

It's time for CLCs

Emerging out of activism and lawyer radicalism, CLCs broke ranks with the charity model of professional (ir)responsibility towards the poor (Rich 2009). During the 1960s and early 1970s, the United States (US) and Australia were controversially involved in the Vietnam War and young men were called to serve amid a storm of protest (York 1987). It was also the heyday of civil rights movements in Australia and the US (Foley 2001). Civil disobedience and clashes with police were common as 'protest and youth became synonymous' (Gerster and Bessett 1991: 43). Rapid cultural change and the unprecedented size of the youth demographic created a (generation) gap between the happening present and the moribund past. The position of women in society also changed dramatically, as feminists demanded a redefinition of the boundary between the public and the private and recognition of women's human rights (Horne 1980: esp. Ch. 3).

Ageing patriarchs and conservative government frustrated the changes demanded by young radicals. Sir Robert Menzies, Australia's longest-serving prime minister, an extreme monarchist and enthusiastic Cold War warrior, dominated politics from 1949 until he retired in 1966, aged in his 70s (Brett 1992). Conservative rule finally ended with the election of the Whitlam Labor government on 2 December 1972 under the slogan 'It's Time' (Hocking 2008). Within three weeks, the FLS opened its doors. John Finlayson recalls:

> You need to probably see it in a political context. In the late '60s and early '70s we'd had a very conservative legal system, a living system. Under successive Liberal Party governments that were very conservative ... and the structures were conservative, the financial markets were conservative, everything was very straight ... there was a lot of anger and frustration out there, and a lot of people wanting to cause or be part of social change.[10]

Challenge to exclusion through alliance

While anger was one element fuelling the emergence of CLCs, the forging of novel alliances was crucial in turning that anger into action. As Ash (2009: 375) points out, alliances between normally separate social groups are key to effective resistance. The anti-war movement created links between erstwhile strange bedfellows: activists and lawyers. Two of the founders of the FLS, youth worker John Finlayson and barrister Peter Faris, for example, met when the latter represented the former on an anti-conscription related offence. The campaign to prevent the hanging of Ronald Ryan in Victoria in 1967 similarly created important new alliances. Geoff Eames, who was to become a significant figure in CLCs' early years (Neal 1984: 55; Chesterman 1996: 31), was active in that campaign as a law student (Richards 2002: 313–14). Lawyers joined with activists to found CLCs, and once they were up and running more became volunteers. Protests and passion for social change created fertile ground for CLCs and inspired others to join once they were set up.

While local conditions created the alliances that underpinned the beginning of CLCs, international precedents also set the scene. Changes in technology have seen a phenomenal increase in the speed with which information travels, and as a consequence the interconnectedness of protest groups globally. History demonstrates, though, that resistance has always been internationally connected. Mahatma Gandhi, for example, who put civil resistance on the map in the first half of the twentieth century, acknowledged the influence of Ireland's Sinn Fein on his ideas (Townshend 2005: 11). The early CLC movement was aware of protest movements and developments in the US, with at least one CLC pioneer drawing inspiration from Martin Luther King and African American demands for civil rights.[11] Others were aware of law programmes in the US aimed at assisting the poor.[12] Unlike Australia, the US had progressive Democrat presidents during the 1960s. In 1962, President John F. Kennedy set out an agenda for consumer rights and two years later his successor, Lyndon B. Johnson, declared a 'War on Poverty'. As part of this initiative, networks of 'neighborhood law offices' were established in the poorest areas (Sackville, 1975: 5). Julian Gardner observes: 'I partly started thinking about this [CLCs] because I'd read about some of the things that were happening in the States ... it was part of his [Johnson's] initiative that he called his War on Poverty.'[13] The late Phil Molan, involved in CLCs from their inception, was also influenced by 'the shopfront stuff that I had been reading about from America' (Molan quoted in Neal 1984: 61). Remy Van de Wiel, a CLC founder, recalls: '[W]hen I met Faris and he showed me all this literature from America, [I realized] that this was all occurring in America. I mean it was all news to me.'[14] The US programmes were a product of government ideology and funding and thus a layer of the welfare state. CLCs were different because they were a grassroots, bottom-up movement, unstructured, unfunded and fired by a passion for justice.

Bridging the gap: bringing legal power to the people

CLCs worked to create a bridge between ordinary people and the law, and to distinguish themselves from 'the establishment'. The spaces that housed them; their hours of operation; the relationships they fostered between lawyers, clients and non-lawyers; the way they conceived legal problems; the language they used; and their dress codes – all of these were aimed at making law and lawyers accessible and at distancing CLCs from the mainstream profession. In contrast with the mystique and elitism of wider legal culture, CLCs were informal, non-hierarchical and open to all. Out of necessity, CLCs frequently set up in shabby, begged and borrowed spaces, often bunking in with other groups. They opened in the evenings to serve people who worked during the day – which also suited volunteers, who often had day jobs.

CLCs forged new relationships between lawyers and non-lawyers. The involvement of non-lawyers in providing legal services was an innovation closely linked to a holistic approach to legal problems, the benefits of which are discussed by Noone (2007) and Curran (2005). CLCs also changed the relationship between lawyers and clients – in the common language of the day, to 'empower' people to manage their own problems. The approach was *client*-rather than *lawyer*-centred, and focused on a broad spectrum of social justice-related concerns, including police violence, violence against women, tenants' rights, consumer rights and welfare rights. Incomprehensibility of legal language was another barrier CLCs strove to overcome. One of the 'primary points of distinction of early CLCs was that they were going to produce information and tell people about the law'.[15] John Finlayson comments: 'The language you get from lawyers now is much more demystified than the language they used in the early 1970s. ... It was really complex, you know, they used more Latin, phraseology and crap.'[16]

CLCs advertised their services and talked to the media, activities that were considered unethical for lawyers in the 1970s. CLC lawyers also dressed differently. Casual, even outlandish clothes separated them from what had until then been a uniform(ed) 'suits and ties' profession. Sartorial statements were made in technicolour. According to one, 'it was a complete fashion parade at legal service conferences. It was nose rings, earrings, blah blah blah.'[17] CLC couture was striking enough to draw comment from a range of quarters. John Chesterman's book on the history of the FLS includes a chapter on 'Legal culture in blue jeans' (1996: Ch. 7). A headline in the *Women's Day* from April 1973 refers to 'Legal eagles in jumpers and jeans'. The clothes distinguished CLCs from other parts of the legal profession: 'It was using clothing ... like a statement about our cultural and political differences.'[18]

Having something to oppose may be important to the success of resistance movements. Upsetting the establishment did not impede the growth and popularity of CLCs – quite the contrary. Phil Molan thought that 'it was a good thing for us that the profession was against us. It was a good thing to fight back against, it really solidified us' (Molan quoted in Neal 1984: 62). Kerry Greenwood (1994: 5), writing about the early days of the Springvale Legal Service, maintains: 'Every client sent away happy was a blow in the face to the Law Institute, who refused to recognise them and the Victorian Legal Aid Committee which oppressed them.'

Young and fun

The Australian centres were not part of any overriding, articulated model or plan. The early centres, to use key words of the time, were 'unstructured', celebrated 'spontaneity' and operated in the spirit of 'do your own thing' (Horne 1980: 42). Pioneers were making it up as they went along. Things were shambolic and there was a sense of fun. It was 'a very exciting time'.[19] '[I]t was a great time. It was the best of times.'[20] The inaugural FLS newsletter confesses: 'This first edition is largely experimental, and certainly in haste', and readers are extolled to 'contribute, suggest, or complain, whatever your thing is' (1974: 2–3). The title of Greenwood's history of Springvale CLC, *It Seemed Like a Good Idea at the Time*, likewise evokes the spirit of the times, claiming that when it started in 1973 its 'operational principles were basically intuitive and expedient' (Greenwood 1994: 17). CLC pioneers were energized and it was infectious. Renata Alexander recounts:

> We had a speech by Peter Faris [at Monash], who's now a QC, and Peter had just done a stint in the Northern Territory [at the ALS] that a lot of lawyers were doing in the 1970s.... And I remember going home and saying to my parents, I either want to work for Legal Aid, or the Aboriginal Legal Service, or some sort of community legal centre. So he was very inspiring about that.[21]

In sync with the times, the CLC demographic was young. John Finlayson recalls: 'Lots and lots of lawyers and non-lawyers were coming to us. They weren't old lawyers, they were young lawyers that were really wanting to do something and give of their time to this free legal service cause.'[22]

Many of those volunteering were law students, young lawyers and young non-lawyers. The involvement of young people, and particularly students, is frequently an aspect of civil resistance (Ash 2009: 375). Young people are often more fearless and idealistic and some CLC pioneers look back in wonder at how brave, naïve and passionate they were. One remembers she 'wanted to change the world'.[23] Neil Cole, the founder of Flemington/Kensington Legal Service, reflects on his younger self and how his inexperience helped him to tackle issues:

> I was very naïve, and for that reason, because I was naïve, actually quite effective, because you didn't think about [difficulties], you'd just run into brick walls literally and run through the brick wall in order to achieve what you achieved.[24]

Creativity

The early activities of CLCs were highly creative, typical of the pattern of civil resistance. As Ash (2009: 378) puts it, 'the history of civil resistance is also art history'. CLCs were trailblazers in terms of packaging legal information: t-shirts, wallet-sized cards, condom wrappers, comics, posters, music video clips, pamphlets and easy-to-read but detailed guides to the law were among the plethora of groundbreaking legal education tools developed by CLCs.

Julian Gardner describes the stir the first 'Know your rights' t-shirt created:

> Police Standing Orders were the only basis on which you could find the law written out which says you have a right to remain silent. It wasn't written anywhere else. The Police Standing Orders were secret. Now we got a copy that fell off the back of a truck. And I came up with the idea of printing the relevant provisions on the front of a t-shirt. Now, that might not seem radical, but nobody had actually seen words on a t-shirt before, or almost

never. T-shirts in those days were just one colour. And to have what looked like a paragraph on a t-shirt, people said, 'Oh, you've got words on it!' ... I remember standing in a Fitzroy post office in Brunswick Street and all of the customers and all of the staff were having a discussion about your rights under arrest, because I was wearing this t-shirt. It was just magic. That sort of grassroots community education was just so new.[25]

Art was also integrated into the campaign tactics of CLCs. Street theatre was used to make a point. CLC lawyer Dick Gross remembers some of the many cases and stunts designed to attract media attention that he was involved in:

We would do anything to get into a stupid costume. I wore tights on so many occasions it didn't matter. Hanging was the most notorious, on the spurious basis that you might as well hang people as imprison them. It had no nexus to the Imprisonment of Fraudulent Debtors Act whatsoever. I still can't make the nexus in my own mind, but it looked good on the telly.[26]

Pyrrhic victories and glorious failures

In the context of civil resistance 'what constitutes success or failure may have no immediate or obvious answer' (Roberts 2009: 1). It is difficult to measure the impact of strategies and campaigns aimed at achieving justice, and thus difficult to measure the success of CLCs. Apart from the complexity of crediting any particular change to one sector when a movement for change typically includes many actors, sometimes change does not bring the result sought. Significant social change is often achieved incrementally over decades; once it is achieved, the exact meaning of the change – and whether it represents progress or a setback in terms of the original goal – can be difficult to capture with precision, as a whole array of social, political and economic relationships have also changed. Furthermore, many acts of resistance that appeared to challenge the status quo in fundamental ways have been accommodated in unanticipated ways. Some 'successes' masked a deeper failure to grasp the ability of power to adjust to and incorporate even the most radical challenges. Many people interviewed for our project were hesitant to claim CLC success in resisting state crime and quick to acknowledge the ways in which injustice is in some ways graver today than it was 40 years ago.

The history of CLCs, and the stories about justice and resistance it illuminates, suggests that real progress is hard to achieve and difficult to measure. Today, many of the concrete things that inspired CLCs have been achieved to a greater or lesser extent but more profound aspirations remain elusive. For example, legal representation is now far more widely available than it was in the early 1970s when Mick O'Brien organized legal representation for young offenders. If there is a prospect that a defendant will be imprisoned, it is highly likely that legal representation will be provided through legal aid. However, young men from low socioeconomic backgrounds are still being imprisoned at high rates today (see, for example, Australian Bureau of Statistics 2009). Perhaps more widespread legal representation means that association with a lawyer no longer bestows the mark of social respectability that it once did, and no longer acts as effectively as a shield against imprisonment as it did when O'Brien's young offenders were released on appeal. To take another example, there is now far more information publicly available about people's legal rights in relation to the police. Still, over the four decades of CLC operation, those legal rights have diminished significantly as police have gained sweeping new powers. A founding member of the ALS, when asked 20 years later about the impact of the legal service movement on police violence and impunity, answered, 'it's made the police much smarter' (Coe 1993: 17). Access to the law is now much more of a reality than it was in the early 1970s, and CLCs had a large, if difficult to measure, role in achieving this; but access to justice remains just as elusive.

With Paul Schiff Berman (2001), we argue that the *possibilities* of using the law to achieve lasting change must be marked and celebrated, even as we acknowledge the very real difficulties that the law poses as a tool of civil resistance. Where most lawyers in the 1970s aligned themselves, consciously or otherwise, with power and control, CLC lawyers posed and continue to pose a challenge that reminds people that such control is granted by the governed, and that there are ways to revoke it.

That the gains made are not easy to pinpoint does not mean that CLCs have not achieved meaningful change. Before CLCs were established, questions about who or which interests Australian law served were rarely considered. CLCs opened the door to a new set of questions and new ways of seeing the relationship between law and power. According to Judith Peirce, who has been involved in CLCs throughout her 40-year career as a lawyer, CLCs exposed the fallacy of impartial justice:

> [T]he law impacts differently on different groups of people.... And the [CLC] influences on trying to use that law across all people's gender, race, language, disability, mental health issues, is something that the law has to grapple with.... It [the legal system] certainly didn't do it in the '70s, which I think was the genesis of these services. [W]e're exposed to a lot more things these days than we ever were in law school pre-legal services. And ... I'm thinking, for example, of ... issues of family violence, and what happened to women in matrimonial law, which ... is my field ... I think that those issues have taken a generation to be taken seriously, and legal services have had a really big part in all of that.[27]

CLCs made visible the systematic exclusion of the poor and many women from the benefits of the law – an exclusion which had previously masked a range of state crimes, including police violence, the criminalization of young working-class men and the institutionalized failure of the criminal justice system to protect women from male violence. The failure to provide legal remedies or protection from these harms allowed, to use Stanley Cohen's (2001) term, a 'state of denial' to exist in relation to these same harms.

CLCs, particularly through their campaign and law reform work, 'developed that skill of giving a voice and a face to some of the issues that confront everyday people, and issues of justice and injustice'.[28] Many of those once excluded altogether from the narrative of the law and justice found a voice within the spaces of law created by CLCs. Simply by being there, to bear witness, to hear the voiceless and help them be heard, CLCs engaged in resistance against a state that accepted and collaborated in their systematic exclusion from the law's protection. As CLC human rights worker Charandev Singh contends, 'The human voice is really important to healing, as it is to justice. Being listened to, and being able to have a voice, is really fundamental to those things. Being heard, being acknowledged.'[29] From this perspective, CLC-led resistance has been effective. If *recognition* is an aspect of justice, then CLCs have achieved some measure of justice for those once excluded from the stories of the law and justice.

Conclusion

Separated from their history of civil resistance, CLCs might be seen as a cheap or even second-rate service for those who cannot afford 'real lawyers'. We have shown that CLCs have a much broader agenda and display characteristics that meet the criteria of civil resistance. CLCs arose out of the protest movements of the 1960s and early 1970s to challenge the elitism of the law, using it as a force to bring to account previously unquestioned state institutions, such as police forces and court processes. Where these had operated largely without check to compound the marginalization of many women, along with the poorest and most neglected members of society, CLCs highlighted the injustices they perpetrated and helped people voice their demands for change.

CLCs imagined a different way of doing justice that would empower people. They pursued that vision with passion and tenacity despite the obstacles, setbacks, defeats and, perhaps especially, the apparent successes. CLC history is one of experimentation, self-expression and respect for self and others, realized through working *with* others that makes it at heart a creative as well as a legal and political pursuit. The history of legal centres is a history of a determination to 'stand beside',[30] to listen to those denied a voice and, where possible, to provide opportunities for them to speak and act. It is a history of the satisfaction of *taking a side* and *working with*: these bring rewards that cannot easily be measured or articulated, but go beyond simply 'doing good'.

History does not repeat but injustice and state crime frequently do. The history of CLCs fails to provide any simple lessons. It illuminates the myriad possibilities and potential for resisting state crime without discounting the many difficulties. The challenge to state crime through the processes and practices of the law used to resist state abuse has profoundly changed the legal landscape and our understanding of the relationship between the law and justice. The CLC experience suggests that resistance is not so much an action or series of events, but more a way of being where actors are joined through a common acknowledgement of their humanity and the need to recognize this in each other.

Notes

1 Julian Gardner, interview with Jude McCulloch, 30 September 2008.
2 Mary Anne Noone, interview with Jude McCulloch, 4 November 2009.
3 Mick O'Brien, interview with Jude McCulloch, 18 September 2008.
4 Judith Peirce, interview with Jude McCulloch, 7 May 2009.
5 *Dietrich* v. *The Queen 1992* is the case widely accredited with guaranteeing representation in serious criminal cases to ensure a fair trial (although it did not find a common law right to publicly provided legal representation in all cases).
6 O'Brien, interview with McCulloch.
7 Ibid.
8 Ibid.
9 John Finlayson, interview with Jude McCulloch, Mark Peel and Bridget Harris, 30 September 2008.
10 Ibid.
11 Gary Sullivan, interview with Jude McCulloch, 16 September 2008.
12 For example, Gardner (interview with McCulloch); Remy Van de Wiel (interview with Jude McCulloch, 26 February 2009); and Peter Faris (interview with Jude McCulloch, 24 February 2009).
13 Gardner, interview with McCulloch.
14 Van de Wiel, interview with McCulloch.
15 Noone, interview with McCulloch.
16 Finlayson, interview with McCulloch, Peel and Harris.
17 Dick Gross, interview with Jude McCulloch, 24 September 2008.
18 Ibid.
19 Neil Cole, interview with Jude McCulloch, 26 August 2008.
20 Peter Gordon, interview with Mark Peel, 30 September 2008.
21 Renata Alexander, interview with Jude McCulloch, 13 March 2009.
22 Finlayson, interview with McCulloch, Peel and Harris.
23 Alexander, interview with McCulloch.
24 Cole, interview with McCulloch.
25 Gardner, interview with McCulloch.
26 Gross, interview with McCulloch.
27 Peirce, interview with McCulloch.
28 Noone, interview with McCulloch.
29 Charandev Singh, interview with Megan Blair and Bridget Harris, 28 May 2010.
30 Genevieve Nihill, interview with Megan Blair and Bridget Harris, 4 May 2010.

References

Armstrong, S. (1975) 'The expansion of legal aid services: the effects on courts of summary jurisdiction', in J. Newton (ed.), *The Magistrates Court: 1975 and Beyond. Report on Australian Institute of Criminology Seminar, 9–11 May 1975*, Canberra: Australian Institute of Criminology.

Ash, T. (2009) 'A Century of Civil Resistance: Some Lessons and Questions', in A. Roberts and T. Ash (eds), *Civil Resistance and Power Politics: The Experience of Non-Violent Action from Gandhi to the Present*, Oxford: Oxford University Press.

Australian Bureau of Statistics 2009 'Australian Social Trends', available at www.abs.gov.au/AUSSTATS/abs@.nsf/Lookup/4102.0Main+Features60Dec+2009.

Berman, P. S. (2001) 'Telling a Less Suspicious Story: Notes Toward a Non-Skeptical Approach to Legal/Cultural Analysis', *Yale Journal of Law and Humanities*, 13, 95–139.

Brett, J. (1992) *Robert Menzies' Forgotten People*, Sydney: Macmillan.

Brown, D. (1984) 'A Critique of the *Legal Service Bulletin*,' in D. Neal (ed.), *On Tap, Not on Top: Legal Centres in Australia 1972–1982* (pp. 40–8), Clayton: Legal Service Bulletin.

Chesterman, J. (1996) *Poverty, Law and Social Change: The Story of Fitzroy Legal Service*, Carlton: Melbourne University Press.

Coe, P. (1993) Interview in J. Faine (ed.), *Lawyers in the Alice: Aboriginals and Whitefellas's Law*, Sydney: Federation Press.

Cohen, S. (2001) *States of Denial: Knowing about Atrocities and Suffering*, Cambridge: Polity.

Cunneen, C. (1990) *Aboriginal–Police Relations in Redfern: With Special Reference to the 'Police Raid' of 8 February 1990*, Report Commissioned by the National Inquiry into Racist Violence, New South Wales: Human Rights and Equal Opportunity Commission.

Curran, L. (2005) 'Making Connections: The Benefits of Working Holistically to Resolve People's Legal Problems', *E Law – Murdoch University Journal of Law*, 12(1,2), available at www.murdoch.edu.au/elaw/issues/v12n1_2/Curran12_1.html, accessed 10 October 2011.

Erlichster, V. (2007) *From Humble Beginnings: A Brief History of Peninsula Community Legal Centre 1977–2007*, Frankston: Peninsula Community Legal Centre.

Fitzroy Legal Service (1974) *Legal Services Bulletin*, Vol. 1.

Foley, G (2001) *Black Power in Redfern 1968–1972*, The Koori History Website, www.kooriweb.org/foley/essays/essay_1.html; www.kooriweb.org/foley/images/history/1970s/emb72/embassyindex.html, accessed 10 October 2011

Gerster, R. and Bessett, J. (1991) *Seizures of Youth: The Sixties and Australia*, Melbourne: Hyland House.

Green, P. and Ward, T. (2004) *State Crime*, London: Pluto Press.

Greenwood, K. (1994) *It Seemed Like a Good Idea at the Time: A History of the Springvale Legal Service 1973–1993*, Springvale: Monash Legal Service.

Hocking, J. (2008) *Gough Whitlam: A Moment in History*, Carlton: Melbourne University Press.

Horne, D. (1980) *Time of Hope: Australia 1966–72*, London/Sydney: Angus and Robertson.

Neal, D. (ed.) (1984) *On Tap, Not on Top: Legal Centres in Australia, 1972–1982*, Clayton: Legal Service Bulletin.

Noone, M. A. (2007) ' "They All Come in the One Door": The Transformative Potential of an Integrated Service Model: A Study of West Heidelberg Community Legal Service', in P. Pleasence, A. Buck and N. Balmer (eds), *Transforming Lives: Law and Social Process* (pp. 93–112), London: The Stationery Office.

Noone, M. A. and Tomsen, S. (2006) *Lawyers in Conflict: Australian Lawyers and Legal Aid*, Sydney: Federation Press.

Reiner, R. (2009) 'Police Property', in A. Wakefield and J. Fleming (eds), *The Sage Dictionary of Policing* (pp. 230–2), Los Angeles and London: Sage.

Rich, N. (2009) *Reclaiming Community Legal Centres: Maximising our Potential So We Can Help Our Clients Reach Theirs*, Consumer Action Law Centre and Victoria Law Foundation, available at www.consumeraction.org.au/downloads/VLFCLCFellowship07-08reportWebFinal.pdf.

Richards, M. (2002) *The Hanged Man: The Life and Death of Ronald Ryan*, Carlton North: Scribe.

Roberts, A. (2009) 'Civil Resistance and Power Politics', in A. Roberts and T. Ash (eds), *Civil Resistance and Power Politics: The Experience of Non-Violent Action from Gandhi to the Present*, Oxford: Oxford University Press.

Sackville, R. (1975) *Law and Poverty Series: Legal Aid in Australia*, Canberra: Australian Government Commission of Inquiry into Poverty, AGPS.

Sexton, M. and Maher, L. (1982) *The Legal Mystique: The Role of Lawyers in Australian Society*, Sydney: Angus and Robertson.

Townshend, C. (2005) *Easter 1916: The Irish Rebellion*, London: Penguin/Allen Lane.

York, B. (1987) 'Baiting the Tiger: Police and Protest during the Vietnam War', in M. Finnane (ed.), *Policing in Australia: Historical Perspectives* (pp. 171–87), Kensington, NSW: Kensington University Press.

14   Hardening the rule of law and asylum seekers

Exporting risk and the judicial censure of state illegality

Sharon Pickering and Leanne Weber

MARIUS BENSON: Chris Bowen, why did you present a case in the High Court yesterday that the judge – Justice Hayne – found to be 'half-baked'?

CHRIS BOWEN: Marius, I'm not going to comment on what was traversed in the Court yesterday in detail. That would be inappropriate as a minister.

BENSON: But what about that criticism? Half-baked?

BOWEN: Marius, the issue is that we believe that we're on very strong ground. All our legal advice is that the government has followed the *Migration Act* to the letter.

BENSON: But can you rely on your legal advice when the judge says the case you put is unsatisfactory and, again, half-baked?

BOWEN: Well, Marius, we have full confidence in the Australian Government Solicitor and the Solicitor-General; and we will be making that case vigorously. We believe we're on very strong ground.

(Bowen 2011)

In the face of exceptional politics over border protection, Australia is currently experiencing what Dauvergne might term a hardening in the rule of law by the courts, in which 'law becomes more law-like' (2008: 175). With the desire and some capacity to enforce borders, nations of the Global North have witnessed varying forms of interaction between the Executive and the Judiciary with regard to how far governments can go to deter and punish those who cross borders irregularly. In Europe, this was recently seen in the form of a ruling by the European Court of Human Rights which found that Belgium breached its human rights obligations by transferring asylum seekers to Greece for refugee processing.[2] During 2011, Australia was subject to rulings on the legality of Executive actions in its deportation of non-citizens. Most recently, the United Nations (UN) Human Rights Committee came to a decision in relation to the case of Nystrom that deportation of a long-standing legal resident on character grounds was disproportionate and arbitrary (*Nystrom* v. *Australia*).[3] However, this case has gone almost unremarked in the national press. Perhaps this is because it occurred at a time of high combat between the Executive and the Judiciary over deportation in relation to the Malaysia Arrangement,[4] whereby the Australian government attempted to export 800 asylum seekers in an offshore processing exchange of non-citizens.

The use of deportation to export risks in the form of non-citizens has brought the Australian government under the full glare of judicial censure in both domestic and international jurisdictions as to the lawfulness of its actions against non-citizens. It would seem that the Judiciary may be the last bastion of protection for non-citizens in an age of hyper-sovereignty characterized by the desire of the Global North to 'juridically other' undesirable non-citizens (cf. Jamieson and McEvoy 2005).

This chapter undertakes a reading of state illegality in relation to the capacity of audiences 'from above' (Green and Ward 2004) to censure state harms. The study of state crime has historically overlooked the possibility of resistance, especially resistance from within the state itself, to state harms and violence. This chapter is concerned with exploring the potential for censure from above, but also from within the apparatus of the state, namely the Judiciary, the complicity of which has often been regarded as crucial to the perpetuation of state harms (Jamieson and McEvoy 2005). Specifically, the chapter considers the capacity of the juridical process to name state illegality, dispute dominant narratives of border protection and produce counter-narratives. It does so by examining the ways the human rights and legal protections of asylum seekers and other non-citizens limit the actions of the state and how judicial censure operationalizes discourses of human rights. The tension between the sovereign rights of states and the individual rights of refugees has been played out in restrictive interpretations of protection, deferral, withholding and avoidance of refugee protection (Dauvergne 2008), which renders 'failed asylum seekers' liable to removal. These legal and political conflicts are not without risks for governments, which stand to be criticized by different constituencies for stances that are considered either too restrictive or too permissive.

The architecture of risk

This discussion focuses on the legality of the state exporting 'risks', in this case the risk posed by asylum seekers seeking protection after arriving by boat in Australia.[5] In this sense, we understand the desire to deport asylum seekers in the Malaysia Arrangement to be part of what we have called elsewhere 'the ambiguous architecture of risk' (Weber and Pickering 2011). Risk is not a single or unitary category of analysis but rather is made up of a range of often complementary and competing forms of risk. The ultimate risk to asylum seekers is the risk of failing to obtain protection, coupled with the dangers of illegalized travel, which can be exacerbated by the actions of governments, facilitators and asylum seekers themselves. However, in this discussion, we concentrate on the political risks experienced and generated by governments, as a way to conceptualize how and why the Australian state sought to use the Malaysia Arrangement to make a political risk go away.

Understanding the governmental rationale for exporting risks, state illegality and judicial censure needs to take account of the high-octane political debate around migration and in particular the 'commonsense' position that the logic of deterrence, disruption and detention has come to occupy in driving government rhetoric and policy (Pickering and Lambert 2002). For more than a decade, successive conservative and Labour governments in Australia have increasingly relied on deterrence to explain the aims and objectives of border control policies and legislation (Grewcock 2009). Notably this has occurred in a context in which the problems of unauthorized migration and people smuggling – an illicit market in the movement of people significantly shaped by the universal visa system whereby legal avenues of entry to Australia are denied for high-risk groups – have been constructed as an unmanageable threat and a national security issue, with a concomitant increase in material and political resources allocated to government agencies and private contractors involved in border protection, detention and compliance (Pickering 2005).

As is well documented, the numbers of people arriving in Australia by boat without valid visas is low in comparison to similar countries (UNHCR 2010). Moreover, the numbers ebb and flow in ways that suggest that a range of contributing factors underpin irregular maritime migration from Indonesia to Australia, which cannot comprehensively be erased by the rhetoric and realities of Australian border protection policies.

These risk-driven policies have seriously diminished the spaces available for the operation of human rights paradigms, although legal challenges framed with reference to international human rights and humanitarian law have at times challenged this hegemonic political position. Notably there are current court proceedings underway to determine whether it is legal to prosecute people smugglers for bringing people without visas to Australia, as this would seem to at best compromise and at worst directly contravene the provisions of the UN *Convention Relating to the Status of Refugees 1951* (hereafter, the Refugee Convention).[6]

A history of combat

In 2004, High Court Justice Mary Gaudron described the excising of Australian territory for the purposes of migration as 'a cute legal fiction' (Munro 2004). This step was taken by the former conservative government of John Howard to deny access to refugee determination procedures to those arriving by boat without visas. This judicial ridicule of statute indicated that in the field of migration the law has bifurcated. On the one hand, aspects of migration law continue to be subject to the full scrutiny of judicial review where prominence is given to the application of established legal principles, including habeas corpus, natural justice and the rule of law. Reliance on grand and enduring legal principles foundational to the security of the legal subject (particularly a non-citizen) are particularly noteworthy as tools of legal resistance in the Australian context, where there is no national Bill of Rights. On the other hand, a raft of migration legislation has been developed that is precisely designed to be removed from judicial review (Pickering 2005). Recent recourse to the courts as a check on state power in migration matters has again highlighted varying degrees of political and judicial discomfort with external (and even internal) reference to human rights standards.

The Malaysia Arrangement was brought into being under s 198A of the *Migration Act 1958* – an amendment to the Migration Act that was introduced in the wake of the Tampa crisis and the establishment of the much criticized Pacific Solution. In 2001, the *MV Tampa* rescued 433 asylum seekers and brought them into Australian waters. The Australian government took extraordinary steps to prevent the asylum seekers from disembarking from the vessel, which resulted in a case being brought before the Federal Court of Australia, the *Victorian Council for Civil Liberties* v. *Minister for Immigration and Multicultural Affairs*, and in appeal, *Ruddick* v. *Vadarlis* in the Full Court of the Federal Court.[7] The case, an application for a writ of habeas corpus, argued on the basis that by not allowing the asylum seekers to disembark from the *MV Tampa*, the Australian government was unlawfully detaining them. Moreover, the applicants contended that the Executive had no independent power to detain non-citizens for the purposes of expulsion because the Migration Act contained no such power. The application was successful in the Federal Court but overturned on appeal on the morning of 11 September 2001. The Full Court asserted that determining entry to a country is so central to the operation of a sovereign nation that a court could not legitimately limit those powers. Thus, it found the prerogative power to exclude and detain for those purposes to be legitimate and that the government was not illegally detaining asylum seekers on the Tampa. As this case unfolded, the government was entering into extensive arrangements with Papua New Guinea and Nauru to admit and detain the asylum seekers for the purposes of offshore processing, which came to be known as the Pacific Solution (Marr and Wilkinson 2004).

Looking back, this development might be regarded as 'Exporting Asylum Risks Mark I'. The Immigration Minister at the time, Philip Ruddock, was reportedly furious that some Federal Court judges continued to overturn Executive decisions by applying a narrow interpretation of various privative clauses which had been introduced to 'judge-proof' ministerial discretion (Brennan 2007). At the heart of the dispute was intense political and legal exchange over the rights of the sovereign nation to control its borders without reference to either the human rights of asylum seekers or long-accepted judicial principles, such as habeas corpus, due process and natural justice. The core concern of this chapter is to consider the Malaysia Arrangement and the extent to which the Australian Judiciary has once again engaged discourses of human rights to limit state power in the case of what might be termed as 'Exporting Asylum Risks Mark II'.

The Malaysia Arrangement

In 2011, the Australian Federal Government sought to establish offshore processing of asylum seekers arriving by boat in an effort to achieve what the Prime Minister and Minister for Immigration described as 'breaking the people smuggler's business model' (Rout 2011). Under the deal, Australia would transport 800 'irregular maritime arrivals' to Malaysia where they would have their applications for refugee status considered. In return, the Australian government undertook to resettle 4000 recognized refugees living in Malaysia. This aspect of the proposal led many commentators to refer to the deal as a 'refugee swap'. The deterrent effect of this policy was purported to be its ability to influence asylum seekers not to board vessels bound for Australia because they could end up in Malaysia, thereby reducing the number of boat arrivals, which in turn would lower the number of onshore applications for refugee protection. The policy has been described as effectively 'contracting out' Australia's protection obligations (McAdam *et al.* 2011). Moreover, the government described it repeatedly as an initiative to reduce the human cost of making the journey, making continual references to the Christmas Island shipwreck of December 2010 in which up to 50 asylum seekers died when the vessel they were travelling on broke up on rocks off the island. As emerging research suggests, claims of the effectiveness of deterrence as an antidote to arrivals and in particular to the risk of death are, at best, disingenuous (Weber and Pickering 2011).

The Arrangement was characterized by aspirational statements regarding refugee processing, protections and human rights. Significant public debate followed the announcement of the policy, with opposition and coalition parties rejecting the deal on a variety of grounds, and political commentators signalling significant concerns. Malaysia is not a signatory to the Refugee Convention and does not undertake refugee processing or protection. Instead, as noted in the legal arguments, Malaysia 'usually' cooperates with the UN High Commissioner for Refugees to undertake these activities. As a result, Malaysia is host to large numbers of asylum seekers, most of whom are trying to move on to other destinations (Weber and Grewcock 2011). Malaysia is also not a party to the *International Covenant on Civil and Political Rights*, the *International Covenant on Economic, Social and Cultural Rights* or the *Convention Against Torture and Other Cruel, Inhuman or Degrading Treatment or Punishment*, and punishments such as caning for illegal entry are reportedly routine. Moreover, despite Australian government assurances to the contrary, those asylum seekers subject to the arrangement who had transited through Malaysia on their way to Australia could be subject to criminal sanctions under Malaysian domestic law.

The High Court case

In August 2011, in response to the imminent implementation of the Malaysia Arrangement, an injunction was sought to prevent the removal of asylum seekers from Australia to Malaysia. An action was filed in the High Court by two plaintiffs seeking to challenge the powers of the government to remove people from Australia to Malaysia under the terms of the Arrangement. The plaintiffs alleged they could not lawfully be taken from Christmas Island to Malaysia. Plaintiff M70 sought to clarify the legality and status of declarations[8] made under s 198A of the Migration Act and to elicit some indication of the legal parameters of any future declarations with respect to the offshore processing of asylum seekers (Karlsen 2011). Plaintiff M106 sought to challenge the legality of Australia sending unaccompanied minors to another country, arguably in violation of its guardianship obligations.

In its substantive judgement, the High Court made permanent the earlier injunctions preventing the Minister from sending asylum seekers to Malaysia. The Court held as invalid the ministerial declaration of Malaysia as a country to which asylum seekers who entered Australia can be taken for the processing of their claims. In relation to the unaccompanied minor, the Court found that an unaccompanied minor (under 18 years old) may not lawfully be taken from Australia without written consent under the relevant guardianship legislation.

The legal discourse of censure

Importantly, the case again raised the issue of the impact of judicial review on the development and implementation of migration policy as was seen in the legal challenge within the Tampa case. The Judiciary in both cases was at pains to emphasize its role in relation to law rather than policy. Distancing the courts from the politicization of migration policy and the heat of arguably the most high-profile and vitriolic national debate, Chief Justice French noted in the 2011 Malaysia case:

> Courts exercising federal jurisdiction for the last two decades in particular have had to decide many judicial review applications in respect of administrative decisions affecting asylum seekers. Some of their decisions, including decisions of this Court, have had practical consequences for the implementation of government policy. It is a function of a court when asked to decide a matter which is within its jurisdiction to decide that matter according to law. The jurisdiction to determine the two applications presently before the Court authorises no more and requires no less.
>
> (French CJ at 2)

Notably, Justice North in the 2001 Tampa case noted:

> The question of Australia's policy towards refugees is a matter of great current debate in our community. It is important for me to stress that the role of the Court is to determine questions of law which are brought to it. That is what I have done in this case.... It is not part of the function of the Court to interfere in the policy decisions made by government. But it is part of the function of the Court to determine if the government respondents have acted within the law.
>
> (Summary at [7])

These statements limiting the role of the courts may be read as an attempt to neutralize any accusations of politicization in relation to a decision that is adverse to government policy. However, there is a notable distinction between the two cases, which points to the very different ways the courts approach the task of censuring government action. The Tampa case was specifically concerned with naming government action as illegal – that is, that the government was illegally detaining asylum seekers on board the vessel. The role of the Court, as quoted above, was said to be 'to determine whether the government respondents have acted within the law'. This goes to the heart of a writ of habeas corpus which is about illegal imprisonment. However, the more recent case on the Malaysia Arrangement couched its role specifically in relation to a more administrative interpretation of law – one which in effect concerned the legality or illegality of government policy, but which was expressed in procedural terms. What was at issue in that case was whether or not the Minister had the legal power to make the declaration that was made under section 198 of the Migration Act. While this may reflect the differences in the two cases – the Tampa being about a specific act of wrongful detention of non-citizens and their planned expulsion, and the Malaysian case being about the intended expulsion of non-citizens on an ongoing basis for the purposes of offshore processing – it is also indicative of how in the latter case the Judiciary rather carefully avoided direct combat with the Executive as an explicitly designated illegal actor.

The Malaysia case turned on whether a declaration made under section 198A was lawful if the declared country was not bound by statute and in practice to meet three criteria: that the country must be legally bound by international law or its own domestic law to provide access for asylum seekers to effective processes for assessing their need for protection; it must provide protection for asylum seekers pending determination of their refugee status; and it must provide protection for persons given refugee status pending their voluntary return to their country of origin or their resettlement in another country. The Migration Act additionally requires that the country meet certain human rights standards in providing protection. Importantly, the Court also held, similar to the conclusion of Justice North in the Tampa case, that under the Migration Act the Minister had no other power (other than s 198) to remove asylum seekers from Australia whose claims for protection have not been determined. The Court stated:

> The general powers of removal of 'unlawful non-citizens' given by the Migration Act (in particular s 198) cannot be used when the Migration Act has made specific provision for the taking of asylum seekers who are offshore entry persons and whose claims have not been processed to another country, and has specified particular criteria that the country of removal must meet.
>
> (High Court of Australia 2011: 1)

The destabilization of government policy in the judgement was both explicit and implicit. Implicitly, the quotation marks at least question the designation of unlawful non-citizen as an accepted categorization of asylum seekers within the legislation, and notably then goes on to use the term asylum seekers. This framing appears to draw on critiques made of government terminology applied to asylum seekers, which has been viewed as dehumanizing and placing them outside an inclusive social and legal imagination (Pickering 2005).

Both the plaintiffs and the government agreed that, under the terms of the Agreement, Malaysia was not legally bound to provide the access and protections stipulated by the Migration Act for a declaration to be made. The difference between the parties was that the government considered a non-binding arrangement sufficient under the legislation. The Agreement was not legally binding on Malaysia to conduct any of the usual processes of refugee processing, determination or protection that are expected under the Australian Migration Act. That the Agreement was not legally binding eventuated in it being found to be in breach of section 198A of the Migration Act as drafted. Ironically, perhaps, according to the terms of the legislation hastily enacted by the previous government in the wake of the Tampa crisis, the Executive could not simply deal directly with another government and develop a refugee processing framework insecurely tethered to processes and applications of established human rights provisions.

The drafting of the Malaysia Agreement demonstrated a limited commitment to the human rights of asylum seekers subject to the arrangement. The Agreement was notable for the language used within it: for example, that the Minister 'has regard' for human rights is not a legal condition – if it were meant as a condition then the Agreement would have explicitly included this. While it has been asserted that there are core and periphery conditions regarding the operation of the Refugee Convention (notably the provision that all nations, not only signatories, must avoid refouling a person to conditions of persecution), the High Court determined that the state must look at the whole of the Refugee Convention and not solely on these non-refoulement provisions. This is a more comprehensive reading and application of the Convention in relation to the rights and indeed the wellbeing of asylum seekers. The Court also confirmed that the rights of refugees cannot be subject to non-binding arrangements between nations which effectively result in the abdication of the rule of law at the national level.

The judgement also established that a critical starting point for considering the criteria as to whether a declaration can be made is not only that the receiving country needs to be a signatory to the Refugee Convention, and indeed to other relevant human rights treaties. Instead, the High Court found that protection is only protection if it is required by law – otherwise the operation of protection is really a matter of good fortune rather than legal and procedural design. The Chief Justice was also emphatic that a written arrangement between two nations does not amount to refugee protection, but rather protection must be measured by what actually happens on the ground. Even the fact that a country is a signatory to the Refugee Convention is not enough to assert that there will be protection. Rather, the Court asserted that the signing of the Refugee Convention (or other treaties) produces frameworks of accountability but not actual processes of protection. Protection was considered a matter not just of law but of law combined with effective practice. This asserts the role of policy and policy implementation (practice) in giving life to laws of protection.

Chief Justice French gave early consideration to how the government had satisfied itself that Malaysia was an acceptable destination for asylum seekers who had arrived in Australia. The Chief Justice (at 29) picked through the Minister's affidavit to censure the government for the tenuous assessment it offered:

> The Minister formed an 'understanding' from his conversations with the Malaysian Minister of Home Affairs and other Malaysian officials that the Malaysian Government 'was keen to improve its treatment of refugees and asylum seekers'. The Minister considered this to be a 'clear theme of the discussions'.

In a clear, but relatively mild rebuke of ministerial decision-making, the High Court roundly rejected aspirational arrangements as a basis for Australia abdicating its role in processing asylum seekers. Therefore, it clearly established, without a single reference to human rights (in the case of the first plaintiff), that refugee determination needed to occur in a predictable and proven system of refugee protection as prescribed by international law:

> It is a misconstruction of the criteria to make a declaration of their subsistence based upon an understanding that the executive government of the specified country is 'keen to improve its treatment of refugees and asylum seekers'. Nor could a declaration rest upon a belief that the government of the specified country has 'made a significant conceptual shift in its thinking about how it wanted to treat refugees and asylum seekers' or that it had 'begun the process of improving the protection offered to such persons'.
>
> (French CJ at 62)

Importantly, the High Court highlighted that the Executive, aware of these limitations in the Agreement, determined such conditions to be acceptable. That is, the insufficient protections afforded to asylum seekers subject to the Arrangement were not unintended consequences but rather core elements of the deal:

> Having regard to the Minister's concession and what appears, in any event, from the submissions upon which the Minister acted and his affidavit, it is clear that he did not look to, and did not find, any basis for his declaration in Malaysia's international obligations or relevant domestic laws.
>
> (French CJ at 66)

Arguably, the most noteworthy aspect of this passage is the reference to human rights standards as a measure of *another* nation's acceptable processing and protection of the rights of refugees as part of an enduring legal framework. While legal commentators have noted that the decision did not assess conditions in Malaysia or whether Malaysia meets human rights standards (McAdam *et al.* 2011), it nonetheless gave some prominence to international human rights norms:

> The Minister must ask himself the questions required by the criteria on the assumption that the terms 'provide' and 'meet' require consideration of

the extent to which the specified country adheres to those of its international obligations, constitutional guarantees and domestic statutes which are relevant to the criteria.

(French CJ at 67)

Human rights are discursively used as a measure of Malaysia's suitability as a destination for asylum seekers who are removed from Australia, which in turn is used to consider Australia's treatment of asylum seekers potentially subject to the arrangement. In effect, this mobilizes human rights norms in relation to Australia's treatment of asylum seekers but it does so at arm's length. It disrupts dominant narratives of national security and state sovereignty but does not explicitly produce a loud counter-narrative of human rights. This attempt to use human rights as a legal discourse of censure took Australia a small step closer to a robust and nuanced legal engagement with human rights as a means of resistance to state power, but it was a tentative step.

Law as a protective force

The High Court became more explicit in its application of international human rights norms in determining the lawfulness of the Malaysia Arrangement when it turned to the question of whether offshore processing compromised Australia's own international protection obligations. This was not a question of whether Malaysia sufficiently met the definition of a declared country as per the required criteria under domestic law, but whether in and of itself failing to process asylum seekers' claims in Australia was unlawful. The Court considered whether Australia would be acting in breach of its international obligations under refugee protection and core human rights instruments were it to expel or return 'in any manner whatsoever' a person with a well-founded fear of persecution 'to the frontiers of territories where his life or freedom would be threatened on account of his race, religion, nationality, membership of a particular social group or political opinion':

> Accordingly, for Australia to remove a person from its territory, whether to the person's country of nationality or to some third country willing to receive the person, without Australia first having decided whether the person concerned has a well-founded fear of persecution for a Convention reason may put Australia in breach of the obligations it undertook as party to the Refugee Convention and the Refugees Protocol, in particular the non-refoulement obligations undertaken in Art 33(1) of the Refugee Convention.
>
> (Majority Judgement at 94)

This part of the judgement found that Australia cannot readily on-sell its protection obligations, enabling commentators to roundly conclude that the Malaysia Arrangement was illegal (Hathaway 2011).

The sole dissenting Judge, Heydon J, excused the Court from the role of Executive oversight. While confirming the primacy of parliament, Heydon's dissenting opinion is notable for its criticism of the President of the Australian Human Rights Commission for seemingly overstating to the Court the standing of the Commission. This judgement also asserted that Australia can expel people prior to their application for refugee protection being processed – a conclusion that is at odds with the majority. The dissenting judgement was notable in that human rights standards and mechanisms were only mentioned in order to be sidelined.

The High Court judgement censured the power of the Executive by clarifying statute and making it the conduit for applying Australia's human rights obligations. In fact, some analysts have gone so far as to suggest that the judgement asserted the supremacy of Australia's international legal obligations (Karlsen 2011) over the desire or need for Executive discretion. Domestic legislation coupled with a political agreement between two nations were found to be insufficient grounds by which to remove asylum seekers from mandated protections provided to asylum seekers processed onshore. Moreover, reference to those obligations by the Court neutralized the effect of political rhetoric which stated that the Malaysia Arrangement would reduce the risks for those seeking to come to Australia by boat. In so doing, it attracted stinging criticism from the Prime Minister.

The political response to judicial censure

[W]e live under the rule of law and that applies to prime ministers as well as everybody else.

(PM John Howard during the Tampa court case, 2001)[9]

The Malaysia Arrangement decision by the High Court simply interpreted a statute which had not been considered previously by the courts. Legal commentators were unanimous that the High Court decision did not amount to a radical judgement or a case of judicial activism. In fact, it was noted that, had the opportunity arisen for the legality of the former government's Pacific Solution to be tested, it would have also run afoul of section 198. However, the Prime Minister and Minister for Immigration roundly criticized the High Court for its interpretation of section 198A, and most importantly the effect of this judgement on policy:

Now yesterday the High Court changed from interpretations of the past, and to give you just a flavour of that because I think it's important, the current Chief Justice of the High Court, His Honour Mr Justice French, considered comparable legal questions when he was a judge of the Federal Court and made different decisions to the one that the High Court made yesterday.

(Gillard 2011)

On 12 September 2011, almost exactly ten years after the Tampa incident, which was the catalyst for the legislative provisions in question, the Prime Minister announced that the government would be introducing new legislation to enable the transfer of irregular maritime arrivals to third countries for the processing of their asylum claims. The proposed legislation would enable the government to make a valid declaration in relation to Malaysia and thus proceed with the transfer of asylum seekers.

In a move that mirrored the much-criticized use of privative clauses by the former conservative government, the proposed amendments under subsections 198AB(5) and (6) would mean that a designation made by the Minister would not be a legislative instrument, and that the rules of natural justice would not apply to the exercise of the power. In order to make the Malaysia Arrangement 'legal', the government sought to erase basic and fundamental principles of justice. The intention to place the legislation beyond the view of judicial censure was unequivocal:

> the purpose of this provision is to make clear that the Minister is not required to give a right to be heard to individuals who may be taken to a country, in relation to the designation of that country as an offshore processing country, or the revocation of such a designation.
>
> (Karlsen 2011)

The proposed legislation did not garner support from the cross benches or the opposition and was not introduced into parliament, thus returning to the onshore processing of asylum seekers and casting doubt over the legality of offshore processing arrangements generally. This outcome depended on judicial and parliamentary arrangements that are characterized by judicial independence and dispersed party political power. It is a tentative limitation on state power, but it is the fragile mechanism on which liberal democracy ultimately relies. In this case, judicial censure combined with a lack of parliamentary majority sustained the censure of the Court. The independence of the Judiciary proved in this case to be a sufficient constraint on state power and repression, and did function as a protective force for those who were to be subject to removal. However, this success was dependent on political arrangements in place at the time, which paralysed political attempts to undo this protection. Should the composition of the federal parliament, or that of the High Court, have been different, this censure may have been countered with relative ease by legislative provisions. Moreover, since the framing of the relevant statute enabled an adverse judgement to be made on the basis of statutory interpretation, rather than via a wholesale incorporation of international legal principles by the Court, the extent to which international human rights protections might be relied upon to uphold the rights of non-citizens under similar circumstances in the future remains unanswered.

Conclusion

When the Minister for Immigration remarked in the media interview quoted at the start of this chapter that his legal advice was sound and that he was working within the provisions of the Migration Act, he did not effectively countenance that the very mundane business of judicial review – interpreting statute – could result in an adverse decision for the government. Moreover, he had discounted the extent to which the drafting of the domestic legislation had opened up a role for international human rights in flavouring the interpretation of domestic law, especially considering the very narrow legal avenues for non-citizens to assert themselves as legal subjects. The Prime Minister attracted widespread criticism for her stinging and personal attack on Chief Justice French and the High Court. The dissenting judgement abrogated the role of the Courts in checking government power even through the interpretation of statute. By contrast, the majority judgement was very 'law-like' in its interpretation of statute. It was quite simply law behaving 'as it ought' (Dauvergne 2008). While the rule of law was not an overriding trope in the majority judgement, the judgement is arguably an indication of the kind of hardening in the rule of law referred to earlier. Indeed, the vitriolic response of the Prime Minister could be read as indicative not only of an unanticipated result, but also of one of displeasure at the applied legal limits through the basic interpretation of statute.

In the 2001 Tampa case, the Courts engaged directly and deeply with the idea that the Australian government had acted illegally in relation to non-citizens. The writ of habeas corpus found that the government had acted illegally in refusing to allow the asylum seekers to disembark, but this was overturned on appeal to the full Federal Court. The case and the judgements detail the historical combat between the observance of individual human rights and the rights of the sovereign state to exclude non-citizens (Pickering 2005). By contrast, the High Court case considering the Malaysia Agreement drills down to a level of detail and complex legal argument about the nature and extent of a declaration made under a domestic statute, and found by a six to one majority that the Executive had exceeded its powers in attempting to remove non-citizens from Australia before considering their claims for protection. The judgement does reference human rights, but in ways that do not incite direct combat with the sovereignty of the nation-state or use human rights as a blunt instrument to counter Executive power. Rather, this reference is used to texture the Court's interpretation of the relevant domestic statute in determining whether Malaysia satisfies the criteria of acceptability for a declared country as required by domestic law, but importantly assessed with reference to international standards. Arguably, human rights were thus used to contextualize the potential actions/inactions of other states, but more indirectly to assess Australia's own treatment of asylum seekers. In so doing, the High Court's judgement reads as a bureaucratic clarification, rather than a stronger censure of state harm in relation to human rights. Yet the effect – to immobilize the arrangement and prevent the export of asylum seekers to Malaysia – was abrupt, damning and a clear expression of the potential for state harm.

In response to what is effectively internal resistance from the Judiciary, the state has once again required the removal of law from the decision-making arena. We might speculate that the adoption of this overtly illiberal strategy reflects an anxiety on the part of government, that any attempts to redraft the provisions of section 198 so as to remove consideration about the refugee protection and human rights records of proposed offshore processing countries might still be overturned, this time through the direct application of international legal principles by the Court. In other words, it seems that 'judge-proofing' was seen as a more secure strategy than 'human rights proofing'. Seemingly, state management of undesirable non-citizens requires circumstances where the rule of law evaporates. Courts are by their very nature rule-bound and their potential is limited, but they nonetheless remain a form of internal resistance to illegal state action.

The Malaysia Arrangement was an attempt to physically remove the largely politically constructed problem of asylum seekers arriving by boat in Australia, through the exporting of political risk. The means was to transfer them to another country where media attention, human rights obligations and Australian domestic law were all but absent. The government response to the High Court ruling was not only to force this physical othering but also to enshrine the legal othering of non-citizens in a series of legislative measures that would have resulted in the removal of non-citizens from the reaches of Australian law. The impact would have been to locate asylum seekers beyond legal protection or place them in what Jamieson and McEvoy (2005) describe as an 'extra-territorial black hole'. However, following the High Court decision, the government could not muster sufficient cross-bench and opposition support in the parliament to progress this regressive legislative package. Although offering only a fragile protection, democratic processes played out to designate the reactionary legislation itself as a political risk, eventually forcing the withdrawal of the proposal. Instead, in an important watershed in limiting state power, asylum seekers are now to be processed exclusively onshore in Australia.

Notes

1 The Honourable Chris Bowen, Minister for Immigration and Citizenship.
2 *MSS* v. *Belgium and Greece*, App No 30696/09 (21 January 2011).
3 Human Rights Committee communication No. 1557/2007, adopted 18 July 2011.
4 *Plaintiff M70/2011* v. *Minister for Immigration and Citizenship* and Plaintiff M106 of 2011 by his Litigation Guardian, *[2011] HCA 32*.
5 As is often noted, many more asylum seekers have arrived in Australia by plane or been settled from offshore. These groups have not been subject to political and administrative arrangements of the same nature and extent as those who arrive by boat (see www.immi.gov.au).
6 The case of Jeky Payara was referred to the Victorian Court of Appeal in September 2011.
7 *Victorian Council for Civil Liberties Inc.* v. *Minister for Immigration & Multicultural Affairs* [2001] FCA 1297. *Ruddock* v. *Vadarlis* [2001] FCA 1329.
8 Section 198A(3) of the Migration Act says that the Minister may:
   (a) declare in writing that a specified country:
      (i) provides access, for persons seeking asylum, to effective procedures for assessing their need for protection; and

   (ii) provides protection for persons seeking asylum, pending determination of their refugee status; and

   (iii) provides protection to persons who are given refugee status, pending their voluntary repatriation to their country of origin or resettlement in another country; and

   (iv) meets relevant human rights standards in providing that protection; and

  (b) in writing, revoke a declaration made under paragraph (a).

9 From an interview carried out on Radio 2UE with the then Prime Minister, John Howard, 3 September 2011.

Postscript

In July 2012, after the writing of this chapter, and in response to a series of drownings, the Australian Government established the 'Expert Panel on Asylum Seekers' to develop recommendations to reduce the loss of life at sea. Politically, the Panel operated to help break a deadlock between political parties. The Panel's Report recommended the re-establishment of offshore processing on Nauru and Papua New Guinea. It also recommended that the

> 2011 Arrangement between the Government of Australia and the Government of Malaysia on Transfer and Resettlement (Malaysia Agreement) be built on further, rather than being discarded or neglected, and that this be achieved through high-level bilateral engagement focused on strengthening safeguards and accountability as a positive basis for the Australian Parliament's reconsideration of new legislation that would be necessary.
>
> (Houston, L'Strange and Aristotle, 2012, *Report of the Expert Panel on Asylum Seekers*, Canberra: Australian Government).

The Expert Panel recommended a series of additional safeguards (including a 'more effective monitoring mechanism') be put in place and, in particular, attention be paid to arrangements for unaccompanied minors and other vulnerable groups. This recommendation, regarded as urgent by the Panel, did not fundamentally address the concerns of the High Court ruling, but rather mapped out elements it believed would enable legislation to move through Parliament which would effectively exclude future High Court review.

The resulting amendments to the Migration Act were subsequently described by the Australian Human Rights Commission as 'Violat[ing] one of the first recommendations of the expert panel report, that adherence by Australia to its international obligations should be one of the guiding principles shaping Australian policy on asylum seeker issues' [http://www.humanrights.gov.au/about/media/media_releases/2012/64_12.html].

These amendments open the way for a wider range of destinations to be used for offshore processing and leave responsibility for ensuring human rights compliance in the hands of parliament and administrative officers rather than the courts.

References

Bowen, C. (2011) *Malaysia Transfer Arrangement, High Court Case*, interview transcript with Marius Benson, ABC Newsradio, available at www.minister.immi.gov.au/media/cb/2011/cb169959.htm.

Brennan, F. (2007) *Tampering with Asylum* (revised edition), St Lucia: University of Queensland Press.

Dauvergne, C. (2008) *Making People Illegal*, New York: Cambridge University Press.

Gillard, J. (2011) *Malaysia Agreement*, Joint Press Conference with Julia Gillard and Chris Bowen, media release, available at www.minister.immi.gov.au/media/cb/2011/cb171279.htm.

Green, P. and Ward, T. (2004) *State Crime: Governments, Violence and Corruption*, London: Pluto Press.

Grewcock, M. (2009) *Border Crimes: Australia's War against Illegal Migration*, Sydney: Institute of Criminology Monograph Series.

Hathaway, J. (2011) *Refugee Expert Says Australia/Malaysia Swap Illegal*, media interview, 10 June, available at www.abc.net.au.

High Court of Australia (2011) Summary of Plaintiff M70/2011 v. Minister for Immigration and Citizenship Plaintiff M106 of 2011 by His Litigation Guardian, *Plaintiff M70/2011* v. *Minister for Immigration and Citizenship*, [2011] HCA 32, 31 August, available at www.hcourt.gov.au.

Jamieson, R. and McEvoy, K. (2005) 'State Crime by Proxy and Juridical Othering', *British Journal of Criminology*, 45, 504–27.

Karlsen, E. (2011) *Migration Legislation Amendment (Offshore Processing and Other Measures) Bill 2011, Bills Dige*st no. 53 2011–2012, available at www.aph.gov.au/About_Parliament/Parliamentary_Departments/Parliamentary_Library/pubs/BN/2011-2012/RefugeeLaw.

McAdam J., Foster, M., Mathew, P., Wood, T., Taylor, S., Zagor, M., Kenny, M. A., Crock, M., Saul, B., Harris-Rimmer, S., Farlenbaum, B., Francis, A., Grewcock, M. and Berg, L. (2011) *Submission to Senate Standing Committee on Legal and Constitutional Affairs, Parliament of Australia*, available at www.google.com.au/url?sa=t&rct=j&q=&esrc=s&source=web&cd=1&ved=0CE4QFjAA&url=http%3A%2F%2Ffreilich.anu.edu.au%2Fsites%2Ffreilich.anu.edu.au%2Ffiles%2Fimages%2FMalaysia%2520submission%252015.9.11%2520FINAL.pdf&ei=M34MUJG4EbGtiQfj86S0DQ&usg=AFQjCNE4_teJFy11FHN3qeo2JIBhIcRMAg, accessed 26 July 2012.

Marr, D. and Wilkinson, M. (2004) *Dark Victory* (2nd edition), Sydney: Allen and Unwin.

Munro, I. (2004) 'Asylum Law is a Fiction: Ex-judge', *The Age*, 5 March.

Pickering, S. (2005) *Refugees and State Crime*, Sydney: Federation Press.

Pickering, S. and Lambert, C. (2002) 'Deterrence: Australia's Refugee Policy', *Current Issues in Criminal Justice: Refugee Issues and Criminology*, 14(1), 65–86.

Rout, M. (2011) 'Another Boat as Bowen Signs Deal', *The Australian*, 25 July.

UNHCR, United Nations High Commissioner for Human Rights (2010) *All in the Same Boat: The Challenges of Mixed Migration*, available at www.unhcr.org/pages/4a1d406060.html, accessed 24 July 2012.

Weber, L. and Grewcock, M. (2011) 'Criminalising People Smuggling: Preventing or Globalizing Harm?', in F. Allum and S. Gilmour (eds), *The Routledge Handbook of Transnational Organized Crime* (pp. 379–90), London: Routledge.

Weber, L. and Pickering, S. (2011) *Globalization and Borders: Deaths at the Global Frontier*, London: Palgrave Macmillan.

15 A global resistance movement?

From human rights to international criminal justice

Dawn L. Rothe[1]

Introduction

Resistance to state crime is an ambitious endeavour, whether at the individual, local or global level, through direct means or more indirect attempts to change a dominant ideology. This chapter argues that global attempts to enhance the protection of human rights – including the development of the Responsibility to Protect (R2P) doctrine, international criminal law and an international criminal justice system – can be seen as mechanisms of resistance to state criminality. It seeks to illustrate how international laws, doctrines and criminal justice systems operate to resist state crime and to promote a new political collective consciousness. I conclude by suggesting that, while still in its infancy and riddled with many problems and contradictions, this effort can be seen as a globally led attempt to resist state crime.

The move towards a global consciousness of human rights

> People are of primary importance. The State is of less importance. The sovereign is of least importance.
>
> (Confucianist Mencius, cited in Glendon 2001: x)

When the development of the United Nations Declaration of Human Rights (UNDHR) began post-World War II, it was viewed as peripheral to other concerns and as a 'paper tiger' in the face of the omnipresent Westphalia philosophy. Discussions of universal human rights were seen by many as a:

> concession to small countries in response to the demands of numerous religious and humanitarian associations that the Allies live up to their war rhetoric by providing assurances that the community of nations would never again countenance such massive violations of human dignity.
>
> (Glendon 2001: xv–xvi)

Still others saw it as an opportunity to establish a moral standard of human dignity; such was the case with the framers of the UNDHR. With the creation of the UN and the UN Charter (1945), the seeds were sown for advancing a new moral agenda and for the beginning of a battle to change the existing consciousness to include the idea of a set of universal human rights.[2]

In June 1946, the Human Rights Commission was established with representatives from 18 UN member states.[3] Yet the concept of universal human rights, at this point, was wedged in a complex web of power and state interests. This web was reflected in the long and arduous debates over whether a declaration or a treaty was in order. Politics and self-interest weighed heavily in the process of developing the doctrine of human rights. The result was a declaration limited to a 'moral value' (Roosevelt 1947, cited in Glendon 2001: 255). In other words, as a declaration for human rights was gaining momentum, it was viewed in the same vein as Abraham Lincoln's inclusion of the term 'equality' in the United States (US) Declaration of Independence: intended not to instantaneously achieve these rights, but to begin the process whereby some day they would crystallize and become enforceable. As noted by Lincoln, during debates involving the Declaration:

> They did not mean to assert the obvious untruth that all were then actually enjoying that equality, nor yet that they were about to confer it immediately upon them. In fact, they had no power to confer such a boon. They meant simply to declare the right, so that enforcement of it might follow as fast as circumstances should permit. They meant to set up a standard maxim for free society, which should be familiar to all, and revered by all; constantly looked to, constantly labored for, and, even though never perfectly attained, constantly approximated, and thereby constantly spreading and deepening its influence and augmenting the happiness and value of life to all people of all colors everywhere.
>
> (Lincoln 1857: 112)

At the end of 1948, the UNDHR was adopted by the UN General Assembly. Work then began on the Covenants[4] to implement the Declaration. While this moment was seen as 'an epoch-making development in international law' (Evatt 1948, cited in Glendon 2001: 163), there was an acute awareness that the doctrine and subsequent Covenants remained entrenched in politics, required a long period of time to be recognized and implemented, and had to be accompanied by a changing global consciousness (Evans 2007).

Although the UNDHR lacked enforcement, it served as more than a 'paper-tiger'. It represented the onset of a changing global consciousness which, I argue, continues today, as evidenced by the codification of human rights into various Covenants, national and international legal systems as well as the emergence of the UN monitoring and enforcement groups and a host of non-governmental organizations. The UNDHR, which began with little value beyond a 'moral' call, has now gained legitimacy and come to be seen as containing necessary and enforceable rights for all of humanity. While the principles of human rights are far from universally applied, they have increasingly acquired justiciable force through international treaties, conventions, judicial bodies and national legal systems.

Development of formal enforcement

> Until recently, it seemed that if you killed one person, you went to jail, but if you slaughtered thousands, you usually got away with it. Times change...
>
> (Brody 1999: 1)

While efforts to create an international criminal court date back to the late 1800s, the onset of the current movement is linked to the end of World War II, the Nuremberg Principles and the establishment of the UN. The UN Charter continued a precedent formulated by the League of Nations[5] to develop international law and its codification, though the universality of any criminal court remained a political issue. The development of the Nuremberg Principles conveyed a cultural message of accountability and the rule of law for crimes, including crimes against peace, war crimes and crimes against humanity. Even though there were no mechanisms for enforcement beyond selective, ad hoc means, the Nuremberg Principles reflected a changing ideology that included the notion that heads of state and high-ranking officials are also accountable for their actions to their own populations. Further, the Statutes of the Nuremberg Tribunal and the 'Tokyo Trials' brought substantive changes in the realm of law, including new classes of international crimes. Thus, in 1945, crimes against humanity and crimes against peace (chiefly wars of aggression) were added (Cassese 2008). These courts served as a catalyst for continuing attempts to codify international criminal law and as a shift in action behind the ideology of ending 'impunity' for heads of state.

Likewise, with the adoption of the 1948 *Convention on Genocide* and the 1949 Geneva Conventions, the first set of principles supporting universal jurisdiction emerged (Cassese 2008). However, the efforts advanced by some international organizations to create an international criminal court as part of the Genocide Convention ended in 1948 due to the lack of political will among major global powers (Rothe and Mullins 2006).

In 1954, the International Law Commission completed the draft Code of Crimes against Peace and Security; yet a consensus could not be reached on a draft for a permanent international criminal court to enforce these newly emerging conventions (Hampson 2002). As noted by the then UN Secretary General, Dag Hammarkj'ld (1959: 3):

> The work of today within and for the United Nations is a work through which the basis may be laid for increasingly satisfying forms of international cooperation and for a future international system of law and order, for which the world is not yet ripe.

Nearly two decades later, two Additional Protocols were added to the Geneva Conventions that provided protections during armed conflict, increasing efforts to enhance a universal set of prohibited behaviours that were enforceable, although at the time no enforcement mechanism was sought given the chill of the Cold War era. During the 1990s, with the International Criminal Tribunal for Former Yugoslavia and the International Criminal Tribunal for Rwanda, the push for accountability and the advancement of an international system of criminal justice gained momentum. However, these remained ad hoc courts due to the lack of political support for a permanent universal criminal court. Central to the development of these institutions has been a contradiction between the ideological and legal image of fully sovereign nation-states and the real need for the external regulation of those polities. This critical tension has played out strongly in the movement to create an international court and to date remains the key strain in the implementation of the court itself and its mission (Rothe and Mullins 2006).

Nevertheless, discussions and work continued on what is now known as the Rome Statute for the International Criminal Court (ICC). During this process, there was great resistance from several states (for example, the US, China and India), centred on the issues of sovereignty and the role of the UN's Security Council. As stated by former US Senator John Ashcroft (1998: 8):

> If there is one critical component of sovereignty, it is the authority to define crimes and punishment. This court [ICC] strikes at the heart of sovereignty by taking this fundamental power away from individual countries and giving it to international bureaucrats.

Consider US Ambassador John Bolton's statement (2002: 1): 'the ICC is an organization whose precepts go against fundamental American notions of sovereignty, checks and balances, and national independence. It is ... harmful to the national interests of the United States, and harmful to our presence abroad.'

Yet many states supported the universal jurisdiction of the ICC, ensuring a universal justice, while other states (mainly the US and China) insisted that the acceptance of the ICC's jurisdiction by states was a necessary precondition to jurisdiction. These two positions were heavily debated and resulted in a compromise that was not fully satisfactory to either side.

At the end of this long and arduous debate over powers of enforcement and jurisdiction, the first permanent international criminal court was established, as were other ad hoc international courts subsequently (such as in Sierra Leone and Timor-Leste). From the 1990s, the formation of a full body of criminal law has emerged that applies to individuals, including heads of state, most notably those orchestrating the gravest offences a state can commit against citizens – genocide, crimes against humanity and massive human rights violations.

Admittedly, the 'force of law'[6] can be destructive in its selective enforcement linked to issues of power.[7] Yet this is not intrinsic, and the law can be used to provide resistance. After all, the extant literature on controls for state crime suggests that a need for perceived and/or real accountability mechanisms is central to constraining these types of crimes. As such, international criminal justice can serve as *jus post bellum* (translated as 'justice after war') and can not only contribute to ending impunity but also act as a potential deterrent mechanism (Mullins and Rothe 2010).

While there is no doubt that the movement towards an international system of accountability is far from a reality, great strides have been made. Since the 1990s, heads of state have found that they are no longer immune from international criminal law (for example, Charles Taylor in 2004, Augusto Pinochet in 1998 and Omar al Bashir in 2009). The broader objective of ending impunity is grounded in a moral and ethical goal for which current efforts to prosecute will serve as a means to achieve a future where heads of states no longer commit crimes of aggression, genocide, crimes against humanity or massive human rights abuses and where the international political community will have an obligatory duty to respond. As noted by the ICC (2002: 1), 'we hope it [the Court] will deter future war criminals, and bring nearer the day when no ruler, no State, no junta and no army anywhere will be able to abuse human rights'.

Consequently, there has been some, albeit limited, resistance to state crime through the advancement of an international criminal justice 'system' and international criminal law. However, as expected, there has been and continues to be opposition to these developments. At the heart of this 'counter-resistance' lies the issue of sovereignty.

The 's' word

> If all states claim to be sovereign, then there can be no higher authority, no international law, or restraint of any kind.
>
> (Ziegler 1977: 103)

As with the development of human rights back in the early 1940s, sovereignty has remained a contentious issue from the onset within all discussions and promotion of a rights-enforcement system. As a result, the international criminal justice system is framed by a selective enforcement of the rule of law. Attempts to universally apply legal and/or moral regulations have been hindered by states' reliance on sovereignty and the sacrosanct nature of national frontiers. Consequently, sovereignty generally becomes a central wedge used by political leaders to ensure that international regulation is limited. To relinquish territorial domestic law to a universality of international law would require states to accept universal jurisdiction and to turn over some of their power to an international system of control, much like the mandatory social contract we all live by which is guided by domestic laws.

The contradiction between state sovereignty structuring an international atomistic system and the ideology of a unified international society has resulted in ineffective means to control those states that violate the moral and legal framework. Put simply, at the core of the matter is the contradiction between the ideal type of rule of law (for all) and the issue of sovereign rule. Further, as the criminological research on state crime has shown, states with the most at risk economically, politically and ideologically, such as the US, are highly unlikely to allow themselves to be regulated by outside agencies (Rothe 2009).

Just as state compliance is unlikely by highly empowered states, those same countries sit on, or have allies on, the UN Security Council, utilizing their veto power in accordance with their political, economic and ideological interests. Indeed, the realpolitik of international relations is still grounded in state sovereignty, hindering efforts to create any concrete system of resistance or control.

Nonetheless, there remains a strong push to continue to change the political and ideological ethos of sovereignty towards states being accountable and responsible to human rights and international criminal law. Nowhere is this more evident than in the recent doctrine of the Responsibility to Protect (R2P). The following section provides a brief overview of R2P and how it can be seen as a significant move towards resisting state crime.

Responsibility to protect

Laws alone are not sufficient to bring about results by themselves.

(Chang 1947: 10)

The R2P is grounded in the realization that states and the 'international political community' have failed to protect citizens around the globe, within and external to their own countries, from massive human rights violations. In 2005, during the UN World Summit, members of the UN made a verbal commitment to the doctrine. This was followed by the 2009 Report by the Secretary-General as well as a long debate in the General Assembly, which resulted in a Resolution (International Coalition for the Responsibility to Protect 2009; UN General Assembly 2009). There are two key passages from this Resolution that merit noting:

138. Each individual State has the responsibility to protect its populations from genocide, war crimes, ethnic cleansing and crimes against humanity. This responsibility entails the prevention of such crimes, including their incitement, through appropriate and necessary means. We accept that responsibility and will act in accordance with it. The international community should, as appropriate, encourage and help States to exercise this responsibility and support the United Nations in establishing an early warning capability.

139. The international community, through the United Nations, also has the responsibility to use appropriate diplomatic, humanitarian and other peaceful means ... to help protect populations from genocide, war crimes, ethnic cleansing and crimes against humanity. In this context, we are prepared to take collective action, in a timely and decisive manner, through the Security Council ... should peaceful means be inadequate and national authorities manifestly fail to protect their populations. ... We also intend to commit ourselves, as necessary and appropriate, to helping States build capacity to protect their populations from genocide, war crimes, ethnic cleansing and crimes against humanity and to assisting those which are under stress before crises and conflicts break out.

Of particular significance in this passage is the 'agreement' and 'commitment' to provide assistance to other states as a *preventative* measure prior to a state engaging in massive human rights violations. Additionally, states have agreed, in principle, to act in a collective and timely way to respond to any country that is in violation of its responsibility to protect its citizenry. Here, the issue of *sovereignty is secondary* to the rights of a population to be protected from human rights violations and international crimes perpetrated by their own government. This is a major step towards changing the historically dogmatic posits of sovereignty by political leaders.

However, as was the case with talks during the development of international legal enforcement mechanisms, there were dissenting views and opposition to the R2P, centred on issues of sovereignty (UN General Assembly 2005). Political preoccupations have also dominated the promotion, and first 'use', of the R2P doctrine (see, for example, the case of Libya). Some members of the Security Council remained sceptical and had political concerns that R2P would encroach on state sovereignty, while giving their reserved support for the doctrine. For example, China stated that, 'All activities pertaining to protection should not … infringe upon the sovereignty and territorial integrity of Member States.' Likewise, the US objected under the guise of sovereignty: 'We would like to stress, however, that the primary responsibility for protecting civilians lies with States and their Governments and that international efforts should complement Government efforts rather than assume responsibility for them.' Here the message is less direct, but the issue remains that a state's business is its own and its population and internal matters should remain a matter for that state rather than the international community. This is also reflected in Egypt's comment, expressing its reservations over the involvement of the Security Council potentially violating the key precept of sovereignty:

> The Council should not expand its authority by establishing general policies for dealing with humanitarian issues and human rights … we are concerned … of the possible role of the Security Council in legislating and taking action under the so-called responsibility to protect.
>
> (UN General Assembly 2005: para 138–45)

As with the human rights doctrine, R2P was seen as a threat to state sovereignty and an intrusion into the private matters of a state.

Nonetheless, no 'state made any kind of formal reservation … R2P is therefore a concept that is supported in principle by all member states of the UN' (Bohlander 2012). The following section attempts to explore how human rights, international criminal justice and the R2P doctrine are interconnected and can be seen as formal efforts to resist state crime.

Connecting the dots

The development of international criminal law and a criminal justice system has formally extended the early human rights movement, by providing the enforcement mechanism as first envisioned by the framers of the human rights declaration. In this regard, the human rights movement has changed the socio-legal landscape. After all, '[n]early every international dispute today sooner or later implicates human rights' (Glendon 2001: xviii). Likewise, the cases currently under the jurisdiction of the ICC all contain charges of crimes that have come out of the human rights movement, including those listed under crimes against humanity. In this sense, the emerging international criminal justice system is more than a political process for the few; it is the continuation of the first steps towards developing a standard of living for humanity and reflects the pragmatic realization that a shift in ideology needed to be accompanied by enforcement mechanisms (that is, policy and legislation).

However, as previously noted, the greatest obstacle to a more balanced and universal application of the rule of law and enforcement of human rights continues to be sovereignty. Yet, I suggest that sovereignty itself is not the barrier, but that states' continuing to be wedded to fulfilling their self-interests (realpolitik) rather than the greater collective good is at the heart of the 'counter-resistance'. In other words, sovereignty is an easy umbrella for political leaders to use to fulfil their own selective interests that may be in contradiction to the broader movement. The obvious question, then, is whether or not this will ever change.

Given that human rights were once seen as meaningless paper and lofty idealism, and today rights abuses are now a commonly cited area of concern, I see R2P as a similar glimmer of hope. Specifically, while we now have international enforcement mechanisms that are far from ideal or universal in force, the ideology of R2P symbolizes what the UNDHR did back in the early and mid-1940s. It 'serves as a potent critic of existing practice' and could transform the reality of today where realpolitik and sovereignty guide foreign policy choices, including humanitarian interventions and aid (Glendon 2001: 165). Put simply, just as the human rights doctrine 'challenged the long-standing view that a sovereign state's treatment of its own citizens was that nation's business and no one else's', one can view R2P as a challenge to state sovereignty (Glendon 2001: xvi). Given the verbal commitment of all UN member states at this time, we may well see the day where this 'lofty set of principles' becomes justiciable and is reflected in the broader socio-legal landscape.

Concluding thoughts

The suggestion here is that the development of human rights and subsequent mechanisms of control that began nearly 70 years ago are a reflection of a broader ideological shift of an international ethos that includes strengthening an international moral solidarity against massive human rights violations, genocide, crimes against humanity, crimes of aggression and war crimes. As this ideological shift and the notion of human rights began to take form, the first movement towards formal resistance to state crime began. We now have a permanent international court that deals exclusively with heads of state and high-ranking officials that commit the most egregious crimes, and the R2P doctrine has gained momentum to which all states have, in principle, accepted and committed. Admittedly, such proclamations that international criminal law or even international criminal justice is or can become a powerful tool of resistance to state crime may appear overly utopian or idealistic. Nonetheless, as the universal human rights principles were developed in the mid-1940s through the UN, their impact on states' policies, legislation and implementation into justiciable treaties remained a distant dream for the founders, but today has crystallized into a reality (Glendon 2001). Consequently, the aim to end impunity and the development of international criminal law and its tenets of control over the past decades is a step forward and represents efforts to resist state crime.

Nonetheless, we should remain sceptical that a universal moral, ethical or legal obligation that takes primacy over states' self-interests will be a reality in the near future. Nor is it likely that we will see an end to state crime, or human rights for all being respected universally. Eradication of impunity or an end to the selective enforcement for heads of state and other high-ranking officials that orchestrate and/or mastermind the worst crimes is highly unlikely in the immediate future, given the historical record. A law for all and an end to impunity are not likely to occur over the course of the next few decades, and nor will the moral and ethical ideology to which these are embedded fully materialize within this timeframe. However, efforts to reduce and resist state crime should be the focus rather than complete eradication, given that most, if not all, criminologists would concur that there will not be a day where there is no crime of any sort, whether that be street crime or state crime.

Notes

1 I wish to thank Jeffrey Ian Ross, Elizabeth Stanley and Jude McCulloch for their comments on an earlier draft.
2 While human rights are often said to be a Westernized concept, the primary framers of the human rights doctrine included Carlos Romulo (a Filipino journalist and Pulitzer Prize winner), John Humphrey (Canadian director of the UN's Human Rights Division), Hansa Mehta (a feminist from India), Alexandre Bogomolov/Alexei Pavlov (delegates from the Soviet Union), Hernán Santa Cruz (from Chile), Peng-chun Chang (a Chinese philosopher and diplomat), René Cassin (a French jurist), Charles Malik (a Lebanese philosopher and diplomat) and Eleanor Roosevelt (first lady of the US). See Glendon (2001) for a detailed historical overview.
3 This included Australia, Belgium, Byelorussia, Chile, China, Egypt, France, India, Iran, Lebanon, Panama, the Philippines, Ukraine, the United Kingdom (UK), the United States (US), the former Union of Soviet Socialist Republics, Uruguay and Yugoslavia.
4 Namely the *International Covenant on Economic, Social and Cultural Rights 1966* and the *International Covenant on Civil and Political Rights 1966*.
5 In 1937, the League of Nations attempted to establish an International Criminal Court (ICC). Two International Conventions were concluded in Geneva on 16 November: the 'Prevention and Repression of Terrorism' and the 'Creation of an International Criminal Court' (League of Nations Document Archived C.547.m.384. 1937). A Diplomatic Conference was held for the proposed Charters that included 35 nation-state delegates; however, neither Convention obtained sufficient numbers for ratification (see Ferencz 1980; Rothe and Mullins 2006).

6 Additionally, we must not forget that the *raison d'être* of the retributive form of 'justice' is to establish the criminal responsibility of perpetrators.

7 Selective enforcement practices continue as the US and the UK remain free from prosecution and formal accountability for crimes committed in Iraq, and as Israel continues to illegally occupy Palestine while committing crimes against humanity, including political assassinations, among other violations. The process of accountability more often than not continues to 'run afoul of pragmatic concerns and the practices of realpolitik' (Guinn 2008: 5). After all, realpolitik plays an important role in regimes' decision-making processes for the support and/or application of the rule of law internally, as well as in relation to other regimes (Bassiouni 2008; Mullins and Rothe 2008). International political players more often than not 'provoke justice, but they may also be more willing to make compromises about justice to fulfill economic, strategic, or political motives' (Stanley 2008: 16). This, along with a host of other factors operating at the state level (such as claims of sovereignty) and international levels (such as a lack of jurisdictional cooperation or juristic interpretations of case law), has a direct impact, not only on enforcement but on the efficacy of international criminal justice.

References

Ashcroft, J. (1998) 'Is a UN International Criminal Court in the U.S. National Interest?', in *Hearing before the Subcommittee on Foreign Relations United States Senate: One Hundred Fifth Congress, 2nd Session*, 23 July, Washington: US Government Printing Office: S HRG, 105–724.

Bassiouni, M. C. (2008) *The Perennial Conflict between Realpolitik and the Pursuit of International Criminal Justice*, public speech, 2 April, University of Northern Iowa.

Bohlander, M. (2012) ' "There Is No Compulsion in Religion": Freedom of Religion, R2P and Crimes against Humanity at the Example of the Islamic Blasphemy Laws of Pakistan', *Journal of Islamic State Practice and International Law*, 8(1), 36–66.

Bolton, J. (2002) *The United States and the International Criminal Court*, Remarks to the Federalist Society, Washington, DC, 14 November, available at http://news.lp.findlaw.com/hdocs/docs/dos/dos111402wcstmnt.html.

Brody, R. (1999) 'One Year Later, The "Pinochet Precedent" Puts Tyrants on Notice', *The Boston Globe*, 15 October, available at www.hrw.org/news/1999/10/14/one-year-later-pinochet-precedent-puts-tyrants-notice, accessed 10 July 2012.

Cassese, A. (2008) *International Criminal Law* (2nd edition), New York: Oxford University Press.

Chang, P. (1947) *Human Rights Commission*, Drafting Committee, Second Session, E/CN./4/AC.1/SR.11, pp. 10.

Evans, D. G. (2007) 'Human Rights: Four Generations of Practice and Development', in A. Abdi and L. Schultz (eds), *Educating for Human Rights and Global Citizenship* (pp. 1–12), Albany, NY: State University of New York Press.

Ferencz, B. (1980) *An International Criminal Court, a Step Toward Peace: a Documentary Analysis. Vol. II: The Beginning of Wisdom.* New York: Oceana Publications.

Glendon, M. A. (2001) *A World Made New: Eleanor Roosevelt and The Universal Declaration of Human Rights*, New York, NY: Random House Publishing.

Guinn, D. (2008) *Human Rights Education: The Third Leg of Post-Conflict/Transitional Justice*, working paper available from Legal Scholars Research Network (p. 5), available at http://ssrn.com/author=199608.

Hampson, F. O. (2002) 'Preventive Diplomacy at the United Nations and Beyond', in F. O. Hampson and D. M. Malone (eds), *From Reaction to Conflict Prevention*, Boulder, CO: Lynne Rienner Publishers.

International Coalition for the Responsibility to Protect (2009) *Report on the General Assembly Plenary Debate on the Responsibility to Protect*, available at www.responsibilitytoprotect.org/ICRtoP%20Report-General_Assembly_Debate_on_the_Responsibility_to_Protect%20FINAL%209_22_09.pdf.

International Criminal Court (2002) *Note to Correspondents, Ceremony Marking Expected Establishment of International Criminal Court*, available at www.un.org/News/Press/docs/2002/note5725.doc.htm, accessed 12 July 2012.

League of Nations Document (1937) *Prevention and Repression of Terrorism and the Creation of an International Criminal Court*, archived C.547.m.384. 1937.

Lincoln, A. (1857) *The Writings of Abraham Lincoln* (vol. 2), available at www.classic-literature.co.uk/american-authors/19th-century/abraham-lincoln/the-writings-of-abraham-lincoln-02/ebook-page-112.asp.

Mullins, C. W. and Rothe, D. L. (2008) *Blood, Power, and Bedlam: International Criminal Law Violations in Post-colonial Africa*, New York, NY: Peter Lang Publishing.

Mullins, C. W. and Rothe, D. L. (2010) 'The Ability of the International Criminal Court to Deter Violations of International Criminal Law: A Theoretical Assessment', *International Criminal Law Review*, 10(5), 771–86.

Rothe, D. L. (2009) *State Criminality: The Crime of All Crimes*, Manham, MD: Lexington/Roman and Littlefield.

Rothe, D. L. and Mullins, C. W. (2006) 'The International Criminal Court and United States Opposition', *Crime, Law, and Social Change*, 45(3), 201–26.

Stanley, E. (2008) 'The Political Economy of Transitional Justice in Timor-Leste', in K. McEvoy and L. McGregor (eds), *Transitional Justice from Below*, Oxford: Hart Publishing.

UN Charter (1945) *Charter of the United Nations*, available at www.un.org/en/documents/charter/.

UN Declaration of Human Rights (1948) *The Universal Declaration of Human Rights*, available at www.un.org/en/documents/udhr/.

UN General Assembly (2005) *Resolution Adopted by the General Assembly*, 60/1 2005 World Summit Outcome, A/60/1, available at www.un.org/depts/dhl/resguide/r60.htm.

UN General Assembly (2009) *Resolution Adopted by the General Assembly: 63/308 The Responsibility to Protect*, A/RES/63/308, available at www.un.org/en/ga/63/resolutions.shtml.

UN Secretary General Dag Hammarkj'ld (1959) *United Nations Report of the Secretary General on the Work of the Organization*, General Assembly, Official Records: First through Fifty-Ninth Session, Supplement No. I. (A/14/1), United Nations.

United States Declaration of Independence (1776) *The Declaration of Independence: The Want, Will, and Hopes of the People*, available at www.ushistory.org/declaration/document/.

Ziegler, D. (1977) *War, Peace, and International Politics*, Boston, Toronto: Little, Brown and Company.

16 The master's tools

Can supranational law confront crimes of powerful states?

Raymond Michalowski

International judicial efforts to confront state crime have grown significantly in the last 20 years. Building on precedents established by the Nuremberg and Tokyo war crimes trials, in the 1990s the United Nations (UN) began using special tribunals to adjudicate claims of genocide, war crimes and crimes against humanity in the former Yugoslavia, Rwanda, Sierra Leone and Lebanon. In 2002, the UN took a further step by inaugurating the International Criminal Court (ICC) as a permanent, independent global court with jurisdiction over these crimes as defined by the Rome Statute (UN 1998).

The goals of this emergent supranational judicial system are to deny impunity to state actors suspected of, in the words of the Rome Statute, the 'most serious crimes of concern to the international community' and to deter similar crimes in other nations (Sands 2003). The existence of this Court is no small matter because it challenges the core image, and possibly the substance, of the Westphalian state – internal sovereignty (Krasner 1996).

Have we finally picked the lock behind which states have long inflicted grievous social injuries with impunity? Before determining the answer to this question, I suggest we give some consideration to Audre Lorde's (1984: 1) observation that 'the master's tools will never dismantle the master's house'. More specifically, can a legal apparatus designed by powerful capitalist states address the social harms, particularly the systemic social harms, committed by those states? I suggest that the current tendencies of supranational law may help remodel the master's house, creating a bit more room for a few who are now outside it. This, however, will still leave intact the basic structure that guarantees relative immunity for powerful states, and the targets of those states exposed to the chilly winds of relative disregard for their human rights. If this is the case, what new tools might help us build a new house, a new world, in which systemic crimes of powerful capitalist states, not just the crimes associated with war by weak states or extreme internal brutality, are confronted by an effective legal apparatus?

I will approach these questions outlined above from three vantage points: first, the conceptual challenges state crime poses for criminology; second, the relationship between state power and state criminality as reflected in current supranational law; and, third, the current necropolitics of international immigration control in the United States (US) as one example of the limits of the master's tools to confront state crime committed by powerful nations.

My concern with the third issue is more than academic. Since 2002, my research and work as a public criminologist has been focused on immigration-related conflicts in Arizona. These efforts have included ongoing ethnographic study of both anti-immigration and immigration rights organizations in the state and serving as a board member for the largest membership-based immigration rights non-government organization in Arizona. My role as an 'engaged observer' (Sanford *et al.* 2006) has given me a first-hand understanding of the challenge of confronting the state crimes of one of the world's most powerful nations.

I contend that newly emerged supranational judicial bodies suffer many of the same limitations as do national courts when it comes to confronting the systemic harms initiated or facilitated by powerful states. Since the rise of the modern state 10,000 years ago, law in all its forms has been indexed to the worldview of, and sometimes directly according to, the interests of dominant class factions in those states (Turk 1969; Chambliss and Siedman 1971; Michalowski 1985). Insofar as the systemic harms characteristic of any particular social formation are usually the collateral damage of the interests and/or worldview of those with the power to make law, it is predictable that many, if not most, of these harms will not only avoid being defined as crimes, but they will fall outside the under-standing of wrongfulness.

I am not suggesting a mechanistic relationship between dominant interests and legal outcomes. While instrumentalist (Quinney 1977) and structuralist (Althusser 1971) conceptions of the law helped fracture the hegemonic vision of law as social consensus, they left a number of sociological questions unanswered. Key concerns relate to how dominant consciousness becomes broadly accepted legal consciousness (Balbus 1977), how repressive social ideologies and practices become broadly normative (Foucault 1977) and how middling classes in modern capitalist societies come to align with elites in a shared project of repressing the most disadvantaged (Evans 2006; Frank 2005).

Given the historic dominance of elites in making law and shaping legal con-sciousness, I ground my analysis here on two propositions. First, insofar as con-temporary institutions of supranational law operate largely according to conceptions of individualism, property rights and human rights consistent with the dominant ideology of the world's most powerful capitalist states, the legal consciousness and legal mechanisms that serve as the foundation for supra-national law are ill equipped to address state crimes other than egregious acts that mimic routine crimes of greed or violence that can be blamed on individual wrongdoers. That is, supranational law, like national laws, is limited in its ability to address organizational deviance and the systemic harms that flow from it.

Second, even where powerful nations are held responsible for state crimes under international law, the enforcement mechanisms of the current suprana-tional justice system are weak relative to powerful states. Certainly, international courts may occasionally condemn the wrongful actions of powerful states. Those states, however, are relatively free to ignore these condemnations. A case in point was the ability of the US to ignore the ruling of the International Court of Justice that the US violated international law when it mined Nicaragua's main harbour during the Contra war (ICJ 1986).

The historic record suggests that powerful nations are relatively free from condemnation of their harmful acts, at least by formal institutions of supranational justice. For instance, the international community did little in the 1970s and 1980s as the US facilitated the overthrow of governments and promoted military dictatorships in a number of countries in Central and South America at a cost of hundreds of thousands of civilian deaths. While it is arguable that the US violated international law repeatedly in Latin America during these decades, the consequences were nil.

Examining a more contemporary context, as I will show, beginning in 2005, right-wing organizations in the US gave birth to the idea of 'attrition through enforcement', forming an increasingly successful political movement aimed at ethnically cleansing individual states of Latino immigrants under the guise of enforcing immigration law. Although attrition through enforcement bears important resemblances to the crime of ethnic cleansing, the architects and enforcers of this policy have little to fear from supranational institutions of justice.

In short, the current system of supranational justice is ill equipped to confront the systemic crimes of powerful states. To do so effectively will require a fundamental redesign of the existing system for global governance which removes impunity from powerful states and their leaders. The existing framework of human rights laws and conventions may serve as a foundation for such a rethinking. However, the current system for ensuring that all states are held to these laws and conventions leaves much to be desired.

State crime and the limits of criminology

The growth in supranational instruments for prosecuting criminal state actors has spawned a parallel growth in what has been termed 'supranational criminology', which offers 'a criminological approach to international crimes such as war crimes, crimes against humanity, torture, genocide and other gross human rights violations that do not readily fall within the contemporary definitional scope of international crimes' (Supranational Criminology 2011). One of the challenges to building a supranational criminology of state crime that can address 'violations that do not readily fall within the contemporary definitional scope of international crimes' is the legalist baggage of criminology.

As a method of inquiry, criminology is organically ill suited to address either the causes or the control of state crimes. The reason for this is deeply embedded in the basic understanding of criminology as 'the scientific study of the making of laws, the breaking of laws, and society's reaction to the breaking of law' (Sutherland and Cressy 1992: 4). This definition limits criminological inquiry both conceptually and operationally. Conceptually, the standard definition of crime is entirely juridical. That is, every element is indexed to law, as in *law*-making, *law*-breaking and *law* enforcement. Operationally, it has focused primarily on the making, breaking and enforcement of laws governing prosaic crimes committed by members of disadvantaged classes. The making of laws, not to mention the systems and processes that lie behind law-making, are largely lost from view.

Supranational criminologists have broken with the operational history of criminology by focusing on crimes committed at the uppermost rather than the lower reaches of nation-states. For them, 'crime' involves the commission of state actions prohibited by international human rights laws and standards. Like more orthodox criminologists, however, the questions of 'Why these laws?' 'Why these institutions?' and 'Why these particular defendants?' have received less attention. By focusing on violations of existing laws rather than questions of how and why laws get made, criminology blinds itself to the political essence of law, and therefore the political character of all crime. This reliance on law within criminology has influenced the study of state crime.

While more critical of states than orthodox criminologists, supranational criminologists also tend to *begin* with laws made by states or states acting in concert through international treaties. This reliance on *some* legal warrant is deeply ingrained in the study of state crime. In 1989, for instance, William Chambliss (1989: 183) characterized state crimes as 'acts *defined by law* as criminal and committed by state officials in the pursuit of their jobs as representatives of the state' (emphasis added). By relying on the state to determine what fits under the state crime umbrella, this definition risks falling into what I have elsewhere termed the 'juridical trap' of allowing states to determine the subject matter of supranational criminology (Michalowski 2009). This point was originally made about criminology in general by the pioneering criminologist Thorsten Sellin (1938) over 70 years ago, and served as a foundation for the rise of what Cohen (1986) termed anti-criminology in the US and Britain (see, for example, Platt 1974; Schwendinger and Schwendinger 1970; Taylor *et al.* 1975). Its most recent expression can be found in efforts to establish a new field of zemiology, that is, the study of harm (Hillyard *et al.* 2004). Yet for all this, critical criminological inquiry remains on the margins of criminological consciousness (Agnew 2011).

Both international law and supranational criminology are further limited by apprehending crime as *individual* behaviour and defining the task of criminology as unravelling the aetiology of that behaviour. Some analysts have argued that the study of criminal aetiology is the only topic of criminology (Siegel 2009: 4–5). Whether in law or in criminology, an emphasis on individual behaviour means that deviant state or corporate *organizations* will not receive an equal share of attention, despite the breadth of the social injuries they cause.

Following the precedents of the war crimes trials held after World War II, contemporary international prosecutions of state crime target governmental leaders who can be identified as directly responsible for discrete violations of international laws. Like the legal systems of the nation-states that are their foundation, supranational institutions of justice have little warrant to target *systems* that produce grave chronic harms, whether it is the destruction of life ways and cultures due to resource exploitation, the massive transfer of wealth into the hands of a small global financial class through 'structural adjustments', or the deaths and injuries resulting from militarization of the boundaries between the Global North and the Global South.

By focusing on discrete violations of international law, supranational juridical bodies have generated a defendant pool whose racial composition mirrors that found in many national criminal courts in the Global North. A visit to the 'current cases' page of the ICC website reveals an array of dark-skinned defendants similar to a 'perp walk' in any US criminal court (ICC 2011). I am not arguing that the ICC is a consciously racist court. It is, however, a court whose parameters and legal warrant make it far easier to take action against leaders of 'failed' African or Middle Eastern states than leaders of powerful states responsible for equal or greater harm.

Admittedly, under contemporary legal consciousness, it is easier to recognize the immediate and brutal deaths and social injuries suffered by the victims of dictatorial leaders in failing states than those caused by technocrats in powerful ones who design and implement wars of choice, global torture networks or planet-killing systems of production in pursuit of the continued political-economic dominance of the Global North (see Kramer, Chapter 4, this volume). This, however, is a consequence of politically constructed consciousness, not a reflection of an objective comparison of the number of bodies broken or lives destroyed by failed state dictators as compared to First World technocrats.

As a positivist mode of inquiry, criminology, much like modern legal systems, tends to search for linear cause-effect relationships between offenders and victims. This results in a central paradigm whose primary questions are whether and why individuals will or will not break the law. There is little room within this paradigm for questions about political-economic or cultural processes that precede and shape law-making, for examining organizations as key actors or for interrogating the underlying nature of the state. Insofar as it is difficult to address the causes and control of state crime without considering each of these un- or anti-criminological questions, criminologists seeking to confront state crime must, perforce, seek to fashion new intellectual tools that differ from those of the master.

The master's supranational tools

Tilly (1985: 169) contends that states are the 'largest examples of organized crime' insofar as state-making and its essential corollary, war-making, are 'quintessential protection rackets with the advantage of legitimacy'. States, however, are more than criminal enterprises. They also facilitate the creation and operation of infrastructures that enable some, and often many, to access public goods such as water, waste disposal, power and transportation networks, education, some degree of healthcare, public protection and arenas (such as courts) for non-violent dispute resolution. That is, states are contradictory social processes.

The core function of any state is to manage the conflict between elites and masses while preserving the central contours of an existing political-economic order that creates those elites (Jessop 1990). Where this conflict is between ruling and subordinate tribes, proto-states manage conflict through apparent adherence to 'custom' (Diamond 1981). When it is between serfs and landholders, these class tensions are funnelled through laws of vassalage and courts of the manor (Cam 1962). Since the mid-twentieth century, conflicts between capital and labour in capitalist states have been most often managed through actual or notional democracy, relief policies designed to ameliorate the worst consequences of the boom-and-bust cycles characteristic of capitalism, and strategic mixtures of social welfare and criminalization to control surplus populations (Rusche and Kirchheimer 1939; Michalowski 1985; Gordon *et al.* 1982; Michalowski and Carlson 1999).

A key question for supranational criminologists is whether international law can intervene in these state-mediated conflicts between capital and labour in ways that minimize the crimes of power that emerge from core political-economic arrangements in powerful states. That is, to what extent can supranational law control the harms resulting from the dominant arrangements in the core states that serve as the primary architects and funders of supranational institutions of justice?

I am not positing a strict instrumentalist vision of the state or of international law. In capitalist political economies, juridical measures have long been used, often over the objections or fractions of economic or political elites, to ameliorate the troublesome consequences of capitalism. These include deep recessions (such as bank bailouts or economic stimuli), political or economic corruption (such as the prosecutions of influence peddling or dishonest accounting practices) and embarrassing uses of state power (such as prosecutions of soldiers for the torture or execution of non-combatants). However, these controls typically leave the core processes of private sector accumulation and the state's monopoly over violence in place. Insofar as they do not transform core processes, legal controls over harms inflicted by elites rarely prevent the harms from reoccurring.

State or supranational laws that punish wrongful behaviours committed under colour of state law (such as torture, non-judicial execution or the maltreatment of prisoners of war) may threaten a particular *government*. They do not, however, challenge the *state* itself. Rather, they help preserve the legitimacy of the extant state form by dramatizing that the state will not tolerate certain wrongful behaviours. It is the political equivalent of the magician who keeps her audience watching her left hand while the right one actually performs the trick.

States commit all manner of inhumanities. States and the international judicial systems they create, however, only prosecute a small fraction of them. Through aerial strikes and destruction of material, social and legal infrastructures, for instance, the US killed, caused to be killed or caused to die at least one million civilians in Iraq and Afghanistan during the invasion and occupation of these countries (Mapreport 2011; Kramer and Michalowski 2005). Nevertheless,

I doubt that any US leader will ever have to answer to any national or international court for these deaths. By contrast, in response to embarrassing reports of torture and brutality at the Abu Ghraib prison in occupied Iraq, the US government moved quickly to punish low-level guards for their depredations (Human Rights Watch 2011). Much like staring at pictures of a train wreck, many people were captivated by the media reportage of the Abu Ghraib tortures and subsequent prosecutions, with Lindy England and Charles Graner serving as poster children for US soldiers gone bad (Zernike 2005). Like a magician, this widely publicized selective prosecution of a few 'bad soldiers' directed attention away from the larger criminal enterprise of the Iraq war itself by dramatizing the US government as a defender of international norms governing the treatment of prisoners.

The new institutions of supranational justice face the danger of becoming a similar magician's trick. To date, they have directed attention exclusively to high-ranking civilian and military leaders of failed or weak states. By prosecuting a small number of offenders from weak states, these courts unwittingly reaffirm that state crime is largely a problem of bad leaders. This focus on failed or collapsing states leaves the social harms committed by leaders of powerful nations not only out of legal range, but out of public consciousness as well.

If leaders of powerful nations who kill and destroy are immune from prosecution *as individuals*, the harms caused by the larger *systems* they manage are even further beyond the reach of supranational legal control. As I write this at the beginning of 2012, a small group of financiers and political leaders representing the interests of finance capital in Europe and the US are deciding how much more 'austerity' they will demand the Greek government impose on its citizens to ensure that the Greek state will not default on its debt – that is, that it will not begin a process that could significantly harm international finance capital (Worstall 2011). The reality is that ordinary Greeks, just like people in every other country subjected to the 'structural adjustments' demanded by finance capital, are being asked to accept punishing economic losses to ensure the continued profitability of international finance.

Greece is but one example of how states in cooperation with global finance capital force an upward distribution of wealth in the contemporary global order. There is, however, neither legal consciousness nor legal mechanisms adequate to address economic tyranny as criminal activity. This gap between harm and legal condemnation is not new.

State crime, past and prologue

What has been the history of efforts to confront state crime? Certainly, many forms of political and economic brutality have fallen under the control of state law in the last 200 years. However, many of these depredations have been outlawed only after they were no longer essential for economic growth or the preservation of state power, or they had become anachronistic impediments to new trajectories for the development of state and capital.

The British outlawed international slavery only after they had secured their own empire, and found slavery in other countries, particularly the US, to be threatening Britain's competitive edge in the global marketplace. Slavery was outlawed in the US only after a brutal internecine war that pitted the new trajectory of machine capitalism against the dying remnants of an anachronistic agrarian capitalism that stood as a material and cultural impediment to an emergent industrial system based on wage rather than chattel slavery (Drescher 2009). The government-endorsed and sometimes government-executed brutalities against workers in factories, fields, mines and ships during the early decades of industrial capitalism gave way to unionization and a degree of labour rights only after industries had been fully capitalized through the brutal extraction of surplus value, and the subsequent growth in productive capacity required the working class to be transformed into a consuming class (Sklar 1988).

Leaders in the US and Britain eventually condemned the genocidal killings in Bosnia, Rwanda, Darfur or East Timor. However, there is no similar condemnation of their own mass murder of civilians in Iraq for the most heinous of motives: securing Western access to oil (Klare 2005). Nor do they condemn the brutalities of other nations as long as those brutalities are consistent with the goals of the US or United Kingdom (UK). The slaughter of a half-million Indonesians in a US- and UK-supported anti-communist pogrom in the 1950s was not called brutality but political progress (Nevins 2008). The killings and disappearances of tens of thousands of Argentineans, Chileans, Guatemalans, Nicaraguans and El Salvadorans at the hands of US-supported dictatorships, instead of being condemned as crimes against humanity, were portrayed by the US government as a justifiable part of the fight against communism (Hermann 1999). Similarly, even though the illegal US war in Vietnam caused over a million civilian deaths, it is increasingly the focus of a revisionist history that claims it was a 'good war' that began the unravelling of communism worldwide (Michalowski and Dubisch 2001).

Since the mid-sixteenth century, the systemic engine of social order in the Global North has been the accumulation of capital. There have been many political-economic variants of capitalism, ranging from *laissez-faire* to state capitalism. Nevertheless, whatever capitalism's particular institutional manifestation, capitalist states, acting individually or in concert, will rarely criminalize harmful actions by state actors or key operatives of the capitalist social order if doing so would seriously threaten either capital accumulation or state legitimacy. This extends to the international arena as well. To the extent that institutions of supranational justice are created by powerful states acting in concert, they will rarely criminalize harmful actions by powerful states that are part of that law-making process. The current efforts of the world's wealthiest and most powerful nations to close their borders to migrants from the Global South are a telling case in point.

The necropolitics of immigration control

When it comes to state crime, national leaders in the US, European Union (EU) and Australia are rhetorical hypocrites. A key, contemporary example of this hypocrisy is their immigration control policies. National leaders in these countries condemn genocide and war crimes in poor nations while simultaneously deploying strategies of border militarization and internal immigration enforcement that result in deaths, injuries and dehumanization for millions of immigrants seeking to escape the 'severe breakdowns of economic, political and social structures' resulting from the neoliberal global economic policies of the very nations to which displaced people are now fleeing (Tactaquin 2011).

This normalization of state violence against immigrants is a vivid example of what Mbmebe (2003) termed 'necropolitics' – the subjugation of the power of life to the power of death. Combining Foucault's (2003) concept of 'governmentality' with Schmitt's (1932/2004) concept of the 'state of exception', Mbembe (2003: 11) contends that the essence of the political state is the power to determine 'who may live and who must die'. As I have noted elsewhere (Michalowski 2010: 28), necropolitics in advanced capitalist societies means that:

1   Capital accumulation is privileged above life.
2   A culture of limitlessness pervades dominant consciousness.
3   Geography and human worth are racialized.
4   Racialization justifies the dispossession, subjugation and 'letting die' of devalued races.
5   Dominant class interests are defined as national interests.
6   Nationalism justifies violence to protect 'the homeland'.
7   The use of nationalist violence relies on 'states of exception'.

When applied to the growing challenges posed by irregular immigration, the necropolitics of advanced capitalist states have brutal consequences. One is an increasing number of lives lost and bodies injured as desperate people seek to cross increasingly dangerous militarized boundary lines around affluent geopolitical spaces such as the US, the EU and Australia (Michalowski 2007; Weber and Pickering 2011).

Unlike the targets of special tribunals and the ICC, the wealthy nations of the North are not bombing, gassing or directly slaughtering masses of immigrants – though they do sometimes shoot them, as the tragic case of Spanish-bound immigrants in Morocco demonstrated (Tremlett 2005). These states, however, combine neoliberal economic policies that destroy traditional livelihoods with militarized boundaries and restrictive immigration policies to create a perfect storm of human suffering.

Many people die, are injured or are reduced to almost nothing in their efforts to flee the inadequate economies and sometimes failing governments of their home countries. The harm done to immigrants is not inevitable. It is the direct result of the intensifying and increasingly militarized efforts of wealthy nations to keep them out. The justifications for doing so are many, ranging from economic protectionism of the domestic working class; to protection of national culture, values and language; to protection against a rising tide of foreign-bred crime and disease; to stopping the infiltration of terrorists (Beck 1996; Dougherty

2004; Hanson 2003; Hayworth 2006). The necropolitics of immigration policy rely on claims that these exceptional threats warrant exceptional measures – that is, they justify the death and suffering of immigrants as 'necessary' in order to preserve national integrity. This is, of course, the same logic that has been used repeatedly to justify genocide (Alvarez 2001).

Another consequence of the necropolitics of immigration is widespread violation of the fundamental rights set forth in the UN Declaration of Human Rights and other international covenants and standards, such as those set by the International Labour Organization and the UN Committee on Economic, Social and Cultural Rights. While space does not permit a full consideration of this issue here, I suggest that the immigration control policies of many nations of the Global North routinely violate Article 6 (personhood before law), Article 9 (prohibition against arbitrary arrest, detention or exile), Article 11 (presumption of innocence), Article 13 (freedom of movement), Article 14 (right to asylum) and Article 23 (right to work) of the UN Declaration of Human Rights.

The normalization of ethnic cleansing

In recent years, an ominous trend has emerged in the US necropolitics of immigration in the form of 'attrition through enforcement'. This policy first emerged in 2005 in response to the possibility that the Kennedy–McCain 'Comprehensive Immigration Reform Bill' become law. Although nearly all of the Bill's 11 separate headings promoted increased enforcement of immigration laws, Title VII would have established a new visa category, H-5B. This visa would have provided access to a seven-year pathway to citizenship for irregular migrants without criminal records who had been residing in the US prior to the law's passage (Visalaw 2005).

Anti-immigration activists reacted quickly, labelling the Bill an 'amnesty' for criminal immigrants. Mark Kirkorian (2005), the head of the restrictionist Center for Immigration Studies, responded by proposing a 'Third Way', which he called 'attrition through enforcement'. He argued that it would be possible to shrink the population of illegal immigrants through a combination of consistent enforcement of immigration law, increased deportations and *'most importantly*, by increasing the number of illegals already here who give up and deport themselves' (emphasis added). Several months later, Kirkorian (2006) expanded on how to convince illegal immigrants to 'give up and deport themselves'. The strategy would:

> Prevent illegals from being able to embed themselves in our society [by] denying them access to jobs, identification, housing, and in general making it as difficult as possible for an illegal immigrant to live a normal life here, so as to persuade a large number of them to give up and self-deport.

While 'facially neutral', this policy has significant racial impacts. In 2005, 5.6 million of the estimated 11.5 million irregular migrants in the US came from

Mexico and another 2.5 million came from other countries in Latin America. At the time the attrition through enforcement strategy was devised, Latinos comprised 78 per cent of Kirkorian's target population of 'illegal immigrants' (Pew Hispanic Center 2006). Insofar as it is designed to drive a significant proportion of a targeted ethnic population out of the country, attrition through enforcement, I argue, is a form of ethnic cleansing. To those who claim that the strategy of attrition through enforcement involves nothing more than enforcing existing law, I would note that the pre-Holocaust narrowing of social life for Jews in Nazi Germany was justified as simply enforcing the Nuremburg Laws (Evans 2006). I want to be clear that I am not saying attrition through enforcement and the Nazi Nuremburg Laws are equivalent. They are, however, similar in their general design to change the ethnic composition of a society by making life unlivable for an ethnically identifiable population.

In April 2010, with the support of White America groups such as the Council of Conservative Citizens that has its origins in the White Citizens Councils of the 1960s, anti-immigration activists and legislators in Arizona were able to transform the idea of attrition through enforcement into law by passing the *Support Our Law Enforcement and Safe Neighborhoods Act*, colloquially known as SB 1070 (Doty 2010). SB 1070 sought to drive irregular Latino migrants from the state by: (1) defining the federal civil violation of failing to possess appropriate immigration documents as a criminal act under Arizona state law; (2) authorizing local police to question and detain anyone they suspected of being an illegal immigrant; (3) making it a crime to 'harbour' or 'transport' unauthorized immigrants, thus criminalizing many of the everyday social relations between irregular migrants and citizens or legal residents; and (4) prohibiting cities from passing laws that would limit the powers of their police departments to enforce immigration law.

In May 2010, Federal District Judge Susan Bolton placed sections of the law under temporary injunction. By that time, however, the virulent anti-immigration rhetoric from legislators and anti-immigrant activists leading up to the Bill's passage had already changed the social landscape. While unauthorized residents of Arizona may feel the greatest threat from SB 1070, there are few everyday markers that distinguish an unauthorized Mexican, Guatemalan or other Latino from a US citizen or legal resident of similar ethnic heritage. As a result, Latino residents, whatever their citizenship status, feel the stigma of Arizona's anti-immigration laws inscribed on their skin.

The fear surrounding SB 1070 has already resulted in a significant narrowing of life space within many Arizona Latino communities. Citizens and legal residents, as well as unauthorized migrants, have increasingly come to perceive public space not as safe space, but as dangerous places filled with risks of unpleasant and possibly life-altering encounters (McDowell and Wonders 2009). The result is that a growing portion of Arizona's Latino population has elected to live 'deeper in the social shadows', shadows increasingly devoid of many of the normal components of routine existence, such as work, education, healthcare, police protection, public services, public recreation, a driver's licence and the ability to shop for healthy food or to take one's children to play in a local park (Hardy *et al.* 2012; McDowell and Wonders 2009). This is the kind of narrowed life that supporters of attrition through enforcement hope will lead to widespread self-deportation.

Arizona's campaign of ethnic cleansing was only the first. In 2011, the states of Alabama and Georgia followed suit with even harsher copycat laws. However, because this particular exercise of necropolitics is being committed within a powerful capitalist nation, it is not recognized as a topic for scrutiny by supranational institutions of justice. In this case, the master's tools lie unused, while brutalization continues.

In conclusion

Based on the analysis above, I suspect that effective resistance to normalized state deviance cannot come from the current institutions of supranational justice. It can only come from mass social movements that demand not simply after-the-fact punishment of state criminals, but rather a recalibration of the political-economic structures that facilitate systemic state crime.

The Occupy Wall Street movement that emerged in September 2011 represents one such example, although its efficacy remains unknown at the time of writing. What it does point to, however, is that effectively challenging systemic state crime will require structural change rather than reliance on international courts created by the very states we are seeking to restrain. Systemic state crimes in the contemporary world demand that we challenge and change the structure of state power and the neoliberal consciousness on which it rests.

As Polyani (1944) noted almost 70 years ago, economies grounded in self-interest are guaranteed to produce state brutalities, either to protect capitalist markets from the people or to protect the people from capitalist markets. Criminologists of state crime need to think long and hard about how to escape this trap. Relying on existing governmental institutions to suppress the worst predations of states or markets, I argue, is not the way. Rather, the way leads through fundamental reconsiderations of power in both government and economy, and probably the devolution of both those forms of power to smaller social units in which economic life and civic life are linked into a coherent whole.

In the meantime, critical criminologists of state crime can continue to play an important role by using existing human rights frameworks to call attention to the normalized destruction of human bodies and human spirits in the name of 'economic growth' and 'national interests'. Our role may be much like that of the boy who proclaimed that the emperor has no clothes. However, our efforts may also help increasing numbers of people understand the nakedness of the neoliberal promise and the need to mobilize to create another, better way.

References

Agnew, R. (2011) *Toward a Unified Criminology: Integrating Assumptions about Crime, People and Society*, New York: NYU Press.

Althusser, L. (1971) 'Ideology and Ideological State Apparatuses', in *Lenin and Philosophy, and Other Essays* (trans. B. Brewster) (pp. 127–88), London: New Left Books.

Alvarez, A. (2001) *Governments, Citizens, and Genocide: A Comparative and Interdisciplinary Approach*, Bloomington: Indiana University Press.

Balbus, I. (1977) 'Commodity Form and Legal Form: An Essay on the "Relative Autonomy" of the Law', *Law and Society Review*, 11, 571–88.

Beck, R. (1996) *The Case Against Immigration: The Moral, Economic, Social and Environmental Reasons for Reducing U.S. Immigration Back to Traditional Levels*, New York: W. W. Norton.

Cam, H. (1962) *Law-Finders and Law Makers in Medieval England: Collected Studies in Legal and Constitutional History*, London: A. M. Kelley.

Chambliss, W. (1989) 'State-organized Crime', *Criminology*, 27, 183–208.

Chambliss, W. and Siedman, R. (1971) *Law, Order, and Power*, Reading, MA: Addison-Wesley.

Cohen, S. (1986) *Against Criminology*, New Brunswick, NJ: Transaction Publishers.

Diamond, S. (1981) *In Search of the Primitive*, New Brunswick, NJ: Transaction Publishers.

Doty, R. (2010) 'SB1070 and the Banality of Evil', *Z Magazine*, October, available at www.zcommunications.org/sb1070-and-the-banality-of-evil-by-roxanne-doty, accessed 12 December 2010.

Dougherty, J. (2004) *Illegals: The Imminent Threat Posed by Our Unsecured U.S.–Mexico Border*, Nashville, TN: WND Books.

Drescher, S. (2009) *Abolition: A History of Slavery and Anti-Slavery*, New York: Cambridge University Press.

Evans, R. (2006) *The Third Reich in Power*, New York: Penguin.

Foucault, M. (1977) *Discipline and Punish: The Birth of the Prison*, New York: Vintage.

Foucault, M. (2003) *Security, Territory and Population: Lectures at the College de France, 1977–1978* (trans. G. Burchell), New York: Picador.

Frank, T. (2005) *What's the Matter with Kansas: How Conservatives Won the Heart of America*, New York: Metropolitan Books.

Gordon, D., Edwards, R. and Reich, M. (1982) *Segmented Work: Divided Workers – The Historical Transformation of Labor in the United States*, New York: Cambridge.

Hanson, V. (2003) *Mexifornia: A State of Becoming*, San Francisco: Encounter Books.

Hardy, L., Getrich, C., Quay, A., Quezada, J. and Michalowski, R. (2012) 'A Call for Further Research on the Impact of Immigration Enforcement on Public Health', *American Journal of Public Health*, 102(7), 1250–3.

Hayworth, J. D. (2006) *Whatever It Takes: Illegal Immigration, Border Security and the War on Terror*, Lanham, MD: Regenery Press.

Hermann, E. S. (1999) *The Real Terror Network: Terrorism in Fact and Propaganda*, Boston: South End Press.

Hillyard, P., Pantazis, C., Tombs, S. and Gordon, D. (2004) *Beyond Criminology: Taking Harm Seriously*, London: Pluto Press.

Human Rights Watch (2011) *Getting Away With Torture: The Bush Administration and Mistreatment of Detainees*, New York: Human Rights Watch.

ICC (International Criminal Court) (2011) 'All Cases', available at www.icc-cpi.int/Menus/ICC/Situations+and+Cases/Cases/, accessed 8 October 2011.

ICJ (International Court of Justice) (1986) *Case Concerning The Military and Paramilitary Activities In and Against Nicaragua (Nicaragua* v. *United States Of America)*, Judgment of 27 June 1986, available at www.icj-cij.org/docket/index.php?sum=367&code=nus&p1 =3&p2=3& case=70&k=66&p3=5, accessed 6 May 2008.

Jessop, B. (1990) *State Theory: Putting the Capitalist State in its Place*, London: Pluto Press.

Kirkorian, M. (2005) 'Downsizing Illegal Immigration: A Strategy of Attrition through Enforcement', Center for Immigration Studies (May), available at www.cis.org/articles/2005/back605.html, accessed 24 September 2011.

Kirkorian, M. (2006) 'A Third Way', Center for Immigration Studies, available at www.cis.org/node/419, accessed 24 September 2011.

Klare, M. (2005) *Blood and Oil*, New York: Penguin.

Kramer, R. and Michalowski, R. (2005) 'War, Aggression and State Crime: A Criminological Analysis of the Invasion and Occupation of Iraq', *British Journal of Criminology*, 45, 446–69.

Krasner, S. D. (1996) 'Compromising Westphalia', *International Security*, 20(3) (Winter, 1995–96), 115–51.

Lorde, A. (1984) 'Master's Tools Will Never Dismantle the Master's House', in *Sister Outsider*, New York: The Crossing Press.

McDowell, M. and Wonders, N. (2009) 'Keeping Migrants in Their Place: Technologies of Control and Racialized Public Space in Arizona', *Social Justice*, 36(2), 54–72.

Mapreport (2011) 'Iraq, Collateral Damage Timeline', available at www.mapreport.com/citysubtopics/iraq-w-z.html, accessed 6 September 2011.

Mbembe, A. (2003) 'Necropolitics', *Public Culture*, 15(2), 11–40.

Michalowski, R. (1985) *Order, Law and Crime*, New York: Random House.

Michalowski, R. (2007) 'Border Militarization and Migrant Suffering: A Case of Transnational Social Injury', *Social Justice*, 32(2), 62–76.

Michalowski, R. (2009) 'Power, Crime and Criminology in the New Imperial Age', *Crime, Law and Social Change*, 51(3–4), 303–25.

Michalowski, R. (2010) 'In Search of "State" and "Crime" in State Crime Studies', in W. Chambliss, R. Michalowski and R. Kramer (eds), *State Crime in the Global Age*, London: Willan.

Michalowski, R. and Carlson, S. (1999) 'Unemployment, Imprisonment and Social Structures of Accumulation: Historical Contingency in the Rusche–Kirchheimer Hypothesis', *Criminology*, 37(2), 217–50.

Michalowski, R. and Dubisch, J. (2001) *Run for the Wall: Remembering Vietnam on a Motorcycle Pilgrimage*, New Brunswick, NJ: Rutgers University Press.

Nevins, J. (2008) *Dying to Live: A Story of U.S. Immigration in an Age of Global Apartheid*, San Francisco: City Lights Books.

Pew Hispanic Center (2006) 'The Size and Characteristics of the Unauthorized Migrant Population in the U.S.', Research Report, 7 March, available at http://pewhispanic.org/files/reports/61.pdf, accessed 25 October 2010.

Platt, T. (1974) 'Prospects for a Radical Criminology in the United States', *Crime and Social Justice*, 1(1), 2–10.

Polanyi, K. (1944) *The Great Transformation: The Political and Economic Origins of Our Time*, New York: Rinehart.

Quinney, R. (1977) *Class, State and Crime*, Providence, RI: Longman.

Rusche, G. and Kirchheimer, O. (1939) *Punishment and Social Structure*, New York: Russell and Russell.

Sands, P. (2003) *From Nuremburg to The Hague: The Future of International Criminal Justice*, New York: Cambridge.

Sanford, V., Anjel-Ajani, A. and Bourgois, P. (2006) *The Engaged Observer: Anthropology, Advocacy and Activism*, New Brunswick, NJ: Rutgers University Press.

Schmitt, C. (1932/2004) *Legality and Legitimacy* (trans. of original J. Seitzer), Durham, NC: Duke University Press.

Schwendinger, H. and Schwendinger, J. (1970) 'Defenders of Order or Guardians of Human Rights?' *Issues in Criminology*, 5(2), 123–57.

Sellin, T. (1938) *Culture, Conflict and Crime*, New York: Social Science Research Council.

Siegel, L. (2009) *Criminology*, Boston: Wadsworth/Cengage.

Sklar, M. (1988) *The Corporate Reconstruction of American Capitalism, 1890–1916: The Market, the Law, and Politics*, New York: Cambridge University Press.

Supranational Criminology (2011) 'A Platform for Supranational Criminology', available at www.supranationalcriminology.org/framespage.htm, accessed 12 August 2011.

Sutherland, E. and Cressey, D. (1992) *Principles of Criminology* (11th edition), Lanham, MD: AltaMira Press.

Tactaquin, C. (2011) 'Immigration and Globalization: The UN Conference Against Racism Takes on Migrant Issues', *CorpWatch*, available at http://corpwatch.org/article.php?id=375, accessed 2 September 2011.

Taylor, I., Walton, P. and Young, J. (1975) *Critical Criminology*, London: Routledge and Kegan Paul.

Tilly, C. (1985) 'War Making and State Making as Organized Crime', in P. Evans, D. Rueschemeyer, and T. Skocpol (eds), *Bringing the State Back In*, Cambridge: Cambridge University Press.

Tremlett, G. (2005) 'Immigrants Killed by Bullets from Morocco', *Guardian*, 30 September, A17.

Turk, A. (1969) *Criminality and the Legal Order*, New York, NY: Rand McNally.

United Nations (1998) 'Rome Statute', available at www.icc-cpi.int/NR/rdonlyres/ADD16852-AEE9-4757-ABE7-9CDC7CF02886/283503/RomeStatutEng1.pdf, accessed 7 March 2011.

Visalaw (2005) 'Summary of the Secure America and Orderly Immigration Act', available at www.visalaw.com/05may4/3may405.html, accessed 6 October 2010.

Weber, L. and Pickering, S. (2011) *Globalization and Borders: Death at the Global Frontier*, Basingstoke, UK: Palgrave.

Worstall, T. (2011) 'Explaining the Greek Debt Crisis', *Forbes*, 16 August, available at www.forbes.com/sites/timworstall/2011/06/16/explaining-the-greek-debt-crisis/, accessed 30 August 2011.

Zernike, K. (2005) 'Behind Failed Abu Ghraib Plea, a Tangle of Bonds and Betrayals', *New York Times*, 10 May, available at www.nytimes.com/2005/05/10/national/10graner.html?ref=charlesagranerjr, accessed 12 June 2005.

17 Beyond state crime

Jude McCulloch and Elizabeth Stanley

This collection captures only a small sample of the continuing history of resistance to state crime. The chapters reflect on the nature of resistance, its diversity, effectiveness, limitations and ubiquitousness across place and through time. In the past, state crime scholars have made great advances in defining, cataloguing and speaking against state crime. Such endeavours expose, defy or undermine the 'denial' that typically goes hand in hand with such crimes (see Cohen 2001). As we argue in Chapter 1, however, highlighting state crimes runs the danger of representing state power as invincible. Although contrary to intention, state crime scholarship may impact on audiences in ways that erode rather than support people's capacity to resist.

The chapters in this volume demonstrate that state power is not absolute, and when states misuse their power they inevitably produce resistance. State crime and resistance are imbricated in a 'dance' (White) of 'intimate relations' (Sentas and Nadarajah) where each moves, reshapes and reforms in relation to the other. If, as critical criminologists argue, crime and crime control are co-produced (Anthony and Cunneen 2008: 1), such co-production is equally true of state crime and resistance. Remembering, acknowledging and studying resistance to state crime extends state crime literature in ways designed to recognize and support the power of people to resist.

Opposition, as we argue in Chapter 1, is one of the essential criteria of resistance. Likewise, the type of criminology reflected in these chapters is partly defined by what it opposes (see Stubbs 2008: 8). The criminology practised by the contributors to this volume opposes a narrow definition of crime that elides crimes of the powerful and accepts state-centred definitions of crime. Critical criminology and the study of state crime, in particular, have repudiated the mainstream focus on the individual as deviant and focused instead on the grave harms committed by states. State crime and resistance as conceived in this collection are located within broader social and political contexts. In defining, describing and reflecting on resistance to state crime this collection seeks, among other things, to interrogate how criminology can most effectively advance the project of resisting state crime in solidarity with the many social movements, civil society organizations, communities and individuals who challenge state crime and who demand social justice and human rights. The first three chapters of this book consider the type of research criminologists might undertake in relation to state crime and civil society, and how we might position ourselves as criminologists in relation to social movements and contemporary social problems in ways that resist state crime (Friedrichs; Green and Ward; Kramer). The contributors have all been engaged with social movements campaigning for justice, often over many decades and in relation to a host of different issues. While this involvement includes a wide spectrum of activities, such activities are nevertheless heavily accented towards the intellectual, particularly reading, writing and teaching. By focusing on state crime and resistance, we hope to contribute some of the necessary intellectual tools to assist people to prevent, challenge, stop or redress state crimes.

There is some debate about the extent to which intellectual work can contribute to resistance. Karl Marx posited a sharp distinction between understanding and acting, famously stating that 'The philosophers have only interpreted the world in various ways; the point is to change it' (1845 quoted in Roberts 2009: 21). We argue that setting up a binary between interpreting and acting is unproductive and inaccurate. Action without reflection is incapable of achieving positive social change and no clear line can be drawn between the two. Challenging state crime brings with it a host of confronting and morally complex dilemmas: How much are we prepared to risk? Who are we prepared to take risks for? What risks and what level of risk are we prepared to take for family, community, humanity or future generations? What consequences will our actions have? How are we to know whether our actions will be effective, futile or counterproductive? What are the consequences of not acting? Who pays for our (in)action? How should we live in a world full of atrocities, suffering and denial? All of these questions require deep reflection, not least about what it means to be human. Challenging state crime inevitably involves a process where thinking, feeling and acting are bound in ways too complex to disaggregate. There are no easy answers, but asking hard questions must be part of the process.

In the same way that state crime is a process (Green and Ward), resisting state crime is also a process. This is the first book to specifically address state crime and resistance; however, it would have been impossible without the earlier contributions of state crime scholars and critical criminologists. Phil Scraton maps part of this trajectory in his 2002 chapter 'Defining "Power" and Challenging "Knowledge": Critical Analysis as Resistance in the UK'. Scraton argues that criminology has taken up the challenge to 'change the world, not only to study it' (Stanley 1990 quoted in Scraton 2002: 30). He argues that '[c]ritical research, publication and teaching within criminology has a significant role in resisting the political and ideological imperatives of official discourse' (2002: 35). In the decade since that chapter was published, critical criminology has expanded to take on the challenge of the transnational and the global (Stubbs 2008: 8). Criminology is now, more than ever, concerned with issues of global dimensions captured in the type of local case studies set out in this collection, and a focus on issues such as climate change denial and other environmental causes that play out on the global stage (Kramer; White).

As the first to focus on state crime and resistance, this collection opens up as many new questions and areas of study as it addresses. Thus, this is only a beginning in mapping the contours of this area of study. We acknowledge a host of omissions that we hope will form the basis for further research and scholarship. The collection excludes any in-depth focus on corporations (see, however, Stanley). As Green and Ward (2004: 51) maintain, there is little doubt that '[t]ogether, states and corporations are responsible for the vast majority of the human rights violations inflicted on citizens throughout the world'. The need to acknowledge and study the role of corporations in state crime and reflect on resistance in this context is particularly acute under conditions of neoliberal globalization. States now outsource coercive functions such as detention, combat and security to corporations (Singer 2008; Jamieson and McEvoy 2005). In addition, many corporations are now larger and arguably more powerful than many states. Despite this, the domestic and international accountability mechanisms that apply to states, inadequate though they are, do not apply to corporations (Clapham 2006). The study of state–corporate crime and resistance, taking into account the growing influence and power of corporations and the shifting border between states and private functions, is pressing.

In line with state crime literature more broadly, the collection has not thoroughly engaged with how state crimes are experienced, through the structural relations of gender, 'race', age or class. Future scholars could productively pay attention to how state crimes, and attempts to bring states into line, 'will be perceived and experienced differently' (White 2010: 57). The collection barely touches on the links between art, creativity and resistance (see, however, McCulloch and Blair; Morrison; Kauzlarich). This is a significant omission in the face of the central place that art, humour and creativity play in many resistance strategies (Ash 2011: 382). The role of social media and its importance in contemporary protest movements and resistance is also only briefly addressed (see Friedrichs; Green and Ward). Another significant gap is any extended discussion on the line between resistance and co-option – while White and Stanley (this volume) both touch on this, a more extended and nuanced consideration is warranted. While the collection looks specifically at resistance through the lens of criminology, it is clear that future studies could also benefit from dialogue with a whole host of other disciplines, including international relations, area studies, law, anthropology and politics. There are no doubt other omissions or future possibilities that this first extended foray into the realm of state crime and resistance has failed to imagine.

We see this collection as merely a beginning. By providing some of the intellectual tools necessary to challenge state crime, we hope to motivate readers to make history themselves by engaging in resistance. As we argue in Chapter 1, resistant acts may be momentous and involve multitudes, or they may be small and personal. Every reader can choose their own path of resistance, and every resistant act they undertake will connect them to other actions and other resisters. For those of us who live in liberal democracies, the costs of resistance may not be as high as for those in repressive regimes. The contrast between the Arab Spring and the Occupy movement bring this home. In Egypt, in one week alone, 40 protesters were killed (El Rashidi 2012: 21). Occupy protesters, on the other hand, while harshly and brutally policed, were not fired upon and none have been killed (Greenberg 2012; McCulloch and Vakalis 2012). All of the contributors to this volume reside in liberal democracies – the United Kingdom, the United States, Australia and New Zealand. Compared to others, writing in different times and in different places, the risks we have taken in writing as an act of resistance are not great. In other circumstances, lives, freedom and experiences of the worst type of terror, torture and intimidation may be at stake. Livelihoods barely above subsistence may be threatened, along with the most basic benefits of citizenship.

What is clear is that acts of resistance, whether undertaken in defiance of state power directly experienced or in solidarity with others, create new possibilities for a more just future. While the trajectory of resistance and its impact on human history is impossible to know in advance, resisters seek to progress or preserve a future worth living for generations to come. In doing so, they build upon and acknowledge the sacrifices of previous generations who struggled to centre ways of living that value humanity and justice.

References

Anthony, T. and Cunneen, C. (2008) 'Introduction', in T. Anthony and C. Cunneen (eds), *The Critical Criminology Companion* (pp. 1–4), Sydney: Hawkins Press.

Ash, T. (2011) 'A Century of Civil Resistance: Some Lessons and Questions', in A. Roberts and T. Ash (eds), *Civil Resistance and Power Politics: The Experience of Non-violent Action from Gandhi to the Present* (pp. 371–90), Oxford: Oxford University Press.

Clapham, A. (2006) *The Human Rights Obligations of Non-State Actors*, New York: Oxford University Press.

Cohen, S. (2001) *States of Denial: Knowing about Atrocities and Suffering*, Cambridge: Polity Press.

El Rashidi, Y. (2012) 'Egypt on the Edge', *New York Review of Books*, Jan/Feb, 59(1), 21–3.

Green, P. and Ward, T. (2004) *State Crime*, London: Pluto Press.

Greenberg, M. (2012) 'What Future for Occupy Wall Street?' *New York Review of Books*, available at www.nybooks.com/articles/archives/2012/feb/09/what-future-occupy-wall-street/?pagination=false, accessed 30 January 2012.

Jamieson, R. and McEvoy, K. (2005) 'State Crime by Proxy and Juridical Othering', *British Journal of Criminology*, 45(4), 504–27.

McCulloch, J. and Vakalis, D. (2012) 'Something Old, Something New, Something Borrowed, Something Blue: Militarized Policing and Occupy Melbourne', *Overland*, available at http://overland.org.au/previous-issues/issue-occupy/feature-jude-mcculloch-anddavid-vakalis/, accessed 30 January 2012.

Roberts, A. (2009) 'Introduction', in A. Roberts and T. Ash (eds), *Civil Resistance and Power Politics: The Experience of Non-violent Action from Gandhi to the Present* (pp. 1–24), Oxford: Oxford University Press.

Scraton, P. (2002) 'Defining "Power" and Challenging "Knowledge": Critical Analysis as Resistance in the UK', in K. Carrington and R. Hogg (eds), *Critical Criminology: Issues, Debates, Challenges* (pp. 15–40), Cullompton: Willan Publishing.

Singer, P. (2008) *Corporate Warriors: The Rise of the Privatized Military Industry*, Ithaca: Cornell University.

Stubbs, J. (2008) 'Critical Criminological Research', in T. Anthony and C. Cunneen (eds), *The Critical Criminology Companion* (pp. 6–17), Sydney: Hawkins Press.

White, R. (2010) 'Environmental Victims and Resistance to State Crime through Transnational Activism', *Social Justice*, 36(3), 46–60.

Index